WORLD RELIGIONS

WORLD RELIGIONS

ORIGINS HISTORY PRACTICES
BELIEFS WORLDVIEW

FRANJO TERHART

JANINA SCHULZE

p

Contents

OTHER RELIGIONS 254

Foreword

In what do you believe, if you do not believe? *Belief or Nonbelief?* is the apt title of a book jointly published in 1999 by the internationally renowned Italian author Umberto Eco (born 1932) and the Bishop of Milan, Carlo M. Martini (born 1927). In it, they speak of the moral crisis the Christian church is experiencing, and, at the same time, explore the question of whether non-believers are incapable of differentiating right from wrong. Can only belief in God provide people with the help they need to navigate our increasingly complex world? Or, do non-believers, as Umberto Eco maintains, also have a benchmark for differentiating good from evil? And if that is so, is it not true that non-believers have a kind of religion, too?

Religion revolves around this central question of differentiating between good and evil—either following God's commandments or rejecting them. The Latin origin of the word "religion" (*religare*: *re* – again + *ligare* – to connect) quite literally signifies a reconnection with the divine. The term can also be understood as denoting rites and duties (Latin *religio*). In reconnecting with the Creator, individuals freely deliver themselves into the hands of God, surrendering completely to God. This, in turn, is contingent on expectations on both sides: the individuals concerned are expected to subject themselves to God's will and follow his commandments; in return, they expect God's protection and a better life after death. A life focused on God appears to make sense, because it constitutes the aim of life in the belief systems of many religions. This God has many faces. Christians, Jews, and Muslims all recognize God as the personal God of Creation, and by no means a faceless principle as portrayed in Taoism. For modern physicists, such as Stephen Hawkins (born 1942), who ponder the universe and so-called black holes, God is the embodiment of the laws of physics, something that unfolds and reveals itself in and through the world itself.

This book presents the known religions according to the current size of their faith communities. At present, the world is home to around 2 billion Christians, 1.3 billion Muslims, 830 million Hindus, 380 million Taoists, 360 million Buddhists, 12 million Jews, and 6.5 million Confucians. Tao, Brahma, Yahweh, Allah, and God are all terms for the one unfathomable being. At the same time, Indian gurus such as Ramakrishna (1836–1886) emphasize that it is not good to say that only one's own religion is true and all others are false. He sees an analogy in the water of a large lake: some may drink at one location and say the water is so, while others may drink at another location and know the lake's water by quite a different name; but they have all drunk from the same water. Recognizing this fact is precisely what religions find difficult to do, as they are continually striving to define themselves and distinguish the essence of their belief from that of other religions.

It is always important to become informed before making judgments about an unfamiliar religion. For this reason, this book offers anyone interested in doing so the opportunity to acquire the necessary information. Anyone who wishes to understand what is currently taking place in the world, for example, the conflict between Sunni and Shia Muslims in Iraq, cannot do so without knowing the religious-cultural background. The essence of each of the world's great religions—Christianity, Islam, Hinduism, Buddhism, and Judaism—is presented comprehensively, with their origins, history, beliefs, worldview, and practices, as are Confucianism, Taoism, the Baha'i faith, the religion of the Mandeans in southern Iraq, nature religions worldwide, and Japanese Schintoism. In doing so, special attention is drawn to events in the historic development of the religions that were significant to the people of the day and, in the present age of globalization, are of no lesser worldwide significance today.

CHRISTIANITY

✝

1

The Roots of Christianity

A long way

When searching for the roots of the Christian faith, a number of questions arise: when did Christianity as we know it today develop? Is Christianity homogenous, or was it at the beginning? Where are the origins of a faith professed by over two billion people—thereby making Christianity the largest religious community in the world—and how did it develop? Christianity has had an enormous influence on the world. The culture of the Western world would be unthinkable without this faith. But it was a long journey from what once was a small Jewish sect in the Middle East gathered around an itinerant preacher named Jesus to a system of faith that not only spread throughout the original region, the countries of the Mediterranean, but that today includes communities on every continent on Earth.

Herod, king of the Jews

The history of Christianity began in the first century BC in Palestine, before the turn of the era. For about 60 years, Palestine had been a Roman province. The Romans had conceded limited authority to vassal kings to rule the Jewish provinces. One of these was Herod (73–4 BC). In 37 BC he was appointed king of the Jewish state. His family had adopted the Jewish faith just shortly before, so he could not expect too much trust from the people.

A model of Jerusalem in the time of Herod.

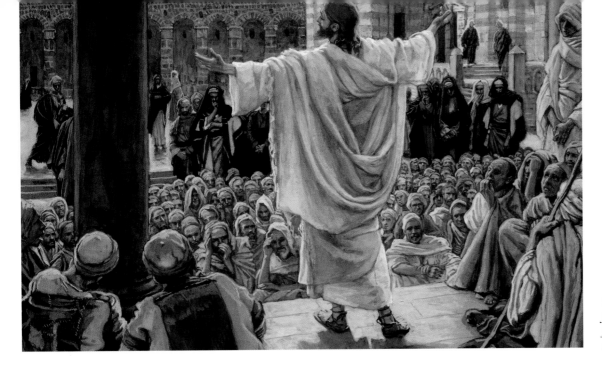

Top left: Jesus preaching in Jerusalem. It was a long way from the original Jewish sect to Christianity.

However, he and his family protected and defended the Jewish faith, though under one condition: while practicing the faith, no criticism should be made of Roman rule.

Pharisees and Sadducees

During Jesus' lifetime, there were two important parties dividing the population of Palestine: Sadducees and Pharisees. The Sadducees belonged to the Jewish upper class. They had great political influence, and the high priest was chosen several times from their ranks. When the second Jewish Temple was destroyed in 70 AD, they lost both their cultic and their economic basis. Until then, they represented the conservative upper class and arranged themselves with the Roman occupiers. Their faith was founded entirely on the Pentateuch and, unlike the Pharisees, they did not acknowledge later oral traditions.

The Pharisees, on the other hand, came from the lower classes. Their ranks consisted mainly of craftsmen and other laborers, though this group also produced some renowned scholars and they were highly regarded at the time of Christ. They considered themselves to be the true Jews and applied the canon of laws of the Jewish faith to their everyday life. They concentrated on interpreting the scriptures, lived very righteously, and accepted only in part the Sadducees' claims to religious leadership. They demanded a separation of religion and state:

the king should have to decide between the throne and the office of high priest.

In addition, the Pharisees felt they were obliged to fulfill two missions: one was to fulfill the laws of God as literally as possible, and the other was to spread their belief in the approaching end of the world and the subsequent Day of Judgment. At the same time, they were expecting the arrival of the Messiah, an anointed ruler who would free Israel from Roman rule.

From 37 BC, Herod ruled over the Jewish people. During his reign, the country blossomed again.

Jesus

The historical Jesus

Around 2000 years ago, a man called Joshua Ben Josef traveled through the desert of Judea as an itinerant preacher. Joshua means

"he will deliver," or also "God helps." Today, there are hardly any reliable facts about his life; only kings and politically important personalities left written accounts of their lives. Jesus was born the son of Joseph, a carpenter in Nazareth, a small town in Galilee with about 200–300 inhabitants. His mother's name was Mary, and, according to the Gospels, she was a "virgin." Today this is considered more of a symbolic means of exaltating a child of God than a physical fact. Jesus' birth can be dated approximately to the year 4 BC, because it coincides with the reign of Herod. These were economically difficult times in which many people feared for their freedom because they suffered from high debts. Those who could not pay off their debts ran the risk of being made slaves.

Herod died four years before the Common Era. The Common Era, a new calendar, was first applied in the 6th century by the Roman monk Dionysius Exiguus; it begins with the birth of Christ (as he understood it; he was off by a few years) and to this day marks the focal point of the entire Christian culture.

What the Gospels relate

The four Gospels, the first four books of the part of the Bible called the New Testament, contain most of the information known to us about the life of Jesus. Nonetheless, they are less historical accounts than documents of faith—reports on the response of the people regarding the life and teachings of Christ. This is why they have to be read in the context of the history of Judaism in the first century. However, certain information about the life of the historical man Jesus can be gleaned: Jesus was born of Jewish parents, so he must have spoken Aramaic, and he was born in the year in which Herod died. His village, Nazareth, was of no particular political importance. Jesus was the firstborn of Mary and had several brothers and sisters.

Youth and first public appearances

It is thought that Jesus learned his father's trade of carpentry. He certainly knew the Jewish scriptures and the demands made by the Pharisees. During that time, many itinerant preachers traveled through the land, exorcising devils, performing miracles, and nourishing the people's belief in the Messiah, a king from the House of David who would bring about better times and free the people of Israel from Roman subjection.

Jesus, too, believed in the forthcoming Kingdom of God. Eventually, Jesus was baptized in the Jordan River by the itinerant preacher John—a ritual which was believed to secure one's survival in the imminent Kingdom of God. Apparently, Jesus became a follower of John the Baptist.

Around the age of 30, Jesus himself began to teach, after John, who had drawn the attention of the Romans, had been put to death. Jesus' teachings spread quickly, in part because they were directed against the Roman occupiers and promised new hope for the people. Jesus oriented his teachings on contemporary Judaism and confirmed that God had spoken through Moses in the Pentateuch, or the first five books of the Bible. But his teachings went further. He appeared publicly in the area around the Lake of Galilee, and his followers steadily grew in number. In contrast to the Pharisees, who were intent on following the laws of God communicated through Moses down to the most minute detail, Jesus emphasized autonomous thought and interpretation of the scriptures.

The name Jesus

The name Jesus is derived from the Hebrew Joshua or Josua. Some countries, in northern Europe for example, rarely use Jesus as a first name or have even prohibited its use, whereas in other regions, such as Spain and Latin America, it is one of the more frequent Christian names for boys.

A new interpretation of the law

The Last Supper was the last time that Jesus ate with his disciples. The Christian sacrament of Communion is today celebrated in memory of that event.

Jesus tried to counteract unthinking obedience to the law. He realized that God and the Jewish faith itself were in danger of being forced into the background by a codex of laws that at the time contained over 600 separate decrees. So he began to reinterpret and, in part, to break the law, as for example in his statement, "The Sabbath was made for man, not man for the Sabbath." (Mark 2:27).

Jesus spread the image of a God who does not measure people by their worldly status, but by the way they treat others. The commandment to love one's enemies, one of the central messages of the Sermon on the Mount, was perceived as a call to break the persistent, evil cycle of violence and counterviolence, but was not fully understood and adopted by everyone. People were

certainly fascinated by the teachings of this itinerant preacher; but at the same time, they viewed his ideas critically.

An explosive teaching

Jesus spread revolutionary ideas, teaching love as a commandment. For him, all people were equal, be they kings, paupers or slaves. But the world was Roman, and social hierarchy and slavery were the order of the day. The freedom that Jesus preached was socially explosive and his ideas threatened to turn the established order upside down. One could hardly expect commandments such as "Love thy neighbor like thyself" to be met with approval by the ruling class of a society built on the suppression and exploitation of subjugated peoples. This becomes especially clear in the Sermon on the Mount (Matthew

How the Gospels developed

After the death of Jesus, the apostles began to write down everything they knew and remembered about him. His followers understood him to be the son of God, which is a perception the Jewish faith does not allow, so the followers of Jesus eventually split away from the Jewish faith. The four Gospels, the first four books of the New Testament, relate the life of Jesus—something like a biography, albeit deeply personalized by the respective author. The Gospels are named after Matthew, Mark, Luke, and John, but whether they are actually their authors cannot be proved.

5–7): the thought of being equal before God instilled the people with new hope. The poor and the sick, the beggars and all those who belonged to lower social classes saw a better future in the Kingdom of God that Jesus preached.

Jesus, the awaited Messiah

The people were yearning to be freed from Roman occupiers and the high taxes they demanded, and thus many believed they had found the Messiah in Jesus and, at the same time, the prophesied son of the family of King David who would bring them freedom. For God had promised King David that rule would remain in the hands of his descend- ants, and this applied to the family of Jesus, who were said to be descendants of David.

Jesus is crucified

Jesus sealed his fate when, probably in the year 30, he decided to go to Jerusalem for the feast of Passover (see the chapter on Judaism). The town was full of pilgrims for the feast, giving him the opportunity to speak to a large audience. But the Romans soon took notice of this agitator from Galilee and made short shrift of him. They placed Jesus under arrest—his sermons were consi- dered jusy as dangerous as those of John the Baptist a few years earlier.

Legend has it that one of his disciples, Judas, betrayed Jesus, who was then handed over to the procurator, Pontius Pilate, who ordered him to be crucified, the usual pun- ishment for rebels at the time. Roman author and politician Cicero (106–43 BC) deemed this method of execution to be the cruelest of all deaths, and Roman citizens were therefore exempt from it. The condemned even had to carry their own cross to the place of execution. According to Roman law, Jesus was duly condemned. Tradition has it that the date of his death was the evening before the Passover feast. He died on the cross, after a few hours. His exact burial place is not known, and has given rise to much speculation up to the present day.

Below, left: As the Roman governor of Judea, Pontius Pilate (on the right, sitting on the elevated seat) was responsible for announcing the death sentence on Jesus of Nazareth.

Below, right: After preach- ing at the Passover feast in Jerusalem, Jesus was arrested and sentenced to death on the cross. Crucifixion was a common penalty for felons; it originated in the Orient and was the usual method of execution in many countries of the ancient world.

Development of the Early Church

From Saul to Paul

Saul (later Paul) of Tarsus became one of the great heralds of Christianity. Being a law-abiding Pharisee with a Hellenistic education, he at first persecuted Christians. He came from the Jewish Diaspora, from a region in Greece where both Jews and Christians lived. On his way to Damascus, he had a vision that made him fall off his horse. Deeply impressed, he asked to be baptized and took on the name Paul ("the little one"). Paul began as a missionary in Asia Minor and

Saul had a vision before the city gates of Damascus. He heard a voice asking him, "Why are you persecuting me?" Deeply moved, he had himself baptized as Paul ("the little one").

decided that heathens should not have to convert to Judaism before becoming Christians. Paul wrote many epistles, originally addressed to the early Christian communities, which today are amongst the oldest documents of the Christian faith. Paul was a missionary in the countries of the Mediterranean region, and the communities of Greeks who had fled from their homeland years before were now welcome starting places for him.

Eventually, Paul felt he had no choice but to entirely reject the codex of laws of the

Hebrew Bible. The reason was the new covenant God had sealed with humankind through Jesus. Paul interpreted the law of love anew: someone who abided by the law of love was not necessarily bound to the secular and traditional law of the Torah. Indeed, God had invited all peoples to join in his new covenant, not just the Hebrews.

Paul's great influence led to a break with the early church, in which Jews and Christians had mingled at first. This new freedom within the faith enlarged the target group for their message of love to include all the heathen peoples, in addition to Jews. This was the basic prerequisite for Christianity to spread to other civilizations.

The spread of Christianity

Christianity now had the opportunity to free itself from its Jewish origins and prove that it could exist as a religion in its own right. It still referred to the holy scripture of the Jews as its basis, but the teaching now went much further. The early Christians saw in Jesus Christ the founder of their religion. He was the Messiah, the Anointed One, who had revealed himself to them in the form of the itinerant preacher Jesus. He was the one they would follow from then on.

Paul's death and the destruction of the Temple

Paul continued his missionary work until he was executed as a martyr under Emperor Nero in the year 64. The center of power in the ruling classes in Jerusalem had once again shifted, and the focus was again on Pharisee obedience to the laws. But Paul had done a good job. In Greece and many regions around the Mediterranean, small Christian communities had been founded that kept in contact with the original community in Jerusalem and were resilient enough to withstand the fatal destruction of the Temple in Jerusalem.

In approximately the year 62, Jerusalem was the scene of an uprising against the Roman occupying forces that had long been in the coming. The Christian communities had to decide whether they would assist the Jews or follow their own law of love and end their solidarity with the Jewish community. It was not an easy choice to make, and, on the horns of a dilemma, the original Christian community decided to flee, settling in eastern Jordan. The uprising, however, ended in a catastrophe: the Jewish Temple was destroyed and the Romans forbade any Jew ever to set foot in Jerusalem again.

Above, left: After his vision and conversion, Paul became one of the most important heralds of Christianity. He was well educated, which meant he could read the scriptures and write letters.

Above, right: Paul, the Diaspora Greek, also preached in Athens, where he found a wide audience.

Persecution of the Christians

A hard time

In the period following the execution of Jesus, the Sadducee high priests tried to bolster their status. A Jewish breakaway sect preaching freedom and independence was a thorn in their flesh. Also, unrest within the population was not welcome and was suppressed with the help of Roman law. Christian teaching was quickly suspected of being subversive, although at first it was tolerated.

During the rule of Festus, Pontius Pilate's successor, the first martyr was stoned to death in the year 36. Stephanus was accused of blasphemy; Paul supervised the execution. This was the beginning of a large-scale persecution. At first, Jews and Christians were persecuted in equal measure. Many Christians fled to the surrounding regions. When the Romans began to honor their emperor as a god, giving sacrifice both to their gods and to the emperor, this directly opposed Christian teaching, which forbade the worship of another human. When the numbers of believers in the Christian faith began to grow steadily, the Romans branded the new cult as dangerous. Eventually, in the year 67, large parts of Rome were burned down, mainly those inhabited by Christians.

Today, it is believed that Emperor Nero was responsible for the arson. But at the time, the Christians were held responsible and publicly executed in the Arena: they were torn apart by wild animals, burned alive, or crucified. Although this mass execution remained a singular event, persecution continued unabated in the ensuing years. Many Christians preferred to face death than renounce their faith, yet their ranks grew continuously over the next centuries. Finally, in 313, Emperor Constantine introduced the general toleration of religion. Christian history knows him as the "thirteenth apostle" because of his promotion of the faith.

State and church in alliance

In 313, Emperor Constantine renewed the edict on religious tolerance that had been proclaimed two years previously, thereby strengthening his commitment to religious tolerance. From then on, diverse faiths co-existed alongside each other. Finally, toward the end of the 4th century, Christianity was proclaimed as the state religion. This was a historically crucial event because it bound faith and politics ever more closely together. What began as the religion of the poor and meek gradually, from generation to generation, became a great instrument of power, wielded by the crown and the ruling classes.

The alliance of ecclesiastical and secular power went so far that in the Middle Ages those who had enough money and influence could buy their way into spiritual positions. Many an aristocrat secured a living for his sons this way, something that also brought secular advantages. Wars were fought and justified in the name of the Church, killing in the name of love: only those who professed the Christian faith could enter the Kingdom of God. The Christian message of love was adulterated to such an extent that even Crusades were accepted as compatible with the Christian faith and blessed by the Church. The original teaching of breaking through the eternal cycle of violence and counterviolence was ignored entirely. The Church had already completed its transformation into a secular power.

Far left: Emperor Nero ruled Rome from 54 to 68. He was notorious for his artistic bent, but had a bad reputation with the Senate.

Left: Saint Stephen is considered the first Christian martyr. However, stoning to death had long been practiced; it was seen as a kind of purification, atoning for the sin of blasphemy.

Christianity is Declared the State Religion

The faith spreads

Far right (box): This statue of Saint Peter was erected in the Vatican City to honor the first pope of the Catholic Church.

Toward the end of the classical age, Emperor Constantine declared Christianity to be the state religion. He convoked three councils, calling all the bishops together to set the basic dogmas of the Christian faith. However, the bishops could not always agree. The question of the divine nature of Jesus already caused some fractions to split. Still, the church grew steadily. At first, emphasis was laid on converting individual towns. Once the inhabitants of a town were converted, bishops spread the faith in the surrounding villages. In this way, separate administrative regions came into being, called *dioceses* (Greek for provinces). In most cases, farmers adopted the faith of their landlords. Particularly influential bishops were called patriarchs in the eastern provinces and popes in

Peter, the first pope

Appointed by Jesus, Peter is accepted as the first pope. St. Peter's Basilica stands on the site of his tomb. Every pope is a successor to St. Peter. He speaks for the college of bishops and is considered infallible when exercising his office as a teacher of dogma concerning the faith or morals. The pope is given divine assistance. The decisions he makes are not contested, they are final and definitive for the Catholic Church.

In 325, Emperor Constantine convoked the Council of Nicaea in order to prevent an impending schism in Christianity.

Rome (derived from the Latin term *pater* for father). The Roman bishops were especially intent on proselytizing and expanding their influence. They converted many members of the ruling classes to Christianity, which brought them great esteem and soon expanded their influence over all of the Roman Empire. Since the members of the Roman community tended to be wealthy, they could financially support other communities.

The First Ecumenical Council

The patriarchs of the East viewed the expansion of the Roman community as a threat to their own decision-making freedom. The quarrels between East and West were ended rather abruptly when, in 312, Constantine defeated Maxentius' army and won the Roman Empire as a result. In the following year, he legalized Christianity, proclaimed it equal to other religions, and began to have churches built. Constantine hoped that Christianity would help him stabilize his newly won empire and tried to unify the Christian churches under one central organization.

However, by then the various teachings had drifted so far apart that they could not easily be brought into line with one another. In order to prevent an impending schism in Christianity, the emperor convoked a council in 325, inviting all 1800 bishops to decide on a uniform profession of faith. In fact, only 300 bishops took part in this first discussion of Christian teaching since the council of the apostles in Jerusalem. It has gone down in history as the First Ecumenical (universal) Nicene Council.

One of the most controversial issues of the Council was the true nature of Jesus: was he a being made by God, in other words, human and transitory, or was he divine and eternal? In the end, the Council affirmed the latter and included the Holy Spirit, formulating the Trinitarian understanding of God that would be dominant from now on. In addition, the exact date of the Easter celebration was bindingly set during this first Council. Although almost all the bishops assembled signed the Nicene Creed, the Church remained divided.

During his battle against Maxentius, the converted Constantine had a vision. The sign of the cross was revealed to him with the words In hoc signo vinces ("under this sign you shall win"). In 313, Emperor Constantine recognized Christianity as an officially tolerated religion.

The Emergence of the Roman Catholic and Orthodox Churches

Rome and Constantinople, two religious centers

Rome was an important center of the Roman Catholic Church in the Middle Ages, and is still the location of the Vatican, an independent enclave and seat of the Catholic pope.

Disagreements between the Byzantine and the Roman bishops about celibacy, ritual, and dogmatic issues remained unsolved and finally led to the Greek-speaking Eastern church splitting from the Latin-speaking West. Henceforth, there were to be two centers of Christian religious life: the Catholic center in Rome, and the Orthodox center in Constantinople, today's Istanbul. In the Byzantine Empire, as the Eastern Roman Empire was called, the monarch remained head of the Church until the 15th century and influenced both ecclesiastical and secu-

The Orthodox Church

In 1054, the Orthodox Church finally separated from its Catholic counterpart. Since then, its head has been the Patriarch, the leader amongst the bishops. The Orthodox Church not only repudiated the pope as head of the Church, it has also rejected the concept of a Holy Trinity. Orthodox Christians celebrate various forms of mass, strictly heeding traditions, and believe themselves to be orthodox, "in the right belief." Once an Orthodox priest is consecrated (done by the bishop), he is entitled to administer six of the seven sacraments. If the priest was married before being ordained, he may remain married. However, the office of bishop can only be held by someone who was previously a monk and has observed celibacy. One characteristic of the Eastern Church is the veneration of icons. The person to be venerated is depicted in a way that conveys their inner being, and by kissing or praying to the image, believers can come into direct contact with the person depicted.

lar matters. But even within the Orthodox Church, there were further divisions, one of which developed into the Coptic Orthodox Church in Egypt.

In 1453, Muslims conquered Constantinople and many people converted to Islam. Consequently, Orthodox missionaries turned to northern and eastern Europe, creating the Cyrillic script for the Slavic languages. It was much easier to spread the biblical doctrine of salvation by way of a script that could represent the language. The political and religious center moved to Kiev, and then on to Moscow, where in the 9th century Christianity was declared the official state religion of Russia. Since all Orthodox lands except Russia eventually fell under Muslim rule, the bishop of Moscow finally adopted the title of patriarch.

The Roman pope takes over the Church

The Roman papacy, too, increased its power. The bishop of Rome took over all the western territories. Missionary work to lands as far flung as the British Isles brought a great number of new followers and vast land hold-

ings, often donated lavishly by landowners. Soon, the papacy was powerful enough to keep even mighty sovereigns under control. Toward the end of the 13th century, Pope Boniface VIII even tried to subjugate the entire secular world to the power of the Church. This nearly led to a united Christendom, but a sense of national identity was just emerging in the various countries of the period, and the Hundred Years' War between England and France (starting around 1337) even led to a schism in the papacy.

Oriental Orthodoxy

The term Oriental Orthodoxy refers to the old Oriental Churches, communities that developed in the East in the 5th and 6th centuries. One that still exists is the Coptic Church in Egypt. When the patriarch of Alexandria was banned by the Catholic Church, the Copts separated and have since been more closely connected to the Orthodox Church. They reject the idea that Jesus is both divine and human. Today there are about three million Copts, mainly in Egypt, the Sudan, in South and East Africa, Palestine, and South America.

Above: Hagia Sophia in Istanbul was, for a time, the main church and center of the Byzantine Empire. Even today, many Orthodox Christians see it as a holy site, although it has in the meantime been converted into a museum. Its architecture has often been replicated.

Opposite page, box: The icons that play a great role in the Orthodox tradition are thought to represent a conduit to the saints, which is why they are venerated.

The Investiture Controversy

Turbulent times

After Pope Gregory excommunicated King Henry IV during the Investiture Controversy, Henry left the German town of Speyer in 1077 and began his pilgrimage of penance to Canossa to ask the pope to lift the ban and once more be granted full freedom of action.

The role of knights, as well as early forms of middle-class life, developed in the 11th century. The old feudal structures began to break apart, and the philosophy of scholasticism launched a way of thinking based on reason. Pope Gregory VII (1073–1085) not only demanded reforms, he also made it clear that the clergy should fulfill their office with greater care. He fought vehemently against clerical marriage and called on people to boycott any mass held by a married priest. Until then it was not unusual for a priest to be married and have children. Now, children of priests were degraded to the status of bondsmen or dependent slaves and were considered the church's property, while priests' wives were reduced to the status of concubines.

Gregory radically pursued his goals and initially met with heavy resistance, especially from the priests. But after a while, people grew to support his reforms. Another controversial point was the investiture of laymen,

Rex rogat Abbatem. Mathildim Supplicat atque;

The Concordat of Worms and the end of the Investiture Controversy

Pope and king continued to quarrel about the coveted offices that promised both revenue and salvation. The Investiture Controversy about the appointment of clergymen was finally resolved in 1122 by the Concordat of Worms. From then on, Emperor Henry IV renounced his right to confer the ring and crosier, ecclesiastical symbols of a bishop's status, and allowed the Church to decide freely on matters of investiture. The Church, in turn, assured the emperor that bishops and abbots would be invested in the presence of an imperial representative, which still gave the emperor a certain control over the affair. Although this agreement ended the dispute, the emperor had lost his spiritual power, and that role and and the papacy were separated.

Left: This medieval painting shows Henry IV kneeling before Abbot Cluny and Countess Matthildis.

Below: Pope Gregory VII was the central figure in the Investiture Controversy. He pilloried abuses in the Church such as clerical marriage and simony, the purchase of ecclesiastical positions.

i. e. the appointment of non-clergy to a bishopric. Gregory VII forbade this in 1075 and immediately attracted the wrath of the Salian king of Germany, Henry IV, eventually leading to Gregory's excommunication of the king. Henry IV then made his famous pilgrimage of penance to Canossa, Italy, and was allowed to rejoin the Church, but the pope was not very impressed and gave his help and support to a rival king, Rudolph of Swabia. After fighting several civil wars, Henry IV returned, deposed Gregory, and had himself crowned the Holy Roman Emperor by Gregory's successor, Clement III. The Church never fully managed to regain its influence over the appointment of bishops.

Gregorian reforms

From the perspective of ecclesiastical history, Pope Gregory VII stands for the Gregorian Reforms, even if they cannot be ascribed to him solely, but were more a result of his times. Apart from the question of how clergy were to be appointed, the main topic in the 11th century was the need to redefine the relationship between church and state. Only those who obeyed the church lived according to God's will. The king was seen as a human whose salvation was constantly imperiled by his earthly and often sordid affairs.

Church, Cross, and State

Right: During the Third Crusade, Richard the Lion-Hearted led the crusaders into the Battle of Arsuf (called Arsur by the Crusaders). The city was conquered in 1101.

The Crusades

The First Crusade was launched after Islamic leader al-Hakim devastated the Holy Sepulchre in Jerusalem, site of Jesus' death and burial, in 1009. The plan was to regain control of Palestine, free the Holy Land of Muslim rule, and convert the "heathens." Under Pope Urban (1088–1099), believers again waged war. They managed to conquer Jerusalem in 1099, but Muslims retook the city just 100 years later. The Fourth Crusade (1202–1204) was aimed against Constantinople.

The pretense of a holy mission gave the Church a weapon for waging war against the entire heathen world, and especially against the Byzantine Empire. Within 200 years, six large and countless smaller Crusades were launched. They altered the political map and led to the establishment of Crusader states in the Middle East, but also cost the lives of many civilians—populations of whole towns were wiped out. What's more, the idea of the Crusades had a lasting effect: it characterized Muslims as barbaric heathens whose death was welcome. This image of a bogeyman proved transferable to other religions, and the first victims of the Crusaders' propaganda

were the Jews living in the Rhine area of Germany. A century later, Crusades were also launched against wayward Christians. The inquisition, too, was born of the practice of crusading. It seems that the devastation of the Holy Sepulchre was used by Christianity as an excuse for centuries of intolerance against members of other religions and apostates. Millions died by the sword wielded in the name of God.

Apart from religious motives, Crusades were also highly important for political and economic reasons. However, they yielded hardly any lasting success.

The emergence of knights' orders

During the Crusades, military orders of knights were founded in Europe, including the Knights Templar and the Order of Saint John of Jerusalem. They took it upon themselves to protect the holy sites and pilgrims, and care for the sick and wounded. The Order of the Knights Templar was founded in 1120 by nine French knights, at the temple on Mount Moria in Jerusalem. Bernard de Clairvaux, later proclaimed a saint, wrote the rules of this order. In 1129, the pope officially sanctioned the order at the Council of Troyes. These knights were unique in that they were both monks and well-trained warriors. They were allowed to kill in the name of Christendom. Their centers of power and lands stretched from Scotland to Spain, Portugal, and Greece, and to the Holy Land itself. The order became extremely wealthy and powerful, and this may be why, in 1312, Pope Clement VI accused them of heresy and immorality and disbanded it. In many cases, Church authorities transferred their possessions to the Order of Saint John. This order was less famous for waging war against enemies of Christianity than for its care of the sick and needy—comparable to the original mission of another order, the Teutonic Order—both firmly in the tradition of knightly ideals.

Opposite page, top: Belief in witchcraft led in many places to public burnings at the stake. The main victims of the witch-hunting craze were women, but men and even children were also executed.

Opposite page, bottom: Use of torture during a trial often left the accused no other choice than to admit their guilt. The inquisition largely used the testimony of witnesses, and gave little validity to factual evidence.

The Inquisition

Belief in magic

Even in the early Middle Ages, the religious fanaticism that culminated in the inquisition was already expressed in persecution of heretics. There was no clear line between heresy, disbelief, and belief in witches and sorcery. Vague notions of pacts with the devil or witches riding broomsticks to their sabbath caused outbreaks of mass hysteria that resulted in countless victims. Accused witches often pleaded guilty to acts never committed to avoid being tortured, for example, using special ointment to enable them to fly on a broomstick to a coven, or having bewitched their neighbor's cow to prevent it giving milk. According to Roman law, using sorcery to commit this kind of damage was a criminal offence. The standard work for witch hunters was the *Malleus Maleficarum*, written by Dominican monk Heinrich Institoris and published in Strasbourg in 1487. This so-called "Witch's Hammer" was used throughout central Europe into the 17th century and translated into many languages. Tests were to be applied to prove the accused's guilt, or not. One was trial by water, where the feet and hands of the accused were chained and the victim then thrown into a body of water. If she drowned, she was innocent, but if the water rejected her, she was declared guilty. Divine judgments of this kind were normal practice at the time, although enforcement gradually became the responsibility of the secular powers.

Witch hunting

One of the causes of the witch-hunting fever was the deep-seated fear of falling prey to someone casting a spell on them. On the other hand, it can also be traced back to historical phenomena such a series of bad harvests and hallucinogens such as ergot. In the 16th century, witch hunting increased dramatically throughout Europe—primarily with the introduction of torture—and continued until the 18th century. The last execution of a witch took place in Switzerland in 1782, but the belief in sorcery persisted despite the Enlightenment. Even today, the Catholic Church still trains exorcists.

The Development of Monasteries and Religious Orders

Ora et labora—Pray and Work

Above, left: The monastery of Subiaco in Italy was the first Benedictine monastery. It was founded in the 6th century by Benedict of Nursia, founder of the Benedictine Order.

Above, right: The Order of Saint John of Jerusalem was the first order of knights founded in Jerusalem, in 1099, and still exists today. The Order of Saint John is known for its medical aid and humanitarian works.

All Christian orders are based on three basic vows of poverty, chastity, and obedience. Apart from that, every order has its own set of rules. Orders for monks or nuns devote themselves either principally to contemplation—meditation and prayer—or they take an active role in society, tending the sick or lending themselves to pastoral care. The members of most orders wear a distinctive garment, called a habit.

One of the first orders was the community of the Italian Benedict of Nursia (480–547), later known as the Benedictine Order. This community had a strictly regulated schedule of work and prayer, and Benedict coined the famous principle, *ora et labora*, pray and work, that is still a duty of monks today. Many more monastic orders were founded from the 11th century onward, such as the Franciscans, a mendicant order, or the Carthusians and Cistercians, both eremitical orders. In the following centuries, the monasteries became the guardians of the written

A new confidence: founding cathedral colleges

The spirit of the Renaissance and budding Humanism led to new self-confidence in the citizens of the mid-14th century. Thus, craftsmen began to leave information about themselves in their works or even include self-portraits in them. Widely understood symbols and sculptures showed biblical scenes. Centers of education grew up around cathedrals, which were previously only found within monastery walls. They taught the Seven Liberal Arts: the *trivium* of grammar, logic, rhetoric; and the *quadrivium* of arithmetic, geometry, astronomy, and music. Some universities also taught theology, law, and medicine. The church's monopoly on education was broken by offering access to knowledge to laypeople, in addition to clergy. These scholarly circles further developed into the first independent universities. The oldest university of the Holy Roman Empire was founded in 1348 by Charles IV in Prague, followed shortly afterwards by one in Vienna, and in 1388 the University of Cologne was founded.

Giving away children

Sometimes, nobles would give one of their sons to a brotherhood. This was usually the case if the inheritance to be distributed evenly among all male offspring wasn't large enough to provide for all. Such a child was usually "given" to a monastery at a very early age, never to leave again. He was thereby provided for, and the church gained a new monk who brought a dowry with him to the brotherhood. In this way, many bonds were forged between the nobility and the Christian brotherhoods and the boundaries between secular and ecclesiastical power dwindled. If the monk had learned to read and write, he was usually employed in the monastery as a scribe, copying biblical texts.

traditions of Christianity: they preserved in their libraries numerous handwritten manuscripts and copies of the Bible and other religious texts. In Germany, for example, this monopoly was only broken with Martin Luther and the invention of the printing press in the 15th century.

The Jesuits are a relatively young Catholic order that was only founded in the modern age, in 1534, and recognized by the pope a few years later. Like the Jesuits, the Order of Saint John considers education to be an integral part of their mission, and has founded a large number of high schools and universities. Even today, new Christian orders are still being founded. For example, in 1950 Mother Theresa founded the Missionaries of Charity, an order of nuns who care for orphans, lepers, and the terminally ill.

The Franciscan Order developed out of the brotherhood gathered around Francis of Assisi. The 'Order of Friars Minor' can be recognized by their white or brown habit and the rope slung around the hip in three knots.

The Reformation

Spiritual Basis: Scholasticism and Humanism

Far right: Legend has it that Luther nailed his ninety-five theses to the door of the castle church of Wittenberg. Today it is thought that his followers spread the theses, making use of the innovation of printing.

Scholasticism, a movement trying to reconcile faith and reason while regarding issues from their various sides, developed in the late 11th century. With its roots in the rationalism of Aristotle (384–322 BC), who had stated that a reliable understanding of matters of thought can be achieved by using reason, scholasticism widely determined the philosophy and science of the Middle Ages. Thomas Aquinas (1225–1274) and William of Ockham (1285–1349) were famous proponents of scholasticism, which held sway from the 9th to the 13th centuries and only ebbed away with the rise of Humanism.

Humanism, which grew out of the Italian Renaissance, once again called for the study of the classic authors and in certain areas did

Right: Martin Luther, an Augustinian monk, is known as one of the great church reformers. He pilloried abuses in the Catholic Church and became the founder of Protestantism.

not refrain from criticizing Christian teaching. All over Europe a desire arose for a moral and religious reform of the Church.

Luther, a protesting monk

Disputes within the Church forced the pope to leave Rome in 1309. Several years later a new pope was enthroned in Rome, but the previous one had fled to Avignon, France where he insisted on his right to lead the Catholic Church. 14th-century Italy saw the rise of the Renaissance, bringing a focus on secular life in the here and now.

A century later, the Augustinian monk Martin Luther (1483–1546) pilloried the abuses within the Catholic Church. While still a young man, Luther was ordained as a priest in 1507 and was appointed professor for Biblical interpretation in Wittenberg only a few years later. To him, the central duty of a Christian was to try and do good, since every human was capable of choosing to do so.

Abuses within the Church

The Church and its dignitaries had to a large extent turned away from what is stated in the Bible and acted in a way that had little to do with the original teachings of Christ. Instead, they were striving for worldly goals. Luther criticized the practice of selling indulgences, remission of punishment for worldly sins through the payment of money, most vehemently because in doing so, God was being pushed increasingly into the background while the Church adopted for itself the role of forgiver of sins.

Luther put together a catalog of points criticizing the Church. Legend has it that he followed an academic tradition when, in 1517, he nailed his ninety-five theses to the door of the castle church in Wittenberg. They found a surprising echo among the public—and heralded the dawn of the Reformation. Modern scholars now suspect that Luther did indeed put together these theses, but hadn't wanted them publicized this way. To commemorate the event, Protestants celebrate Reformation Day on October 31 (most Lutheran churches have transferred the festival so that it falls on the Sunday, called Reformation Sunday, on or before October 31st).

With the help of the printing press, developed in the late 15th century, Luther's theses circulated widely. Since many of his arguments were well founded and many people agreed with them, a split in the Church into Protestants and Catholics resulted. Luther did not react when Rome demanded he recant, but instead publicly burned the papal bull that threatened his excommunication. To him, the Vatican and the papacy were not divine, but of human making, and therefore without divine authority. In 1521, Luther was first excommunicated and then declared an outlaw—a secular punishment that deprived a person of all legal protection.

When Luther was excommunicated by the Church, he publicly burned the papal bull, which led him to fall even further from favor: he was declared an outlaw and thereby stripped of protection by the law.

A new path: the first German Bible

Above: Elector Frederick the Wise afforded Luther protection in the Wartburg castle, where he lived under the name of Junker (nobleman) Jörg and translated the Bible into German.

But Luther was lucky. In the following years he was able to stay in the Wartburg under the protection of elector Frederick the Wise. He worked as a scholar of the German language, wrote many theological treatises, and translated the New Testament into German. This gave many more people—those who could not read Latin—access to the Bible for the first time. When Martin Luther died he bequeathed a new church centered on the word of God, and clearly different from the Catholic Church. The Catholic Church reacted with the Counter-Reformation, changing its practices and reformulating them at the Council of Trent (1545–1563).

Peace and war between the confessions

Right: Gutenberg printed a Bible in two volumes with colored initials for which he cast a total of 290 different figures. Of the original 180 copies, less than fifty are still in existence.

The Peace of Augsburg signed in 1555 brought peace between the Holy Roman emperor and the empire's Protestant princes. Lutherans were no longer heretics, but officially recognized. However, the faith of most people living in the late Middle Ages was dictated by their landowners. The Thirty Years' War raged in the 17th century (1618–1648); caused by conflicts about secular power as well as religious strife between confessions, it had devastating consequences for all of Europe.

Gutenberg's printing press

The Chinese were familiar with printing long before it came to Europe. In the 15th century, Gutenberg invented a technology of movable type. Twenty-six movable letters enabled Gutenberg to print entire texts and to duplicate printed matter in much shorter time than before. Gutenberg's newly-invented press printing technique with movable type was very useful to Luther, because it enabled him to circulate his treatises quickly.

Luther's Bible: a landmark in linguistic development

Luther's translation of the Bible from Latin into German was not the first of its kind. Others before him had failed because they primarily wanted to set the Latin version in the right perspective. Luther went about things differently, and that has made his translation the most successful. He was a very talented preacher who knew how to convince the congregation with his clear and straightforward language. With his new translation, Luther proved that it was possible to express all thoughts, imaginations, and emotions through the German language, which until the 16th century had been mainly the language of the common people. Luther also made the content of the Bible accessible for the common people. It was probably only now that they understood for the first time what the Bible was all about. Luther did not translate word for word, but instead tried to explain the contents of the Bible, as he understood them, in the German language. Luther used a powerful, popular, and gener-

ally understandable language with a lot of imagery, one that the common people could follow. His translation of the Bible decisively forced the development of a standard German language (High German), which was later used in all German-speaking countries alongside regional dialects. This is why linguists see Luther's translation of the Bible as a landmark in the history of the German language. Luther coined many terms and expressions that are used to this day, such as the hymn "A Mighty Fortress is Our God."

His translation became a catalyst for many other scholars throughout Europe to follow his lead and translate the holy scriptures into their own languages, thereby making the Bible accessible to their peoples. Several Protestant rulers sought to standardize and regulate the plethora of translations and interpretations that arose by commissioning and authorizing standard versions to be used in their realms (for example, the King James Bible of 1611 and the Swedish Gustav Vasa Bible of 1540–1541). Such translations also significantly influenced the development of their respective languages.

In his study, Martin Luther translated the New Testament of the Latin Bible into German in only eleven weeks. The study in Wartburg castle has been reconstructed and can be visited.

Christian Confessions in the Modern Age

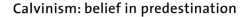

isolation that could only be escaped through work. Success as the visible sign of being chosen by God led to a new dilemma, from which no human consolation could free them. They were forced to work if they feared for their salvation—which presented the entrepreneur with a willing worker.

Sociologist Max Weber (1864–1920) saw this Calvinist view of life as one of the cornerstones of capitalism. In addition, work as a duty to be carried out to the benefit of both the individual and society as a whole was also a way of practicing Christian love, as Martin Luther had already pointed out. At the same time, it helped to build an increasingly effective bridge between religious piety and the budding capitalist economy, with a puritanically modest way of life on the one side and an achievement-oriented quest for success on the other. According to

Calvinism: belief in predestination

Earthly success as a confirmation of a righteous life—this thought, developed upon the foundations of Humanism, was central for the Calvinist community, a religious group that split from Protestantism. The French Humanist and doctor of law John Calvin (1509–1564) developed a doctrine of double predestination, according to which an individual's fate is predestined. The sole purpose of humanity is to glorify God—although one part of humankind is predestined to belong to the chosen that are granted special earthly success, while the rest are threatened with eternal damnation. No one can alter anything that is predestined; hereby Calvin refuted all magic means of influence, once and for all. Individuals had been thrown into a state of

Weber, these two directions helped form modern "economic Man," while economic success, wealth, and even the unequal distribution of goods in the world could be explained as God-determined.

The Anglican Church

When Pope Clement VII (1523–1543) refused to consent to the request of the English King Henry VIII for a divorce, Henry responded without further ado by founding the Anglican State Church. He broke with Rome and had parliament confirm him as the supreme head of the Church of England. The Anglican Church has characteristics of both the Catholic and Calvinist churches. It survived the attempt by Mary Tudor (Queen of England, 1553–1558) to reintroduce Catholicism, and in 1600, Queen Elizabeth I definitively determined that the English Church would be Anglican and quite independent of Rome.

Since then, the Anglican Church has to a great extent retained its beliefs and religious practices, including the office of bishop, although a bishop has no authority to issue directives in any dioceses other than his own. There are, however, four so-called Instruments of Unity (Communion): the Archbishop of Canterbury, the Lambeth Conference (an assembly of all Anglican bishops), the Anglican Consultative Council (the council of the Anglican Church), and the Primates' Meeting of senior archbishops and bishops.

There are many various aspects to Anglican teachings. Some of them are close to those of the Catholic Church, while others are closer to Calvinism and Protestantism. With the British Empire, Anglicanism spread throughout the world; today it is a member of the World Council of Churches. Unlike the Roman Catholic Church, the liturgy has been held in the vernacular since the time of the Reformation and was therefore understood by everyone. Similar to the Catholic Church, the Anglican Church also has religious orders for both men and women.

Other Christian confessions

The religious community of Quakers arose in 17th-century England. Today, they are mainly found in Africa and English-speaking countries.

Quakers, children of the light

Rejecting the English State Church, George Fox founded the Quaker movement in the 17th century. Originally, they called themselves the "Society of Friends." The name "Quaker" derives from the quaking, or shaking, movements they made in their ecstatic experience of God during worship.

Quakers believe that something of God can be found in every one of us, and to them, every believer, male or female, can be a preacher. They emphasize the equality of all believers and strive to find a consensus of all members for decisions that affect the community. Quakers are extremely critical of self-indulgent living.

Although Quakers are not part of the World Council of Churches, they do maintain contacts with other confessions. They are known for their extensive social work.

Jehovah's Witnesses

Jehovah's Witnesses can be traced back to a late 19th-century revivalist movement in the USA with its own interpretation of the Bible. Jehovah's Witnesses believe that doomsday can be predicted. They believe only a small group of the faithful will be allowed to enter heaven; the others will be given a kingdom on earth. Armageddon—according to Revelation (16:16) the location of the final battle against the forces opposed to God—will be the final battle between good and evil, the former commanded by Jesus.

The religious practice of Jehovah's Witnesses is characterized by its worldwide proselytizing; missionaries speak to people, go from door to door, and hand out publications such as *The Watchtower*.

Mormons: The Church of Jesus Christ of Latter-day Saints

The Mormons go back to Joseph Smith (1805–1844), who founded this church in 1830 in Fayette, New York, adding the Book of Mormon to the Holy Scriptures. Today they are called The Church of Jesus Christ of Latter-day Saints.

Their headquarters is in Salt Lake City, Utah. They consider themselves Christians, although they differ in many points from other Christian confessions. Mormons believe that God reveals himself today just as much as in the past. The Bible should therefore not be seen as completed, but open to new additions. Baptism is only possible once a person is capable of consciously choosing the faith. Mormons assume that life is only a passing stage. Before and after life, people are spirit beings who come to earth in order to gain experience.

The original community of Mormons has today split into several divisions, some of which allow polygamy. Central to this faith is a missionary service that can last one to two years and is paid for by the missionaries themselves.

Methodists

Another revival movement is the Methodist church, which believes in the "New Birth." The name of this denomination was originally a nickname used because of their methodical approach to the scriptures and Christian life.

The Methodist Community developed in 18th-century England as a movement within the Anglican Church. Clergyman John Wesley (1703–1791) gathered a group of people around him who tried to do God's will through study of the Bible and charitable work. To Methodists, love is the central message of Christianity.

Baptists

The Baptist church is often viewed as an Evangelical Protestant denomination with its origins in English Puritanism. Theologically, many Baptists emphasize adult baptism by immersion, performed after a profession of faith in Jesus as Lord and Savior. While the congregational form of church governance gives individual Baptist churches autonomy, they often form associations like the Southern Baptist Convention, the largest in the world.

Following a vision in which both God and Jesus appeared to him, Joseph Smith founded an idiosyncratic religious community, the Church of Jesus Christ of Latter-day Saints, or Mormon Church. Today, it is widely spread in the USA.

The Church's Influence Declines

Theology and science

With the dawning of the Industrial Age, a critical and scientific approach began to dominate thought: scientific explanations gained through experience, or empiricism, gradually displaced theological explanations of natural phenomena. Life was no longer a mystery; it was there to be discovered.

This approach influenced theology itself. Philosophers like Friedrich Schleiermacher (1768–1834) and Sören Kierkegaard (1813–1855) increasingly sought to combine science and theology. But Christianity's loss of social relevance could not be stopped. As early as 1805, Ernst Moritz Arndt wrote that "being a nation is the religion of our time," succinctly articulating the spirit of the 19th century. The Catholic Church reacted by convening assemblies of the faithful, a tradition that had been introduced in earlier centuries to improve the sense of community within the church.

Charitable church organizations

Christian Aid

Christian Aid, begun in 1945, was first known as Christian Reconciliation in Europe and changed its name to Christian Aid in 1964. It cooperates with local partners in more than 60 countries to help the world's poorest communities, regardless of religion or race. Christian Aid also works on issues that lie behind world poverty, speaking out on unjust trading practices like tariffs barriers and Third World debt.

Caritas International

Caritas International is a group of 162 Catholic charitable and social service organizations operating in over 200 countries. Their mission is to build a better world for the poor and needy. Caritas was founded in Germany in 1897. Other national Caritas groups soon followed, including the USA (Catholic Charities) in 1910.

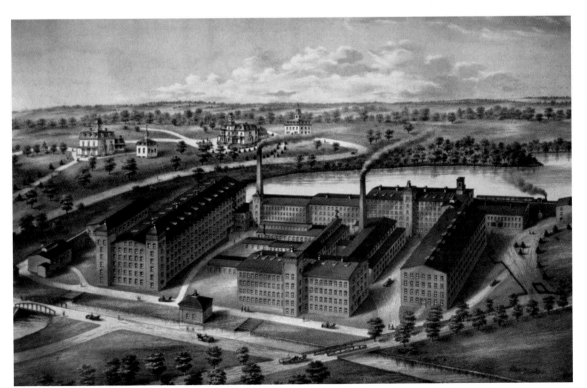

Industrialization drew great numbers of people to the cities. The clear structures of the villages slowly dissolved and many workers felt forlorn in the large and increasingly anonymous surroundings of the cities.

Guiding the Direction of Christianity at the Turn of the Millennium

Pope John Paul II

Above: John Paul II was one of the best-known and most popular popes ever. He was renowned for his charisma and his involvement in politics.

Right: During the last papal election, millions of Christians in Rome, and in front of television sets all over the world, fixed their eyes on the chimney of the Sistine Chapel in anticipation of the rising smoke.

Karol Jozef Wojtyla (1920–2005), born in the Polish town of Wadowice near Kraków, was elected pope and thereby head of the Roman Catholic Church on October 16, 1987. He was famous for his numerous travels and had a lasting influence on global politics, criticizing heads of state if they acted against Christian rights. As a young man, Karol Wojtyla studied literature and philosophy. When the university was shut down during World War II, Karol escaped deportation and imprisonment by taking a job as a stone cutter in a quarry. In 1942, he entered the underground seminary run by the archbishop of Kraków, Car-

dinal Sapieha. Four years later he was ordained a priest. He wrote his doctoral thesis on Saint John of the Cross, a theologian and mystic, and from 1953 taught moral theology at the Catholic University of Lublin. In 1958 he was named suffragan bishop of Kraków, and in 1964 archbishop. In 1967, Karol Jozef Wojtyla was appointed cardinal, and in 1978 was elected successor of Pope John Paul I.

His election came as a shock to communist rulers, especially in his home country of

The papal election

When a pope dies or resigns, the cardinals convene in the Sistine Chapel and—in seclusion from the world outside—they elect the new pope. After every unsuccessful round of voting, the ballot papers are traditionally mixed with dry straw, soaked in pitch, oil, or other, modern chemicals to produce black smoke, and burned. If the ballot has been successful, i.e., one of the candidates has received more than two-thirds of the votes, the ballot papers are burnt with straw only, producing white smoke, which then escapes through the chapel chimney. This is a sign for the faithful that they have a new pope. The phrase *Annuntio vobis gaudium magnum, habemus Papam!* ("I announce a great joy to you: we have a pope!") is used as an introduction to the public proclamation of the elected candidate's name.

Poland. The Polish pope pilloried the communist dictators of the Eastern Bloc, calling for reforms and the observance of human rights. His unswerving zeal, his advocacy of human rights, and the effect of his charisma fortified the young Polish workers' union, Solidarity, led by Lech Walesa. Today, it can justly be said that John Paul II was mainly responsible for the collapse of communism in Eastern Europe. He encouraged the people of Poland, always staunch Catholics, to revolt peacefully against state authority. The seed germinated and spread to other countries. When in 1981 an attempt was made on the life of John Paul II, which has still not been fully explained, the pope forgave the Bulgarian assassin while still on his sickbed and visited him in jail when he had recovered. A year later, his bodyguards managed to prevent a second attempt, this time with a bayonet. After twenty-seven years in office, Pope John Paul II died in April 2005, aged 84. The obsequies were held on Saint Peter's Square in Rome, with many thousands of believers and heads of state from all over the world taking part, once again proving how popular and distinguished this pope was.

Pope Benedict XVI

On April 19, 2005 Josef Alois Ratzinger (born in 1927 in Bavaria) was elected successor to Pope John Paul II. Although he had been a member of the Hitler Youth for a short period, he always held on to his wish of becoming a priest and went on to study the history of religion and philosophy after finishing school. In 1951 he was ordained a priest; in 1953 he earned his doctorate, and four years later became a professor for fundamental theology. In the following years, he taught at various German universities and was soon one of the country's most renowned theologians, repeatedly criticizing the rigid structures of the Catholic Church. In his position as Prefect of the Congregation for the Doctrine of the Faith he was committed to un-adulterated presentation of the core of the Christian message. Early in 2006 he published an encyclical entitled *Deus Caritas Est* ("God is Love"). In it he distinguishes between eros, or passionate and worldly love, and agape, which is giving, unselfish, and spiritual love. Benedict XVI thus returns to the original message and central theme of Christianity.

In April 2005, Pope Benedict XVI succeeded John Paul II, becoming the first German pope in modern times. As Cardinal Josef Ratzinger, he had previously taught as a professor at various German universities before becoming Prefect of the Congregation of the Doctrine of the Faith.

Christian Beliefs and Philosophy
The Bible

The word of God

The Bible (Greek *tà bibla*, the books) is a collection of writings through which God reveals himself. Although written by humans, the Bible is considered the word of God and is of central importance to the Christian faith, one of the "religions of the book." The Christian Bible is divided into two parts, the Old and the New Testaments.

The books of the Old Testament (composed in pre-Christian times) include the five books of Moses, the books of the Prophets, and the Psalms. In general, the contents coincide with the Jewish Torah, although the order of the various sections differs.

The New Testament consists of the four Gospels (Mark, Matthew, Luke, and, slightly later, John). Written ca. 50–70 AD, they recount the life of Jesus. The New Testament

In the 4th century, Hieronymus translated the Bible from Hebrew into Latin (portrait ca. 347-349).

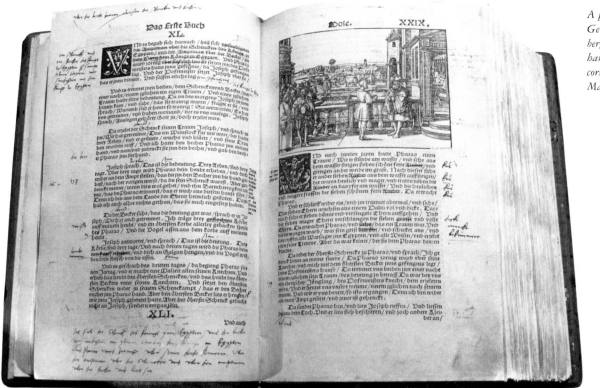

also includes the Acts of the Apostles, letters or "epistles" (including those of Paul), and the Revelation to John (also called the Apocalypse), a graphic description of the Last Days.

A number of other books, called the Apocrypha, were not accepted into the canon of the Christian Bible. They often provide additional insight that contributes to our understanding of the creation of the Bible.

Although the Reformation was a real catalyst for translating the Bible into various vernaculars—i.e. Luther's German (1521); Tyndale's English (1526/1535), and the 1611 King James version—there were earlier versions such as Wycliffe's 1380–1390 English Bible, a Hungarian Hussite Bible in the mid-15th century, and a Spanish edition in 1478.

The Septuagint and Vulgate

The biblical texts were originally composed in three languages: Hebrew, Aramaic, and Hellenistic Greek. One had to know these languages to read the Bible. Between the 3rd and 1st centuries BC the Hellenistic Jews of Alexandria began translating the Torah into Greek to give more people access to it. The result was called the Septuagint (Latin, "the seventy"). The Septuagint is not a unified translation, and the text was altered to make it comprehensible to Hellenistic readers.

A Latin version of the Bible, known as the Vulgate (Latin, "commonly used") was translated directly from the original Hebrew text in the late 4th century. In western Europe, the Vulgate quickly replaced the Septuagint and was long the only valid Bible translation.

At the Council of Trent (1545–1563) the Catholic Church established the Latin Bible (Vulgate) as the authentic and binding version. Books that did not find their way into the Christian canon are termed Apocrypha ("hidden texts").

Key Elements of Christian Theology

The fall from grace

The fall from grace is a central motif in Christian theology. Through their disobedience and turning away from God, the first man and woman brought original sin upon themselves. The story of Adam, Eve, and the serpent is one of the most familiar stories of the Bible.

Key themes in Christian theology are the fall from grace, original sin, and the resultant inborn guilt passed on from generation to generation. In the story of the temptation in the Garden of Eden (Genesis 3:1–24), the serpent (Satan) tempts Eve to eat of the forbidden Tree of Knowledge. God had already warned Adam and Eve: "You shall not eat of it, neither shall you touch it, lest you die." But Satan argues that if Eve eats the apple, she will not die, but rather gain the ability to discern between good and evil: "… and you will be like God, knowing good and evil." Eve and Adam eat the forbidden fruit—and are cast out of Paradise by God.

Important in understanding the Christian concept of original sin is that this act distanced Adam and Eve—representing humanity—from God. The disobedience is a sin due to the guilt that arises from freely choosing evil. By their own free will, people violated God's commandment. As a result, human nature fell into a state of confusion. From this

Angels

Christianity recognizes two angels above all: Michael and Gabriel, who appear both as heralds and as destroyers. The Bible relates that angels already existed before the creation of the world, but it does not go into further detail about their realm. Christians adopted not only the idea of angelic beings, but also the hierarchies of angels from Judaism, a religion that recognizes many more angels. The Book of Moses speaks of angelic guards in Paradise, and angels destroy the city of Sodom; in the New Testament, an angel informs Mary that she will bear a child. The wings typical in images of angels symbolize their nearness to God as well as their ability to ascend beyond the level of mortals. The fallen angel, Satan (also known as Lucifer) is thought to have been a special angel who, however, turned against God. Satan's role is to lead people into temptation and test them. His appointed place is hell, a complete and final separation from God's love and mercy, as punishment for sinners. The other angels' task is to continually reveal God and his will to humanity.

moment on, humanity was no longer living in the sanctifying grace of the Creator, but in a state of freely choosing between good and evil—now weighed down with the indelible stain of Adam and Eve's sin, the original sin, a flaw inherited by all succeeding generations.

The Catholic Church finds a solution to this inherited sin in the crucifixion of Jesus Christ, an event that allows people to regain redemption and be reconciled with God. For Luther, humankind is wicked from the very beginning and lives in a state of sin. We live separated from God and need his grace, or unmerited mercy, for salvation. Augustine of Hippo (354–430), one of the great church teachers, argued that without original sin people would not be able to distinguish be-

tween good and evil. In this sense, according to philosopher Immanuel Kant (1724–1804), the "fall" was a decisive moment on the path to maturity, or the assumption of responsibility for one's own actions. The serpent enticed humans out of a state of immaturity into a life of hope and fear, decision and error.

The Sermon on the Mount

That Jesus actually preached a single sermon before several hundred people on a hill near Jerusalem—as reported by two Gospels—is doubted. Instead, theologians assume the text represents a summary of ideas that Jesus preached most often. The Sermon on the Mount (Matthew 5–7; Luke 6:20–49) brings together the essential ideas of Jesus' religious message and, since the very beginning of Christianity, these extraordinary and unparalleled commands have impressed people with their succinct and paradoxical formulation, their radicalism and uncompromising nature: "Blessed are the merciful, for they shall obtain mercy" and "Blessed are those who are persecuted for righteousness' sake, for theirs is the kingdom of heaven." (Matthew 5:7 and 5:10) These so-called Beatitudes are formulated as moral stipulations. In general, the Sermon on the Mount admonishes to moral behavior, and in particular it presents justice as the highest human duty. "You will know them by their fruits." (Matthew 7:16) Complete devotion to God and the search for his kingdom are the tasks of the faithful believer, who is not to judge, "that you be not judged" (Matthew 7:1). The Sermon on the Mount warns people not to be content with mouthing empty words, but to bear witness to God through their lives.

The Apocalypse of John

The powerful symbolic images of the Apocalypse—the visionary Revelation to John the Evangelist—conclude the New Testament. The only completely prophetical book of the Bible, the Book of Revelation describes the Day of Judgment that Christians have been awaiting since Jesus' ascension to heaven. Even the Sermon on the Mount cannot really be understood without the assertion so often made by Jesus that "the Kingdom of God is at hand." Early Christians expected the imminent arrival of this kingdom. Sharing this expectation, John composed his now famed apocalypse in the 1st century on the Greek island of Patmos. Biblical scholars think this account was meant to comfort to early Christians during their persecution. God will wreak a terrible justice on those who do not believe. His angels will punish the evildoers: "And the second angel poured his bowl into the sea; and it became like the blood of a dead man, and every living thing died that was in the sea." (16:3) According to John's prophecy, however, God causes everything to be created anew: "Then I saw a new heaven and a new earth; for the first heaven and the first earth had passed away … " (21:1)

The Revelation to John should be understood less as a detailed timetable and description of future events, and more as a reference to God's return to earth at an undetermined point in time.

Left: Jesus clarifies the basic principle of his teaching in the Sermon on the Mount. Today, however, it is a matter of dispute whether he actually preached the sermon; instead, it is assumed that the Sermon on the Mount represents a summary of his teachings.

Below: Among the various figures of the Apocalypse are the four horsemen, who ride horses of different colors. They are the heralds of the Day of Judgment, when God himself will judge mankind.

The Holy Sacraments and the Eucharist

The sacraments

Below, left: The preparation of the sacrifice is a central element in Catholic Mass. The transformation of bread and wine into the body and blood of Christ recalls the sacrifice of Jesus, through which he freed humanity from its guilt.

The Catholic Church recognizes seven sacraments (Latin *sacramentum*, "making sacred"): baptism, confirmation, marriage, Communion (Eucharist), penance, anointing of the sick, and the ordination of priests. Anglican Protestant understanding, in contrast, recognizes as a sacrament only what directly emanates from Jesus and presents a visible sign. Protestants therefore recognize only two sacraments as such: baptism and the Eucharist. The others are understood as rites.

Below, right: Babies are usually christened as infants to become part of the Church as soon as possible. Baptists reject infant baptism, requiring profession of faith first. Baptism is a requirement for salvation and a sacrament for most Christian groups.

The Mass

The Catholic Mass consists of several stages: a didactic service, the Eucharist, and sundry hymns and prayers. Normally Mass begins

The Lord's Prayer

The New Testament offers two versions of this prayer attributed to Jesus, in Matthew 6:9–13 and Luke 11:2–4. As the most important prayer for all Christian denominations, it has been incorporated into Christian services of worship since the 5th century.

Our Father, who art in Heaven, hallowed be thy name. Thy kingdom come, thy will be done on Earth as it is in Heaven. Give us this day our daily bread and forgive us our trespasses as we forgive those who trespass against us. Lead us not into temptation, but deliver us from evil. [For thine is the Kingdom, the power and the Glory, for ever.] Amen.

On Sundays, Christians attend church to worship God. No work should be performed on the "Lord's Day."

with a hymn, then a short confession of sins, followed by a reading or Psalm from the Old Testament. A further reading and a Psalm alternate with hymns; then comes the Gospel reading. After a profession of faith, the preparation of the sacrifice is begun with more penance. The priest prays the so-called Consecration of the Host, followed by the holy transubstantiation of the offerings (bread and wine as symbols of the body and blood of Christ, in memory of his sacrifice). After reciting the Lord's Prayer—the most important prayer in all Christian denominations—the faithful receive Communion, but only if they have previously received First Communion and the religious instruction associated with it. Toward the end of the Mass, the congregation usually sings several hymns, after which the priest dismisses them. On special holy days the Mass varies according to the feast. Protestants, by contrast, receive Communion only after they have been confirmed, and the Eucharist is celebrated in a specific Communion service.

The Apostles' Creed

I believe in God the Father Almighty, maker of heaven and earth; And in Jesus Christ his only Son our Lord: who was conceived by the Holy Spirit, born of the Virgin Mary, suffered under Pontius Pilate, was crucified, dead, and buried; the third day he rose from the dead; he ascended into heaven, and sitteth at the right hand of God the Father Almighty; from thence he shall come to judge the quick and the dead. I believe in the Holy Spirit, the holy catholic church, the communion of saints, the forgiveness of sins, the resurrection of the body, and the life everlasting. Amen. (Methodist version)

The Apostles' Creed contains the most important elements of the faith and is recited aloud by the congregation during services of worship in most churches. Although the Creed is generally recognized by all Christian churches, Orthodox congregations recite the Nicene Creed, which only differs from the Apostles' Creed in a few omissions and additions.

Sunday

Sunday is the Christian version of the Jewish Sabbath, the seventh day of the week. This is a day set aside for prayer and the worship of God. In some countries, Sunday observance and the custom of not working on this day has been protected by law and is strictly obeyed, although Sunday working and trading restrictions have increasingly being relaxed or abolished altogether; for example, the Sunday Blue Laws in the USA have been greatly loosened, whereas Sunday trading Laws in Great Britain have practically been repealed altogether.

The Holy Trinity and Mary

Father and the Son as two forms or images of God. This meant Jesus was equivalent to God. Another subordinated Jesus to the Father. The Council could reach no agreement on the issue. The initial debate over the relative positions of the Father and Son soon expanded into a dispute over the nature of the Holy Spirit. Not until the early 5th century was Augustine able to establish the doctrine of the Trinity and its holiness by resorting to the idea of incarnation, and describing the Father, Son, and Holy Spirit as three expressions of one God. In Western Churches, the feast of the Holy Trinity is celebrated the Sunday after Whitsun; in Eastern Orthodox churches, the feast of Whitsun is also the feast of the Trinity.

Marian Apparitions

People occasionally report having personal contact with the Mother of God. The place where these visions have occurred very often becomes the site of a church, monastery or shrine. Among the more famous places are Fatima (Portugal) and Lourdes (France). A number of miraculous healings have occurred at Fatima. According to legend, three children saw the Virgin Mary in 1917 while they were playing. After the children broke their silence about the apparitions, many other people also witnessed miracles at Fatima. In later visions, the children were entrusted with the three secrets of Fatima. In 1930, the bishop of Leiria declared the apparitions credible.

The Trinity: a contradiction in terms?

Above: There are a number of different images of the Holy Trinity. The white dove has become a traditional symbol for the Holy Spirit. God the Father and Jesus are usually illustrated in human form.

Christianity unites monotheism with the idea of "one God in three persons": God the Father, God the Son, and God the Holy Spirit. Historically, this concept has led to problems, because the two ideas appear to be contradictory. The Council of Nicea (312) took up exactly this issue. Although the Trinity was mentioned in many prayers, interpretations of the term differed. One interpretation saw the

Mary, the Holy Mother

According to the Bible, the virgin Mary (Hebrew, Mirjam) conceived Jesus after being informed by an angel that she would bear a child. At the time, Mary was betrothed to her future husband Joseph and lived in Nazareth, in Galilee. The New Testament, especially the Gospel of Luke, has a number of references to Mary, according to which she has several children after Jesus: "Is not this the carpenter, the son of Mary, and brother of James and Joses and Judas and Simon? and are not his sisters here with us?" (Mark 6:3) Mary is also called the Mother of God and the Holy Virgin. Veneration of Mary incorporates heathen notions of a "holy mother" as a symbol of fertility and the renewal of life. For Catholics, Mary is the most highly venerated saint as well as the patron of the Church. Her importance is illustrated by the many holy days dedicated to her. Protestant churches honor Mary as the mother of Jesus, but do not treat her as a holy figure.

Left: Mary is typically represented along with symbols of her "immaculate conception." Lilies, a symbol of purity, are often incorporated into paintings of Mary.

Opposite page, right: Every year hundreds of thousands of pilgrims journey to the Portuguese city of Fatima, where Mary is said to have appeared to three children. Pilgrimage shrines are often built on the sites of Marian apparitions.

The Vatican

The papal state in Rome

Right: In front of Saint Peter's Basilica in Rome is an enormous oval plaza with an obelisk at its center. On solemn occasions—at Easter, for example, when the pope celebrates Mass and pronounces the papal blessing Urbi et Orbi ("to the city and to the world")—the square is filled with people.

Below: Today, Saint Peter's Basilica is the headquarters of the Catholic Church.

The Vatican, the headquarters of the Catholic Church, is a small, independent state inside Rome, the capital of Italy. The Vatican was named after the hill *Mons Vaticanus*, site of an ancient circus where Christians were bloodily executed in the days of the Roman Empire. The apostle Peter is also supposed to be buried here, and Saint Peter's Basilica is named after him. As Rome emerged as the center of Christianity in the 14th century, the Church wanted to underline this supremacy through architecture. Accordingly, over the course of the next two centuries Saint Peter's Basilica and the Apostolic Palace were built on the site of Peter's grave.

Today the Vatican has around 900 inhabitants. The main languages are Italian and

Latin, though other languages are also commonly used. The head of the Vatican is the pope, who is elected by a college of cardinals. Pope Benedict XVI was elected in 2005. He holds judicial, legislative, and executive powers. The pope is considered to be the

Christian symbolism

Over the course of history, the Church has developed numerous symbols, such as the fish or the ship, many of which are still well known and used throughout Christendom today: the dove symbolizes the Holy Spirit; the rose stands for the Christian readiness for martyrdom. The rose—which is also a symbol of Mary—is an important symbol to mystics and many secret organizations, as well. Christianity has also developed a complex symbolism of color, as seen in the use of blue and red for Mary and Jesus. The Mother of God is often portrayed in blue to suggest her uniqueness; and Jesus in red, the color of blood, to reflect his sacrifice. In addition, yellow is a symbol of joy in Christianity, and violet a symbol of penance.

direct successor to Saint Peter. The Swiss Guard, a specially trained security troop, protects the pope and the Vatican.

The history of the Vatican

Originally, the pope was the sovereign of a politically independent church-state. With the Donation of Pippin in 756, the French king promised to cede the areas he conquered in Italy to the Vatican, forming a state that grew into the 15th century. Although the Vatican had been under the protection of the Holy Roman Emperor since the coronation of Charlemagne, it could not always maintain its sovereignty, and thus remained dependent on the powerful within the Empire. During the French Revolution and Napoleonic era, the Vatican's holdings were again reduced. In 1798, the papal state temporarily disappeared when Napoleon created the Roman Republic. Pope Pius VI died in captivity in 1799, but his successor, Pius VII, reached an accord with Napoleon that reestablished the Vatican as a state, and in 1815 the Church even

regained its holdings from 1797. In the 19th century, Rome, like the rest of Europe, faced increasing social and political unrest, which also affected the Vatican. Not until 1929 did Mussolini establish and guarantee the sovereignty of Vatican City in its present form.

The private archives of the Vatican

The private archives of the Vatican currently contain over 30 miles (45 km) of shelving that house all the laws handed down by the Holy See as well as diplomatic correspondence. The archive contains a total of 35,000 volumes including, for example, letters from Michelangelo and Henry VIII. Detached from the Vatican library in the 17th century, the archive remained tightly sealed until the late 19th century. The files through the year 1922 (the year of Pope Benedict XV's death) are now almost completely open to scholars. The late pope John Paul II opened the files between 1922 and 1939 for research—but only insofar as they concerned Germany.

The Swiss Guard is one of the Vatican's official security services. More than two-thirds of the Guard lost their lives during the sack of Rome in 1527. The event is still commemorated by the guards.

Christian Mysticism

Mystics see in Jesus a role model who has succeeded in understanding and living according to the mysteries behind the world. They consider Christ to be the "Great Initiated One."

What is mysticism?

The term mysticism (Greek, *myein*, "to close eyes and lips") refers to how people try to experience the ultimate reality, that is, to undergo a direct experience of the divine. All the great religions of the world have produced schools of mysticism in the course of their theological development. Because mystical experiences are not something that everyone can comprehend, they have always been surrounded by an aura of secrecy and mystery. Whereas the aim of the yoga tradition of Asiatic cultures is to forget the self in order to gain deeper understanding, the Christian mystic retains consciousness of self, and seeks a dialogue between it and divine truth. Christ is regarded as the great teacher by Christian mystics, who begin by focusing not on his death on the cross, but on his life. They see Jesus as having been initiated or consecrated into the secrets of life and

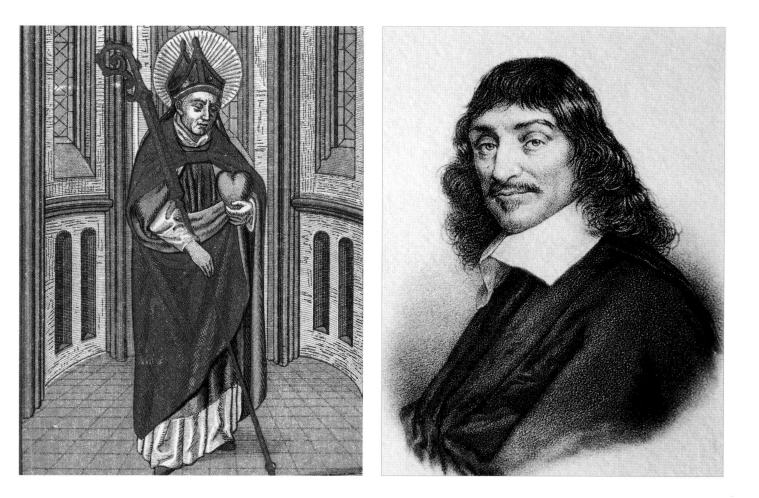

possessing direct experience of the mystery. Christ therefore acts as a pioneer on the path the mystics are attempting to follow.

The search for eternity

Mystics rarely speak of their experiences: someone who has experienced the transcendental cannot often find the words to express it. The mystic is seeking inner perfection along with liberation from earthly bonds in order to overcome the cleft between this world and the world beyond. Christians believe, however, that this can be achieved only with God's help; Christian mystics call this transcendence the *unio mystica*.

Saint Augustine (ca. 350–430)

The theologian and philosopher Augustine (Latin, "the exalted") has been decisive in the formulation of Western thought. He composed both theological and scientific texts, and his philosophy contains Platonic elements. Born to a Christian mother in a North

African city, he himself only accepted baptism and Christianity as an adult. Of decisive importance for the later development of this great teacher of the Church was the fact that he pursued a relatively wild lifestyle, in which he left few sins untried, for decades prior to his conversion to Christianity. In 389, Augustine established a monk-like community on his country estate: the *servi dei* (Latin, "servants of God").

Augustine propounded the notion of the duality of body and soul. In his search for truth, he saw thought itself as proof for his own existence. Later, the French philosopher René Descartes (1596–1650) would express this idea in his famous statement *cogito, ergo sum* ("I think, therefore I am"). Augustine entered the mystic tradition when he began to search for the truth within himself. He came to the conclusion that the ultimate truth rests with God, who grants it to human beings through enlightenment. Augustine understood the Trinity as three equal existences, and considered time a purely subjective phenomenon.

Above, left: After many years of wild living, Augustine let himself be baptized and began to seek the truth within himself. He was an advocate of the concept of the dualism of soul and body.

Above, right: The French philosopher René Descartes (1596–1650) re-expressed Augustine's teaching in his famous formulation, "I think, therefore I am." This statement became the leitmotif of the Enlightenment.

Hildegard of Bingen (1098–1179)

Hildegard of Bingen still remains a fascinating figure today. She was born the tenth child of her family and considered herself a simple and uneducated person, yet became abbess of a cloister near Bingen, Germany, and occupied herself not only with religion, but also politics and medicine. With great care, she collated ancient knowledge about herbs and other plants in her writings. Neither did she shy from recording her visions and, with the help of an amanuensis, published them in Latin. She composed her most important work, *Liber Scivias Domini* (*sci vias Domini*, "Recognize the Lord's Way") over a period of six years, and is said to have healed a blind boy with water, as well as other people through the laying on of hands. Her immense medical knowledge, evident in her writings, places them among the most important works of the 12th century, and far beyond. Already during her lifetime she was considered the "German

prophetess" and a great mystic with supernatural visions. "I am wrapped in the embrace of God's secrets," she declared, explaining that she saw what was hidden as if she had gazed into a great mirror in full consciousness.

Thomas Aquinas (1225–1274)

Aquinas was born in 1225 to Duke Lanulf, who sent him to a monastery as a child in preparation for a later political career. Thomas, however, decided to become a monk, and entered the Dominican order. On his travels, Aquinas also studied with Albertus Magnus. He defined God as pure being; everything else only participates in this being, a tree, for example, to a lesser degree than a person. His writings are not only of importance to religious theory and ethics, but also to politics and philosophy. His pronouncements on religious freedom are especially impressive: for example, that a person who firmly believes that he can find God outside the Catholic Church is justified, not before the Church,

Above left: An illustration from Hildegard of Bingen's renowned work Liber Divinorum Operum. Hildegard occupied herself a great deal with gathering and disseminating medical knowledge.

Above right: The young Cusanus studied various branches of knowledge, and developed the thesis that God is a union of opposites. With this thought, he was way ahead of his time.

but before God: he must make the case for his decision alone before God. Aquinas' proofs of God's existence became well known from his main work, the *Summa Theologica*. In 1323, he was canonized (declared a saint), and in 1879, his work was accepted as a basis of the Catholic school, and has since had a lasting influence on the faith.

Meister Eckhart (1260–1327)

Little is known about Meister Eckhart's actual life. We do know that he entered the Dominican order in 1275. His teachings saw in God the process of life. In his work *Questiones* (Latin, "questions"), Eckhart describes God's outpouring of his being and relating back to himself as a process of creation. Accordingly, creation is omnipresent and without beginning or end. Creation is taking place at all times, and exactly this is the essence of God. For God to be "born" into a person, the person must learn to let go of all material things; in order to live for God's sake, the person must give up their own will. Furthermore, Eckhard declared that God is nothing, possessing none of the characteristics of finite existence, and neither images nor terms can describe him. For this reason, people should not try to form a concept of what God is like. Eckhard argued that people imagine God to be like a cow that they can milk with requests and wishes. But precisely that is mistaken!

Nicolas of Cusa, or Cusanus (1401–1464)

Born the son of the merchant Johann Cryfftz, Nicolas of Cusa initially studied mathematics, physics, philosophy, medicine, and law—and later theology—in Heidelberg, Padua, and Cologne. This universal scholar quickly rose to the position of cardinal and was soon playing a central role in the church politics of the day. He is considered the most important philosopher of the 15th century. His philosophic-mystical thought defines the transition from the Middle Ages to the modern age. He anticipated such physical laws as gravity and the rotation of the Earth. Cusanus, as he was respectfully called, understood God as the Coincidence of Opposites, the *coincidentia oppositorum*. As a result, neither God nor the universe can be understood rationally. Every religion in turn reflects only some portion of divine truth, because each is only able to understand partial aspects of God, in whom all contradictions are united. For the Middle Ages, this was an outrageous and daring thought.

Thomas Aquinas, depicted here standing with an unknown patron, is one of the most important thinkers of the Western world. He emphasized the importance of knowledge in addition to faith.

Life after Death

Awaiting the Day of Judgment

The goal of a Christian life is to live without sin and, as a reward, to spend eternity with God after death. This is supposed to take place in heaven, a place free from cares, where angels praise God, and humans, who have been damned to exercise free choice since their fall from grace in the Garden of Eden, finally experience their long-desired rest. For when the Adam and Eve ate the fruit of the tree of knowledge despite a divine command not to do so, they were expelled from this paradise.

From this time onward, humankind has been burdened by this sin—the human ability to turn against God—the so-called original sin that is passed on from generation to generation. Upon death, Christians fall into a kind of sleep of the dead while they await the Day of Judgment, when God will separate the just from the unjust.

The Son of God and mystics

Jesus is "God become man," and thereby embodies one of the great mysteries of Christianity. Some scholars see Christ chiefly as a model teacher who had incorporated the secret mystic truths so completely that he was regarded as the son of God. With his death on the cross, Jesus symbolically took humanity's guilt onto himself, thereby freeing the human race from original sin and renewing the covenant God had once made with Moses. Life after death opens a whole new perspective for humans by giving them hope that everything does not end with death.

Purgatory and hell

According to Christian understanding, purgatory is a place of purification, of cleansing. Here the soul receives a final chance to cleanse itself of sin and prepare itself for

Christians believe in the Day of Judgment when God will separate the sinners from those who have lived a life free from sin. The former, however, receive a chance to do penance for their sins in purgatory.

A Christian burial

Christians are buried according to precise funeral protocols. Sometimes, church members find their last resting place in a cemetery belonging to their church. According to Christian ritual, the body must be buried as a whole in order to guarantee resurrection at the time of the Last Judgment. Cremation, by contrast, destroys the body; however this practice has become more and more common in recent decades. The ashes of the dead are then placed in an urn and either buried in a cemetery or strewn to the winds. Those attending a funeral usually wear black, the color of mourning. After a short church service, the mourners form a procession to accompany the coffin to the cemetery. There, with a few words of farewell, the coffin is lowered into the earth, and friends and relatives can take their last leave with wreathes of flowers.

Because the body is supposed to remain intact for the Day of Judgment, Christians are traditionally buried in a coffin that is laid in the ground.

heaven. The fires of purgatory are not to be mistaken for hell, however. According to the medieval imagination, purgatory is a crater made by Lucifer as he fell from paradise. In purgatory, sinners repent for their sins and are tormented by devils and other spirits. God's presence can already be felt there, but souls feel unworthy, and therefore cleanse themselves through sorrow and suffering for their sins. Hell, on the other hand, is a place of sheer suffering. It is divided into various areas in which sinners are punished according to the severity of the sins they committed during their lifetime.

Sinners are usually depicted in illustrations of purgatory raising their arms and eyes pleadingly toward Heaven. They still hope to reach heaven. Sinners in hell, by contrast, cannot hope to do so.

Life in the Christian Faith
The Church Building

The structure of a Church

Below, left: Cologne Cathedral is one of the world's most famous Gothic churches. Its many columns and buttresses reduce the burden on its walls, allowing a more filigree structure with many windows.

Below, right: The central nave of Cologne Cathedral is 141 feet (43 m) high; the side aisles, 62 feet (19 m). The cathedral holds around 4000 people.

The church is the place where Christians come together—they believe—in the presence of God to pray and worship. Traditionally, a church that is the seat of the bishop of a city or region is designated a cathedral, from the Greek word *kathedra*, meaning chair. In ancient Greece, the king's throne stood at the far end of a gabled rectangular *basilika*, or king's hall. Early Christians adopted both this basic architectural form and its terminology for their houses of worship.

Earlier European churches, in particular, have many architectural features in common. For example, most were built along an east-west axis with a large central nave flanked by one or more side aisles on each side, separated from one another and the main nave by rows of weight-bearing columns. Often transepts intercepted the main nave in a north-south direction: from a bird's-eye view, the church thus had the form of a cross. The main nave extends into the so-called choir and terminates in the sanctuary, containing the apse and the altar (in place of the throne where the king or judge once sat). Today, important churches are often called basilicas, regardless of their architectural structure.

The Gothic church

Church construction in Europe began to blossom around the year 1000, initially in the

Left: It is no longer possible to recognize many modern churches as such by their architecture, such as Notre-Dame-du-Haut (Ronchamp, France), designed by Le Corbusier. The church was begun in 1950 and dedicated in 1954. To the right, one can recognize the exterior choir, with a freestanding altar and pulpit.

heavier, solid Romanesque style before it was replaced by the medieval Gothic style, with its upward-striving, pointed arches and gables. Many important European churches contain Gothic elements: the Burgundian pointed arch, combined with ribbed vaults, made possible larger windows that flooded the interior with light. The weight was borne by slender columns, aided by exterior flying buttresses. Large stained-glass windows and filigree architecture gave an overall impression of monumental lightness, reaching up to heaven itself. Cologne Cathedral in Germany (begun 1248) epitomizes this style; similarly, Saint Veit's Cathedral in Prague (begun 1344) exhibits the typical Gothic exterior form, separating the interior of the church from the sinful outer world. In many cases, exterior walls are decorated with drain spouts in the form of gargoyles, whose monstrous forms symbolized the threats constantly confronting mankind. In this same period, secular architects began to design sacral buildings, a task that until then had been done by the clergy. Masons' guilds arose and have left their marks and symbols on individual churches.

Below: Salisbury Cathedral in England displays the form of a cross, formed when the middle nave is intersected by two transepts. Originally intended as a means of creating more space inside the church, the cruciform was subsequently adopted for its symbolic character.

Different forms of church buildings

The function of a church determines its designation. A *cathedral* (Greek *kathedra* = chair) is a church that is also the seat of a bishop. The suffix *-minster* (Latin *monasterium* = monastery), as in Westminster Abbey, originally referred to a church that was part of a monastery; later, the original structure sometimes expanded into a large church and became a bishop's seat; thus the word *cathedral* and the suffix *-minster* are often used synonymously. *Chapel* (Latin *capella*) denotes a small structure. It may stand alone or be part of a larger complex, as in a hospital. Large churches often include one or more chapels. In the UK, *chapel* is sometimes used to denote a non-Anglican Protestant house of worship as opposed to an Anglican *church*.

Feasts of the Church Calendar

Above, left: Easter celebrates Christ's resurrection, three days after his death on the cross (Good Friday).

Above, right: Children love to celebrate Easter. Because it coincides with the coming of spring, Easter is usually associated with colored eggs and nests, bunnies and chicks, symbolizing the return of life.

Church holy days

With one exception, the recurring cycle of traditional Church holy days traces the life of Jesus: birth (Christmas); baptism (Epiphany in the Orthodox churches, the Feast of the Magi in the West); Good Friday and Easter (crucifixion and resurrection); Ascension Thursday and Pentecost or Whitsun, (commemorating the descent of the holy Spirit to Jesus' disciples and the founding of the Church). Good Friday and Easter are approximately at the same time as the Jewish feast of Passover; Pentecost and Ascension Thursday also have parallels to Jewish feasts. The original function of baptism as an initiation ceremony into the religious community changed into a ritual to symbolize acceptance into Roman society itself. Formal entry into society now began with baptism, but admittance to the Eucharistic celebration, the Communion, was restricted to those who had undergone religious instruction culminating in Confirmation, a ritual signaling final entry into the Christian community.

Easter, the feast of the resurrection

Easter, which celebrates the mysteries of the crucifixion and resurrection of Jesus, is considered the most important Christian feast. Because the date of Easter is determined by the spring moon, the feast is movable: it falls between the end of March and the third week in April, and is preceded by a forty-day period of fasting. Present-day Easter customs are a mixture of Christian and heathen customs. Easter, the feast of the resurrection, coincides with the awakening of nature in spring; accordingly, fertility symbols, such as rabbits, chickens and eggs, all find a place in the celebrations of various countries.

The Ascension and Pentecost

The Feast of the Ascension is celebrated forty days after Easter, followed ten days later by Pentecost (Whitsun). Historically dating from the year 130, Pentecost celebrates the descent of the Holy Spirit to the disciples and the founding of the Church. Various regional customs for the feast exist, for example decorating a Pentecost pole, or holding a procession. Traditionally, Ascension falls on a Thursday. It celebrates Christ's ascension into heaven without leaving a corpse behind. In some countries, such as Austria, Switzerland and parts of Germany, it is a legal holiday; here Father's Day is celebrated on the same day—again incorporating Christian and non-Christian customs.

Corpus Christi

In June, ten days to two weeks after Pentecost comes the primarily Catholic feast of Corpus Christi, first celebrated in 1264. The date varies from region to region since it is a moveable feast, and in some countries, such as the United States, it is observed on the first Sunday following Trinity Sunday. The Latin word *corpus* means body, and refers to the Eucharistic body of Christ. Traditionally, processions commemorate the feast, with the monstrance—a decorated golden, usually cruciform, container with the Host, or Eucharistic wafer—carried through the streets for all to see. In some regions, Communion children wearing white dresses and suits take part in the procession. The procession halts at four open-air altars along the route. Here the congrega-tion makes so-called intercessional prayers for "a particular person" and the priest imparts God's blessing. The idea behind such processions is that the followers are "God's pilgrims," who gather around Christ, the "Bread of Life."

At the Council of Trent (1545–1563), the feast of Corpus Christi took on the character of a demonstration of power against Protestantism. In reaction, Protestant peasants in areas with a mixed religious population, such as Switzerland, resorted to provocative protests: they spread dung on their fields precisely on this day. Catholic peasants took their revenge by doing likewise on Good Friday, to the annoyance of the Protestants.

In many regions, processions take place on Corpus Christi, in which the Eucharistic body of Christ is carried through the streets.

Above: In Catholic regions, people decorate the graves of their dead with flowers and candles on the feast of All Saints, November 1.

tries, children parade through the streets with lanterns, act out the scene, and ask for sweets, an old tradition. Earlier, a tenth of the annual harvest was delivered to the lord of the manor on this day. The custom of roasting a Martin's goose stems from those days: the lord had the right to the fattest goose and chicken.

Christmas

In winter, Christians observe the birth of Jesus at Christmas (Christ + Mass). Since the date of Christ's birth is unknown, the celebration was set for the birth of the pagan sun god on the evening of December 24 and the following day, December 25.

All Saints' Day, All Souls' Day

In the West, November 1 is a day of collective veneration for all saints, and in some places is a legal holiday. In the Eastern Church, the feast is celebrated a week after Pentecost. All Souls' Day, dedicated to the dead, is the day after All Saints' Day. On this day, the faithful decorate graves with flowers and candles and reflect on those departed. Traditionally, most Protestants celebrate Reformation Day on the day before All Saints' Day. Today, most Lutheran churches have moved this day to the Sunday (called Reformation Sunday) on or before October 31 and transferred All Saints' Day to the Sunday on or after November 1.

Saint Partrick's Day, Saint Martin's Day

Throughout the Church calendar, there are days devoted to various saints. Some are national patrons, such as Saint Patrick of Ireland, and their feast days are often national holidays (Saint Patrick's Day, March 17). In other cases, saints' special deeds are honored on their feast days. For instance, the legend that Martin of Tours (317–397) cut his cloak in half to share with a beggar is celebrated on November 11, Saint Martin's Day. It symbolizes the Christian duty to share with the needy. In some coun-

Right, box: Saint Nicolas is one of the most popular saints in Christendom. Filling shoes or socks with presents refers to the old legend that Saint Nicolas secretly gave gifts to three poor maidens in one night.

Saint Nicolas is coming!

The feast of Saint Nicolas on December 6 commemorates Saint Nicolas of Myra (ca. 270–343). Born in present-day Turkey, Nicolas donated all his wealth to the poor when he became a priest at the age of 19. Many legends surround Nicolas, and he is regarded as one of the most important Catholic saints. The patron saint of merchants and children, Nicolas has also been adopted by seafarers and lawyers. Originally, the feast of Saint Nicolas was the day of gift-giving, rather than Christmas; children made little boats or set their boots in front of the door in the evening, hoping to find them filled with presents the next day.

The Christ Child, the angel and Santa Claus

Until the Reformation, Saint Nicolas was the bringer of gifts. Protestants, however, don't acknowledge the canonization of saints. The day of gift-giving was therefore moved to December 24, so the presents could come from the Christ Child. But the image of the Christ Child soon changed to an angel-like being, whose original companion, the servant Ruprecht, first became Father Christmas and later, Santa Claus. Today, Christmas traditions vary throughout the world, with the Christ Child, the angel, Father Christmas, and Santa Claus all bringing gifts, according to the region.

Christmas celebrates the incarnation of God in the person of his son, Jesus, and has been a Church holy day since 336. Today it is chiefly a family holiday: extended family gathers and gifts are exchanged. In most countries, both December 25 and 26 are legal holidays. Many families decorate a Christmas tree indoors, and Santa Claus, Father Christmas, or the Christmas Angel leaves gifts for the children (see box, left). In some northern European countries, Christmas is combined with the old Germanic Yule Feast celebrating the winter solstice.

The Eastern Orthodox churches celebrate Christmas on January 6. In Catholic countries, this is Epiphany, the feast of the Magi, or Three Wise Men: see Matthew 2:1–12.

Lantern-lit processions take place in many German towns to commemorate Saint Martin. The legend that Martin cut his cloak in half to share it with a poor man is then re-enacted.

The Church in the Third Millennium

The search for the meaning of life

Many people today are searching for something that transcends daily life. As in earlier centuries, people are still plagued by questions about the meaning of life: What do we live for? What happens after death? Many answers are offered; in many ways the Church's answers no longer satisfy people. As a result they seek alternatives, often in the realm of the esoteric, with the promise of a direct religious experience. A mix of various religions, the contents of esotericism are often distant from the original teachings.

Many mainstream churches see their task in the third millennium mainly in the social arena. Where society has failed, there is a pressing need for Christian service to their neighbors. The array of services ranges from programs to counter growing violence among the young (also in schools) by conveying humane and social values, to caring for the poor and troubled, to running hospices, which offer the terminally ill the chance to depart this life in peace, under the psychological care of specially trained personnel. This is an important task that has brought churches growing respect in recent years.

The church worldwide

In recent years, the traditional churches in the West have experienced an unmitigated decline in membership. Many people feel the

Faith in God plays a larger role in the poorer regions of the world than it does in the West. People in the Third World look to the Church as a source of education and political support.

church fails to respect their views and is divorced from everyday life; especially in the area of sexuality, it does not take them seriously. In recent years, themes like abortion, "the pill," celibacy, and the ordination of women have driven many Roman Catholics from their church—though not from faith itself. The result has been too few young people choosing to become priests and the deconsecrating of redundant churches. Despite closures, there is still a veritable dearth of priests to serve the existing church communities. If the Catholic Church were to open itself further to women, the situation would improve. This question is related to the issue of celibacy. It remains to be seen whether Pope Benedict XVI will manage to establish a forum and initiate discussion of this sensitive issue among the cardinals and bishops.

By contrast, so-called Third World countries are moving in the opposite direction: on Sundays, churches are as full as ever. In Latin America, China, and parts of Africa, people see the church as a source of education and political help. In the Philippines, the Catholic Church is a strong force in everyday life and has great political influence. It is no accident that through the engagement of priests like Ernosto Cardenal (born 1925) the churches of Nicaragua are full, for Cardenal represents a Christian religion and a "theology of liberation" that stands up against state oppression and injustice. The same phenomenon seems to be at work in China, even if this is denied by the government in Beijing.

Evangelical missionaries have met with remarkable success in the countries of South America and Africa, and more fundamental forms of Christianity have long been extending their influence and growing in confidence in the developed countries. Born again evangelism has been remarkably successful in setting the social and political agenda in the USA, among other places, while making use of modern technology to spread its message to ever wider audiences.

Above: In recent years, traditional churches have been losing members. Reasons include not only insufficient proselytizing among the young, but also uncompromising and apparently outdated views on such themes as sexuality and contraception.

Left: A hospice provides support for the terminally ill. The expert care they receive often provides relief for the families of the dying, as well, and allows them to spend their last days in pleasant surroundings, which make it easier for them to bear their fate.

Ecumenism

The World Council of Churches (WCC) is the main international ecumenical organization. With its headquarters in Geneva, Switzerland, and a membership of over 340 churches and denominations, it can claim about 550 million Christian members in more than 120 countries. Members of the Council include almost all the world's Orthodox Churches, many Protestant churches—such as the Anglican Communion, some Baptists, many Lutheran, Methodist, and Reformed churches—as well a wide range of independent churches.

The world's largest Christian community, the Roman Catholic Church, is not a member of the council, although it does send representatives to all important Council conferences, meetings of the Central Committee, and General Assemblies. The Catholic Church has worked closely with the Council for many years and the Vatican nominates twelve members to the Faith and Order Commission of the WCC. Although not a member of the WCC itself, the Roman Catholic Church is a member of some of the regional and national ecumenical bodies.

Delegates from member churches meet every seven years in an assembly that elects a Central Committee to govern the Council between assemblies. A wide range of ecumenical, evangelical, and social commissions report to the Central Committee.

Successes

The most significant success of the WCC has been to increase understanding and acceptance between various Christian groups and denominations. The activities of the Faith and Order Commission have fostered mutual understanding and respect. The aim of the WCC has not been to seek the organic union of various Christian denominations, but to facilitate dialogue and support local, national, and regional efforts at cooperation.

The WCC coordinates ecumenical, evangelical, and social actions of both its member churches and other religious and social organizations. The Faith and Order Commission has been successful in moving toward consensus on such issues as baptism, the Eucharist, ministry, the date of Easter, the nature and purpose of the church (ecclesiology), and biblical interpretation. Material for the annual Week of Prayer for Christian Unity is prepared jointly with the Roman Catholic Church.

The YMCA and YWCA sprung up as unions of young Christians who, among various other activities, also spend their free time together.

Current WCC social programs include an international campaign to combat AIDS, "A Decade to Overcome Violence," and an initiative called Justice, Peace and Creation.

Controversy

However, some of the Council's actions have been controversial, including alleged funding of revolutionary groups engaged in violent struggle in the 1970s. The WCC also faced criticism for being biased against Israel, alleging that it had not given other humanitarian crises as much attention as that in Palestine.

Orthodox and Evangelical churches are trying to redefine their relationship with the Council and clarify the WCC's limited authority to speak on their behalf. Some churches have decided not to join the WCC because they regard it to be overly liberal and left-wing.

World Youth Day

Each year, scores of young Christians gather for a few days to celebrate, discuss the basic questions of life, and pray. The event is held in a different city each time, around the world, uniting people from many walks of life in faith.

In the summer of 2005, Pope Benedict XIV attended the 25th annual World Youth Day held in Cologne, Germany. The event drew hundreds of thousands young people from all over the world to share their ideas and be near the pope—even if few came as close as those in the picture.

Missionary Work

At the Sea of Galilee, Jesus preached to his disciples that they must spread his message throughout the world, laying the foundations for Christian missionary work.

"I will make you fishers of men" (Matthew 4:19)

Jesus' command to his disciples on the Sea of Galilee has had a lasting effect on the faithful. In the course of their religion's 2000-year history, Christians have continually sought to spread their faith, to convert heathens and announce God's salvation to unbelievers. Since the Crusades to the Holy Land in the Middle Ages, innumerable "heathens" have fallen victim to Christian missionary zeal: at times, those who didn't want to believe even paid with their lives. Christianization has again and again been coupled with military subjugation. In addition, the Church also appropriated sites holy to other traditions to build its own houses of worship, and heathen feasts were given a Christian meaning.

Today missionary work is combined with economic and social development, especially in countries of the so-called Third World, where wells, hospitals and schools are being built. The Christian message is taught in those schools, albeit accompanied by technical knowledge and ethical values. Today's

Missionary work in Africa

Today, Christian missionaries in African countries are primarily engaged in helping the people to become self-sufficient. They do not attempt to force a "foreign" religion on them, but guide them to help themselves and to stengthen their own economic basis. The missionaries sustain orphanages, schools where people can learn crafts and household skills, primary schools, and even boarding schools. They understand their mission as being called to be servants to the African people and helpers in the name of their church and the love of Jesus to support the growth and independence of local communities.

Above: Mother Theresa was also known as the "Angel of the Poor." She devoted her life to the poor of Calcutta. Shortly after her death, she was officially beatified by Pope John Paul II.

Opposite page, box: In Morogoro, Tanzania, the Faraja Trust founded a project for children and orphans of parents who suffer from AIDS.

missionaries have more often made it their personal credo to avoid arrogance and Christian condescension that those of previous centuries. At the same time, it cannot be denied that missionary work has helped many peoples connect with the scientific and technological world, whose values are largely Christian.

Mother Theresa, the saint of the slums

Born in Skopje, Macedonia, Agnes Gonxha Bojaxhio (1910–1997) was already venerated as a saint by Christians around the world within her own lifetime. Furthermore, the

Catholic nun and founder of the order Missionaries of Charity was awarded the Nobel Peace Prize in 1979. On October 19, 2003, she was beatified by Pope John Paul II. At age 18, she entered the Loreto order, which operated schools in India. For seventeen years, she taught at Saint Mary's School in Calcutta and eventually became the school's director. However, she felt a calling to help the poor. When she founded her own order in 1950, she had already become an Indian citizen. From that point on, she devoted her life to the care of the sick and dying (especially lepers). In the course of her work, Mother Theresa founded both hospices and orphanages for Indian children.

The Search for Peace

A retreat at a monastery

Many people are seeking a way to understand their lives, to find meaning. Staying for a time in a monastery can be an important step to that end. Monasteries, once closed to the public, today offer rooms to those seeking peace of mind. The thick monastery walls are a barrier to stress. Meals are eaten together and, depending on the monastery, guests may also participate in the services. No one, however, is bound to submit to the daily routine of the monastery: many prefer to make sojourns into the surrounding countryside instead. The peaceful and uniform days in a monastery exert a magical effect on stressed contemporaries. Whether one takes a walk in the countryside or shows interest in monastic daily life, many monasteries are now oriented toward visitors and gladly welcome them. Some also offer seminars within their buildings. Cloisters that abide by the oath of silence have been the subject of special interest in recent times.

Pilgrimage to Compostela

Pilgrimages and longer journeys on foot are another way to find spiritual focus. A very popular, ancient route is the pilgrimage to

---

Cloister

The cloister (Latin *claudere*, "to close") refers to the area of a monastery or convent that is accessible only to members of the order. Here, the monks or nuns live among themselves. Their cells, hallways, dormitory, dining room and their rooms for working and reading are normally closed off to outsiders or visitors. Sometimes the monks are also forbidden to leave a certain area. The word cloister can also refer to intense concentration on a goal and the associated withdrawal from the outside world.

the tomb of Saint James, one of Jesus' twelve apostles, in Santiago de Compostela in northern Spain. Pilgrims have been making the journey to his tomb since the Middle Ages: Saint James' shells served as proof that one had actually reached the goal, and they were said to be freed from all their sins.

For some, the route has become a kind of alternative vacation for those wanting to walk a long distance with like-minded souls. In 1987, the European Commission designated the pilgrimage route—actually many routes from all directions of the compass that meet in Campostela—as a European Cultural Route. The final 60 to 120 miles (100–200 km) of the trek are made on foot, horseback, or bicycle, in order to experience what it means to journey as a pilgrim. For many, this this proves to be an intense experience. Pilgrims' participation in stages of the route is confirmed at stations along the way. Many books have been written about the pilgrimage route to Campostella. *The Pilgrimage: A Contemporary Quest for Ancient Wisdom* by Paul Coelho is one recent bestseller.

Opposite page: In recent years, young people are also again showing interest in monastic life. The uninterrupted peace of everyday life in a cloister is attractive to the stress-plagued people of today.

Left: In many places along the way, shells mark the pilgrimage route to Saint James tomb. Usually they are stone markers. Earlier, shells were confirmation that the pilgrimage had been carried out properly: the pilgrims attached them to their clothing.

Below: According to legend, Santiago de Compostela is the final burial site of Saint James. This church has been an important pilgrimage site since the Middle Ages.

ISLAM

The Origins and History of Islam
Introduction

The religion that came out of the desert

Mohammed received his divine revelations at the age of 40 in a cave called Ghar Hira near Mecca, in what is now Saudi Arabia. Before that, the Prophet had been living in the desert for several decades and was fully aware of its dangers. Life in the desert is harsh, and people living in such an environment are aware that they can only survive by following strict rules within a strong community. The desert welds people together because survival requires them to maintain close relationships among themselves.

During the first centuries of the Islamic calendar, i.e. from the 7th century AD onward, this unconditional solidarity within the tribe played an important part in the rise of the Islamized Arabs to become a world power. Conversely, the Islamic belief in a single, powerful God strengthened the confidence of the nomads who had renounced polytheism to become Muslims: functioning communities could be established in a shorter period of time when held together by a single strong God, rather than many gods.

Desert values

One God—Allah—and one law—Sharia—one tribe and one common faith: much of what defines Arabs and their culture has been shaped, if not exclusively, then to a significant extent by the living conditions of the desert. Understanding Islam as it is practiced in the Arab world and its importance in the third millennium of the Common Era requires recognition of the influence of the desert. To name just one aspect, the desert provides the background for the emergence of such timeless values as strong family loyalty and tribal cohesion.

The harsh living conditions in the desert give rise to values such as a strong sense of community and discipline, providing the foundations for the Islamic faith.

The Prophet Mohammed

Mohammed's early life

Mohammed (also Muhammad) was born in approximately 570 AD in Mecca, in present-day Saudi Arabia. Long before Mohammed was born, his mother, Amina, is said to have heard the voice of an angel, who prophesied: "The son you are expecting shall be the Lord and Prophet of your people."

Mohammed's father died shortly before his son was born, and his mother also died when the boy was only 6 years old. Little else is known about Mohammed's childhood, youth, and early adulthood. He is generally described as shy and reserved, but outgoing when among friends. Mohammed is said to have had a warm smile and to have spoken in a precise manner, articulating each individual syllable.

Muslims reject depictions of the Prophet, yet his outward appearance might still be sketched based on the descriptions in the sources that have survived.

Above: Mecca, Mohammed's birthplace, is now one of the most modern cities in Saudi Arabia. It attracts millions of pilgrims every year.

A birthmark the size of a dove's egg

Mohammed was frequently in a hurry, making it hard for people who wanted to accompany him to keep up. His beard became one of the most important religious symbols and a source of many precious relics. A great number of mosques believe they they are in possession of hairs from his beard. These relics are kept in ornate containers and, it goes without saying, are closely guarded.

Mohammed had a birthmark the size of a dove's egg between his shoulder blades. It is said that the monk Bahira was able to identify the boy as the promised Prophet by this distinctive sign.

Left: A Muslim clergyman presents a glass container with a lock of hair from Mohammed's beard to the faithful. It is one of Islam's most precious relics.

Idolatry in a barren land

Mohammed grew up as an orphan in Mecca. According to the Koran, Mecca is located in a "plantless valley." This refers to the largely arid Arabian Peninsula, 1250 miles (2000 km) long and 750 miles (1200 km) wide, which in pre-Islamic times was mainly desert with the occasional oasis. Summers in and around Mecca were, and still are, hot; in winter, the region experiences heavy rainfall and occasional tempestuous storms. Long periods of drought are not unknown. The particular geography of Arabia had considerable influence on Mohammed's life story. He understood at an early age that life here is harsh and unforgiving.

The Days of Ignorance

The people Mohammed encountered as a young man were Arab nomads, most of whom tried to make a living by raising livestock, hunting, and a little trading, which frequently required them to travel at length. During the first half of the 6th century AD, it was common for caravans to be attacked and robbed, except for three particular months.

In the seventh, eleventh, and twelfth months of the lunar year, all warriors of the various tribes convened as pilgrims on Mecca, temporarily setting their quarrels aside. Muslims refer to this pre-Islamic time as the "Days of Ignorance" (*Ayyam al-Jahiliyah*), when the Arabs worshipped many gods and followed various rites, including fertility rituals and rain-making. The religious ideas of the majority of Arabs were only vague, albeit strongly influenced by magic. However, they did not believe in life after death.

Kaaba and Mecca

Before the rise of Islam, the center of the prevailing polytheistic religion was a square temple called Kaaba, which is said to have been built by Abraham as a place for sacrifice. According to the Muslim faith, Abraham was a *hanif*, a seeker of truth (and a precursor to the Muslims in that sense), who during the era of idolatry believed in the one and only God and submitted himself unconditionally to God's commandments. For several generations, the Quraish, Mohammed's tribe, had been the custodians of this sacred site in Mecca, which had already become the

During pre-Islamic times, referred to as the "Days of Ignorance," hostile Arab nomadic tribes gathered peacefully in Mecca three times a year as pilgrims, ceasing hostilities for the duration of their stay.

economic and religious center of the Arab world. The Arab world was not a unified political unit at that time, but was fragmented into a great number of tribal areas.

The Trustworthy One

Even before Mohammed became the Prophet at the age of 40, people who knew him referred to him as the Trustworthy One, because he had proven himself as an arbiter in a religious dispute. The argument was about where to best set up the black stone that is revered at the Kaaba. While one party was pointing this way and the other that way, Mohammed settled the quarrel by placing the black stone on a cloak and giving one of its corners to each of the representatives of the various tribes. This way, they carried the stone to its destination together.

Mohammed's wife

As a young man, Mohammed became an employee of the wealthy widow Khadijah, for whom he undertook several trade journeys to Syria. Khadijah was so impressed by Mohammed that she married him, bearing him seven children—including Fatima, who is revered as the Prophet's favorite daughter in parts of the Islamic world (by Shia Muslims). Mohammed remained faithful to Khadijah as

long as she lived. After her death, however, he is said to have married at least nine other women. A statement ascribed to Mohammed, "Marriage is my Sunnah," became a guiding principle for the relationship of Muslim men and women. Sunnah, the body of traditions and law based on the words and life of Mohammed, is binding for all Muslims. Another saying attributed to Mohammed is, "Paradise lies at the feet of mothers."

Above: The Kaaba, a windowless cubic temple covered by black brocade, is located in the inner courtyard of the Sacred Mosque in Mecca.

Below: The Kaaba is said to have been built by Abraham and his son Ishmael and used by them as a sacrificial site.

Footprints and use of the right hand

In Islamic countries, religious relics are of great importance—including stones said to show the Prophet's footprint. Legend has it that Mohammed's foot left an impression in the rock at the Al-Aqsa Mosque in Jerusalem during his Night Journey on a winged horse.

It should thus come as no surprise that believers continue to find stones with imprints said to resemble the Prophet's footprint. Such stones are revered and often touched, followed by passing one's hand over one's own head and upper body. This way, Mohammed's blessing is passed on to the believer.

It is also important to Muslims that Mohammed is said to have done everything with his right hand, at least as far as eating, drinking and business matters were concerned. The left hand was reserved for cleaning oneself after defecating, which is why to this day, many Muslims won't touch their food with the left hand.

Right: The Al-Aqsa Mosque in Jerusalem. Legend has it that Mohammed left his footprint when he briefly stopped here during his Night Journey on a winged horse.

Below: The cave in which Mohammed experienced his first divine revelation was close to the mountain Hira near Mecca.

Called to be God's Prophet

When Mohammed was about 40 years old, he would regularly retreat to a cave near the mountain Hira outside of Mecca to pray.

Mohammed fasted and meditated, and then received his first revelation from God, an experience he found deeply unsettling and, initially, confusing. He heard a voice that told him: "Arise and warn!" Just like the

prophets of the Old Testament, Mohammed, encouraged by his wife, Khadijah, now considered it his duty to convince people to change and renounce idolatry. Mohammed was strengthened in his duty to fulfill God's will exclusively from then on by visionary experiences: the Archangel Gabriel appeared to him repeatedly, urging him on.

The Prophet's Night Journey

Mohammed's "Night Journey" is another of these visionary experiences. In it, God took the Prophet to Jerusalem, from where he ascended to heaven riding a mythical creature and was instructed to introduce the five daily prayers that have characterized the Muslim ritual of faith ever since.

Mohammed was deeply agitated by this experience and sometimes afraid. For three years, he refused to make public what God had revealed to him; he only spoke about his visions with his family and a small circle of people he trusted. However, his message did not stay confined to this intimate circle for long, and more and more men and women converted to Islam, "until the fame of it spread throughout Mecca, and it began to be talked about." (1)

Mohammed preached that submission to God's will is what God expects from his creatures. He had finally accepted that he was God's Prophet.

Mohammed as a religious leader

Without doubt, Mohammed's achievement lies in his emphasis of the central and exclusive importance of the one God, Allah, to all Arabs and the entire creation. "There is no deity except God," the Prophet says. Everything else is a tin god, an idol, man-made. After realizing this, Mohammed had all the idols that had been set up in the Kaaba destroyed, except for representations of Jesus and Mary. Submission to God's will—the meaning of the word "Islam" (which might also be derived from Arabic *salaam*, meaning peace)—is the Prophet's central message. Consequently, those who submit themselves to God completely call themselves Muslims.

However, it was not long before Mohammed had to leave Mecca: his increasingly

uncompromising nature had turned the brewing conflict with the residents of Mecca, who saw their traditional lifestyle threatened by his message, into open hostility.

God took Mohammed, riding on a mythical creature, on the so-called Night Journey that culminated in Mohammed's ascension to heaven, where he was commanded to establish the practice of the five daily prayers.

The first four caliphs and the spread of Islam

The first four caliphs, or leaders of Islam after the Prophet's death, are known as the Rightly-Guided Caliphs. They emerged from the circle of the Prophet's closest confidants and saw their primary role in the governing of the community and the execution of the law. From this point on, Islam spread like a wildfire: Syria became an Islamic country as early as 636, Egypt followed in 641, and Persia in 642. In 674, Muslims stormed Constantinople, in 696 they conquered Carthage, and in 711 they crossed the Strait of Gibraltar to Spain. In 732, they encountered the Frankish troops of Charles Martel, who defeated them at Poitiers, France, stopping their advance.

Mohammed's Successors

The Shias and the Twelver Shia

Following Mohammed's death, the ensuing dispute about his succession soon led to a split between the Sunni majority and the party (*shia* in Arabic) of Caliph Ali ibn Abi Talib, the Shia. The Sunnis, the largest religious group in the Islamic world (ca. 90 percent), see themselves as followers of the Sunnah (tradition) of the Prophet. The political disagreements that led to a schism among believers, dividing them into two camps after the Prophet's death, led to theological disagreements, as well.

This led to the emergence of Shia, or Shiite, Islam, which today is found mainly in Iraq, Lebanon, and Bahrain. Most Shias are part of the so-called Twelver Shia. This religious group differs from Sunni Islam mostly in that they do not recognize the authority of the first three caliphs: Abu Bakr (632–634), Umar (634–644), and Uthman (644–656).

Hussain, Mohammed's grandson, died in the Battle of Karbala in present-day Iraq. He was a fighter for the faith and is revered as a martyr by Shia Muslims.

Instead, they believe only the direct descendants of Mohammed, twelve in number and called imams, are the legitimate carriers of Islamic tradition and understanding.

The Twelver Shia

The legal succession of the imams is called the Twelver Shia, twelve men descended from Ali, the Prophet's son-in-law. The twelfth imam, Mohammed Al-Muntazar, disappeared as a child in 874 and will remain forever the "hidden imam" to Shia Muslims; some Shia groups even deny he was ever born. From the eleventh imam's death in 873 until 939, four "deputies" claimed to be in contact with the twelfth and to act at his behest, carrying out his instructions. It is said that at the end of time the (twelfth) imam will reappear as the *Mahdi*, the "Rightly-Guided," to restore justice like a messiah.

Other Shia beliefs

Shia Muslims grieve the death of Hussain, Mohammed's grandson, who was killed in a massacre in present-day Iraq in 681. To this day, the martyrdom of Hussain moves his followers to acts of self-mortification. Shias also revere Ali, their religious founder; in fact, their name means "Ali's party" (Ali's *shia*). In everyday life, Shia Muslims—as opposed to Sunnis—are allowed to engage in temporary marriage, thereby making it possible to deny their faith in times of religious persecution.

The Sevener Shia

Another group, the Sevener Shia, recognize just seven imams. They keep their teachings secret. This group includes the Ismailis, who describe God mainly through negative statements: God is neither existent nor non-existent, neither powerful nor powerless, etc. The Ismailis derive their name from the seventh, hidden imam, Mohammed ibn Ismail. They interpret the Koran allegorically rather than literally, which has led to a mystic and esoteric exegetic practice. Today, about 18 million Ismailis live in East Africa, India, Afghanistan, and Central Asia.

Above: For Shia Muslims, the holy shrine of Imam Reza is the most important sanctuary. Every year, about 20 million of the faithful pilgrimage to this site in present-day Iran.

Left: Shia Muslims regard an imam to be the rightful successor to Mohammed. Only imams are considered capable of comprehending the deeper meaning of the Koran.

The Islamic calendar

The Islamic calendar follows the course of the moon over twelve months. It is therefore, ten or eleven days shorter than the sun-based Gregorian calendar, depending on the phases of the moon. Over a period of 32.5 years, it runs in the opposite direction to the Gregorian calendar ("backward," so to speak). Depending on the moon's phase a single month has 29 or 30 days. Since time adjustment occurs at every new moon, the Islamic calendar does not require corrections like leap years.

The Development of Islam

An archway in the Alhambra, a city fortress in Granada, Spain. The Alhambra is an outstanding example of the Moorish style of Islamic architecture.

Baghdad: the center of Islamic theology

After Mohammed's death in 632 AD, close confidants initially ruled over the astonishingly quickly expanding Muslim empire. In numerous conflicts within the Prophet's tribe, the Umayyad family prevailed. They made Damascus the capital of Islam and ruled there from 661 onward, contributing greatly to the continued expansion of Islam. However, their excessive luxury and corruption increasingly gave offense to pious Muslims. Eventually, in 750, the Abbasids violently overturned the Umayyads.

The Abbasids ruled for nearly 500 years from Baghdad, establishing the city both as a mighty bastion of Islam and the cultural center of the world as it was known at the time. Arguably, the most famous Abbasid caliph is Harun al-Rashid (786–809), whose magnificent court is recounted in the "Arabian Nights." Baghdad became a center for literature, science, music, and fashion, but also for philosophical issues, including the questions of man's free will and the nature of God. Such considerations were strictly rejected by the orthodox legal schools. According to them, no one is allowed to debate or philosophize about the nature of God.

The rise of various centers of Islam

Early in the 10th century, the Fatimids rose to power in the Maghreb (Morocco, Tunisia, and Algeria). They refused allegiance to the Abbasid caliphate in Baghdad and declared themselves caliphs. The Fatimids moved their base to Cairo, the newly-founded capital. At the same time, the Seljuk Dynasty conquered the eastern parts of the Islamic Empire, especially those inhabited by Persian and Turkish peoples, while Spain rose to become the most important Islamic center in the West under a branch of the Umayyads. In the coming centuries, Islam enriched numerous areas of life and science throughout the West; from the mid-8th century until the end of the 15th century, cities like Granada, Cordoba, and Seville were important seats for philosophy, literature, science, and mysticism.

Islam on the Iberian Peninsula

In 711, Tarik Ibn Ziyad and his army arrived on the Iberian Peninsula, coming by way of Mauritania (the source of the name "Moors"). The place where he landed has borne his name ever since: Gibraltar, which means "Mountain of Tarik." Within only four years, the Iberian Peninsula was under Islamic rule, with the exception of a narrow strip of land in the north. Islamic Spain was given the name Al-Andalus, and Cordoba became its center. With the exception of the upper class, the population not only welcomed the arrival of the Muslims, they also considered it as a liberation. This was especially true of the Jewish people, who fought alongside the Muslims and later adopted the Arabic language in gratitude.

Culture and science bloom

Islam brought an enormous body of knowledge to Spain, helping the country blossom intellectually and economically. Muslims made fallow land fertile with their irrigation techniques. New plants were imported, such as the orange from Persia. Other profitable activities involved the production of leather, ceramics, paper, and textiles, all of which were luxury goods in Europe, since the knowledge required for their production was lacking. The sciences blossomed under Islam, as well, including mathematics, astronomy, and medicine. Through the Muslims, all of Europe was exposed to scientific progress, which at first was demonized. It was only several centuries later that these advances were put to use, as in the case of street

lighting: while all the other European towns lay in darkness in the evening, the streets of Spanish towns were illuminated after sunset by outdoor pitch lamps. Architecture was also in full bloom, and we can still marvel at its fruits today in towns such as Cordoba or Granada, site of the world-famous Moorish castle, the Alhambra.

Above: The Ibrahim-al-Ibrahim Mosque on the Rock of Gibraltar was a gift to the people of Gibraltar from King Fahd of Saudi Arabia. To this day, the region's population is 7 percent Muslim. The mosque was consecrated in 1997.

Left: Harun al-Rashid, whose magnificent court is legendary, listens to a poet in a scene from the Arabian Nights. Under his rule, the city of Baghdad experienced a golden age.

Light in the Dark Ages

A golden age of science and culture

Islamic rule in Spain was a great blessing for Spain, and the rest of the Occident benefited, as well. By the mid-10th century, Cordoba was the largest and richest city in Europe. Its population is estimated at about half a million, at a time when no European city (with the exception of Constantinople) could muster more than 30,000 inhabitants. Cordoba became a center for science and boasted a respectable public health and education system. Fifty hospitals, eighty public schools, seventeen institutions of higher education, and twenty public libraries made it the undisputed queen of all European cities of culture. In particular, the size of Cordoba's libraries exceeded anything known in Europe. Some contained hundreds of thousands of books—nothing unusual in the Islamic world, but sensational by European standards: the library of the Monastery of Saint Gallen, for instance, had just under 600 books.

The number of libraries in a town was a symbol of its cultural status. Cordoba, with its twenty public libraries, was at that time the undisputed center of science in Europe.

Arabic numerals

The West became acquainted with the numeric system through the Arabs, who in turn had learned it from the Indians (to this day, Arabs refer to them as "Indian numerals"). People in India began to count and calculate with numerals around 300 BC. In an intermediate step, before the full development of positional notation, the value of each position was explicitly indicated (e. g. 6T, 7H, 4T, 2O for 6742). In the 6th century AD, when the Arabs became acquainted with positional notation, the Indians had already fully developed it. From that point forward, written calculation was possible.

Equally important was the invention of the number "zero." When Arabic numerals became known in the West, people had particular difficulty grasping the concept of "zero." In the West, Pope Sylvester II propagated the new numeric system around the year 999 AD; Sylvester had had contact with the caliphate in Cordoba as a young man.

The discovery of zero

Soon after their introduction, some of the Arabic numerals retained their Arabic names in Europe. Four, for instance, was *arbas*, and eight was *temenias*. The zero was not introduced to the West until the 11th century: Arabic *sifr* led to the word "cipher," and "zero" and "decipher" are also derived from it. Numerals were originally called figures, and only zero was referred to as "cipher." But this distinction was confusing, and the common people called all numerals "ciphers." This is why the term *nulla figura*—"not a figure"—was introduced, which turned into "nulla," and eventually became "null."

Left: The West became acquainted with Arabic numerals through the Arabs, though they were actually developed in India. Prior to that, the more complicated Roman numerals were in use.

Below: In 785, Caliph Abd ar-Rahman had a mosque built in Cordoba. It was the third largest mosque in the world. Some 860 marble columns support this arched construction.

Egypt and Mad Al-Hakim

Relations between religions

During the 10th and 11th centuries, Egypt established itself as the strongest power in the Arabic-Islamic world. As late as the 9th century, the majority of the population had still been Christian. In order not to endanger traditional trade relations, good relations with Christians and Jews in other countries were important to Muslims. This is one reason why the Fatimid rulers of Egypt treated their Christian and Jewish subjects with extraordinary consideration. Egypt has retained its own character within the Islamic world to this day.

A mad ruler?

The atmosphere of tolerance was disturbed by the despotic rule of the Fatimid Al-Hakim (996–1021). Al-Hakim implemented draconian measures: he forbid all fermented drinks and certain foods, astrologists were persecuted, and women were not allowed to leave their houses. Disobedience was punishable with death. Around 1008, Al-Hakim started brutal persecution of Jews and Christians. He banned them from drinking wine and eating pork, and re-introduced the discriminatory dress regulations that required Jews to wear a bell around their necks. At the same time, preachers announced that Hakim represented divine reason, the highest incarnation of God outside his unfathomable being. Today, the Druze, a community that lives in modern-day south Lebanon, southwest Syria and northern Israel, still adhere to this doctrine. After Al-Hakim's death, they believed that he had been "hidden" and will return on Judgment Day as the messianic Mahdi.

Followers of the doctrine of Al-Hakim can still be found today among the Druze, a community that lives in Lebanon and elsewhere.

The Hashshashin

The first suicide attackers in history

The Hashshashin were Ismailis, a religious splinter group within Islam. They managed to survive as a secret society from the 11th century onward, until they were expelled by the Mongols in the 13th century. Their fortress was Alamut, located close to the Caspian Sea in present-day Iran. The Hashshashin were the first to establish an efficient and, above all, enduring organization for the purpose of using terrorism as a political weapon. For their assassinations, they always used a dagger, never poison, which often would have been easier. A Hashshashin would not usually try to flee after his action, since surviving a mission was seen as something shameful.

The Old Man of the Mountain

Hashshashin actions were a combination of cold-blooded planning and religious fanaticism. Their precept of absolutely secrecy guaranteed both security from the outside world and internal solidarity. This created strong internal social cohesion, led by a charismatic, coolly calculating leader: Hassan-i-Sabah, known as the "Old Man of the Mountain," who succeeded in gathering an enormous number of followers around him. Many people died for him at his command.

Power and enticement

For centuries, the *Hashshashin* (meaning "hash smokers" in Arabic) have been shrouded in sometimes blood-curdling legends of assassinations (their name survives in the words "to assassinate" in English and *l'assassin* in French), religious fanaticism, and hired killers. There is no doubt that they threatened Islamic princes and Crusaders. Like the devil, the Hashshashin turned into "Angels of Light" (to quote a contemporary description) by imitating the gestures, clothes, language,

Above: Alamut, the mountain located in present-day Iran, where the first suicide attackers in history had their fortress. The fort has been destroyed.

Jihad: the holy war

The "holy war" is mentioned in the Koran, but is interpreted in various ways. Sura 48:13 reads: "Anyone who refuses to believe in God and His messenger, we have prepared for the disbelievers a hellfire." On the one hand, this supreme battle takes place within each person in the form of the individual's struggle on their journey to God, with the goal of purifying oneself and showing charity toward others.

But Mohammed's successors also interpreted the expression in a more literal and deadly sense: the first "holy war" took place in 624 AD with the Battle of Badr. Throughout the history of Islam, "holy wars" have been waged and legitimized in religious terms in order to expand the scope of Islam.

Heavily armed combat and willingness to give up one's life in "holy war" is not the only interpretation of the term "jihad."

customs, and behavior of many nations and peoples in order to achieve their murderous goals. They killed to order. In 1192, for instance, the designated heir to the French throne, Conrad de Montferat, was assassinated. The Hashshashin considered their own lives to be of little value. The Old Man of the Mountain is said to have gave a memorable demonstration of this and his own power in the presence of Crusaders—on

Alamut, his fortress, he ordered two Hashshashin to jump to their deaths. To the horror of the Christian observers, the two men did not hesitate to follow his order.

The Hashshashin and the Crusaders

The Crusaders' mightiest fort was the Krak des Chevaliers near Maysaf in present-day Syria. It was a virtually unconquerable for-

The Krak des Chevaliers (a combination of French and Arabic, meaning "knights' fortress") was the Crusaders' mightiest fort, located near Maysaf in modern-day Syria. The Hashshashin entered into temporary alliances with their European brothers-in-arms.

Drugs and a secret garden

One of the many stories told about the Hashshashin concerns their alleged use of drugs. Many scholars believe that in preparation for an assignment, a Hashshashin would spend the night in a legendary secret garden near Alamut that was praised as a foretaste of paradise by the Old Man of the Mountain. It is assumed that he gave some kind of drugs to his assassins, possibly hashish, to enhance their powers of imagination and make

the garden appear paradisiacally beautiful. Legend has it that a wonderful, refreshing lake enticed them to swim, and there were girls prettier than anything a Hashshashin had seen before. Without doubt this had to be paradise!

Shortly before sunrise, it was time for the men to depart from the garden again. But afterward, they were ready to die for what they had seen and the beauty they had experienced.

Scholars assume that Hassan-i-Sabah gave drugs like hashish to his followers before sending them to the secret garden in order to prepare them for their mission.

tress. Christian crusaders and Islamic Hashshashin became allies in their fight against the Sunni princes in Persia. This pact included the exchange of information, but also strategic alliances for certain targets—such as the conquest plans of the Christian knights. The Old Man of the Mountain, in his shrewdness, had realized that his usual strategy of killing the most important man in an organization, such as a prince, wouldn't have got him anywhere in this case. The Crusaders would have immediately re-assigned the position to someone else from their own ranks. Instead, the Old Man of the Mountain entered a pact with the Crusader knights, and he even paid tribute to them when required to do so.

The end of Alamut

Alamut's walls were stormed in 1256 by a Mongol assault. The Mongols, with their swiftly operating hordes on horseback and powerful composite bows, swept over the country and its people like a hurricane. Almost everything and everyone fell prey to their attacks. The "Eagle's Nest" bitterly resisted them for three long years. Eventually, however, the Mongols stormed the Hashshashin fort and burned Alamut to the ground.

The wealth of Alamut, with its observatory and a collection of scientific, religious, and philosophical writings without match, was destroyed almost completely during the Mongol raid around 1260. Only a few documents were saved by the Sunni secretary of the Mongolian leader, including the autobiography of the Old Man of the Mountain, Hassan-i-Sabah. It would later become the basis of a book on the Hashshashin, written by the secretary.

Today, descendents of the long peaceful Hashshashin still live scattered across the Middle East and Southeast Asia.

The Mongol attack sealed the fate of the Hashshashin. The Mongols swept over the country like a hurricane. After three years of fierce fighting, they eventually stormed the fortress of Alamut and burned it to the ground.

From the Mongols to the Ottomans

The Mongol reign

In 1258, the last Abbasid caliph of Baghdad fell to the Mongols, who had begun raiding the Islamic Empire in that century. The Crusades also took place during this period. The Crusaders had held Jerusalem since 1099 and had successfully stood their ground against the Muslims for many years. Their eventual conqueror was Salah al-Din (1137–1193). A descendent of the Kurdish Ayyubid Dynasty, he became sultan of Greater Syria and Egypt, and drove the Crusaders from the Holy Land. The Mongols, on the other hand, were not defeated; they were instead Islamized. Previously to this, they had almost broken the power of Islam—not least due to the support of neighboring Christian countries—bringing Islamic culture to the verge of extinction. As a result of their wide-ranging conquests, the Mongols opened trade routes from one end of Asia to the other.

The Mongols ruled the land for hundreds of years before the Ottomans finally invaded and brought their empire to an end.

Far left: Crusaders had occupied Jerusalem ever since the battle of 1099. Eventually, the Mongols defeated them and drove them from the Holy Land.

Left: Selim I, also known as Selim "The Grim," was sultan of the Ottoman Empire from 1512 to 1520 after deposing his own father.

The Ottomans assume power

In Egypt, the Ayyubid were superseded by the Mamluks, whose 75-year-long reign of Egypt as the center of the Islamic world guaranteed a certain amount of military stability. However, discovery of the Americas at the end of the 15th century and the newly established sea route between Portugal and India were major setbacks for the Mamluk rule. In 1516/17 their state fell to the Ottomans, who had been steadily expanding since the 14th century. What was more, from 1550 on, Islam completed its expansion in the countries around the Indian Ocean. In 1453, Byzantium (Constantinople) was conquered by Mehmed II, ending the thousand-year existence of the Eastern Roman Empire.

The Ottoman reign

Under Ottoman leadership, Asia Minor slowly became unified again. Early in the 16th century, the Ottomans successfully made themselves the rulers of all of Mesopotamia, the Land of the Two Rivers between the Euphrates and the Tigris. In 1517, Selim (1512–1520) and his superior firearms put an end to the Mamluk state. Under Selim (1512–1520) and Süleyman (1520–1566), the Ottoman Empire reached the peak of its power. When the Ottomans advanced as far as Yemen and Algeria, the empire spanned the entire Arabic-speaking world, and with the conquest of Rhodes (1522), Cyprus (1570), and Crete (1669), they also gained control over sea travel and trade in the Mediterranean. Although the Islamic kingdom of Granada was forced back into the European Christian fold in 1492, Islam nevertheless gained new ground in the cultures of Black Africa and Southeast Asia.

Islam 1502–1668

1502: Reign of the Safavid Dynasty in Persia. The Shia faith becomes the state religion.

1529: The Turks, under the leadership of Süleyman the Magnificent, besiege Vienna.

1550 onward: Spread of Islam to India and Indonesia.

1571: Victory of the Venetians and Spaniards over the Turks at the Battle of Lepanto.

1666: Sabbatai Zevi (1626–1676), Jew and self-proclaimed messiah, converts to Islam when Ottoman authorities present him with the choice between execution or conversion. This was interpreted as the *tikkun* ("repairing") of the Islamic world that had been captured by evil powers.

1668: Second siege of Vienna and Turkish threat to Central Europe.

Islam in Modern Times

The West and Islam

From the 18th century onward, the influence of the West and its culture and political structures in formerly Islamic countries steadily increased. A strict separation of state and religion is entirely foreign to Islam; yet this is precisely what was attempted under Western influence. European laws were applied to Islamic states in a form that was to some extent unacceptable to Muslims. Only Turkey, under Kemal Atatürk, has adopted a form of government close to the Western model.

Since 1975, Islamic countries have often tried to repel Western influence. At the same time, fundamentalism, showing its murderous face in the form of terrorism, has awoken. By its very principles, Islam is a faith based on peace, which is why it is important for

In 1979, Ayatollah Khomeini proclaimed the Islamic Republic of Iran, following the overthrow of the Shah of Iran. He installed a theocracy and introduced the rule of the Sharia in Iran. Was this the beginning of Islamic fundamentalism?

the Western world to take a good look at the justification of those who revolt against Western dominance, how it is done, and for what reasons.

Between Islamism and separation from the West

Twenty-first century Islam is still finding its way, searching for a means to come to terms with Western values without losing its own compass. What is called laicism in Western societies, namely the strict separation of church and state, has thus far been difficult to conceive of in the Islamic countries, because that would necessarily mean keeping Allah's laws out of significant aspects of human life. One exception is Turkey, which has codified secularization (understood there as the subordination of religion to the secular government) in its constitution. On the other hand, civil law (called *kanun madani*) exists alongside religious law (Sharia) in many Islamic countries.

Differences between Western and Islamic ways of thinking are also evident in other areas, for example, in Islamic banking. The Koran forbids Muslims to collect or be paid interest. It is a point of debate whether this

applies only to unreasonably high interest, which is known as usury, or to any and all interest. Islamic modernists favor the former interpretation of the prohibition, in order not to have to exclude themselves from international business practices However, the majority of Muslims clearly understand it to have a deeper meaning. In fact, an entire system of Islamic banking that complies with Sharia has developed to accomodate Muslims, who might otherwise be unable to purchase a car or a house, for example.

With regards to the situation of women, in a large number of Islamic countries—including Pakistan, for instance—there are increasing numbers of women in academia, and Muslim girls and young women have access to schooling and professional training in broad sections of the Islamic world. Nonetheless, the rate of illiteracy

among Muslim women remains significantly higher than it is among their brothers in the faith.

Since the devastating attacks of September 11, 2001, Islamic fundamentalism has shown itself to be a force for global terrorism in a series of violent and deadly attacks in many countries, not only in the West, but also in Turkey, Bali, Iraq, Afghanistan, Saudi Arabia, and more. As a result, the West is extensively supporting those Islamic countries that are in the process of building up democratic structures. The vision of a more dynamic Islam, one that adapts to the actualities of the twenty-first century and even changes with respect to democracy and human rights, does not have to remain a utopian vision. As it says in the Koran, "Thus, God does not change the condition of any people unless they themselves make the decision to change." (sura 13:11)

Political events in the Islamic world from 1770 to the present

From 1770 until about 1950, a slow process of conquest and subjugation of the Muslim peoples of North Africa, Saudi Arabia, India, and the Middle East through the French and the British took place. In the countries affected, Islam was strongly imprinted with European-Christian culture.

1745: The sect of Wahhabism is established by Mohammed Ibn Abd al Wahhab, who reforms Islam in Arabia from 1780 onward.

19th century: Development of the schismatic schools of the (Sunni) Ahmadiyya and Baha'i religions (see pages 294–297). Weakening of the Ottoman Empire through Western powers. Establishment of European colonies and protectorates in Islamic territories (India, Egypt, North Africa).

1878: British occupation of Egypt.

1880–1920: Rise of Pan-Islamism.

1881–1898: Revolt of the Mahdi (sees himself as Islamic leader sent to prepare people for the end of the world and Last Judgment) in the Sudan.

The Shah of Iran—Mohammed Reza Pahlavi— established a police system that terrorized people.

1900 onward: Settlement of Palestine by Jewish immigrants.

1916: The Middle East is divided by France and Great Britain into spheres of interest; Palestine comes under international, Syria under French, and Mesopotamia under British administration.

1917: The Balfour Declaration: during World War I, Britain promises the Jews a "national homeland" in Palestine.

1921: Faisal I appointed King of Iraq by the British. Abdullah, his brother, becomes King of Transjordan.

1922: Kemal Atatürk (1923–1938) implements the separation of state and religion in Turkey and abolishes the Ottoman sultanate. End of the Ottoman Empire.

1924: The Turkish caliphate is abolished.

1926: The Turkish National Assembly decides to adopt Swiss civil law.

1940 onward: Gradual liberation of Islamic states from European hegemony in the countries of Jordan, Syria, Egypt, and Algeria.

1945: Founding of the Arab League in Cairo.

1947: The UN issues a recommendation to split the British mandated territory of Palestine into a Jewish and a Palestinian-Arabic state. The consequence: beginning of heavy fighting between Arabs and Jews. Pakistan becomes an independent Islamic state.

1948: Founding of the state of Israel, proclaimed by David Ben Gurion. First Arab-Israeli War.

1948: New civil law in Egypt, based on a Western model.

1949: New civil law in Syria.

1950 onward: Gradual spread of Islam to central Africa.

1963: Reforms known as the "White Revolution" by Shah Reza Pahlavi in Iran. A military coup in Syria brings the Ba'ath Party to power.

1967 and 1973: Wars of the Arab-Islamic states against Israel.

1969: Colonel Muammar Gaddafi organizes a coup in Libya and becomes president of the Libyan Arab Republic.

1971: Hafez al-Assad becomes president of Syria after a coup. Establishment of the United Arab Emirates.

1975 onward: Increasing suppression of Western European and Christian culture in Islamic states. Awakening of radical Islamic fundamentalism.

1979: Shah's regime in Iran is overthrown; "Islamic Republic of Iran" proclaimed by Ayatollah Khomeini. The establishment of a theocratic state and the reintroduction of the Sharia in Iran made the general public in the West aware of Islamic fundamentalism as a movement opposed to Western culture, religion, and civilization.

1980–1988: First Gulf War, outbreak of war between Iran and Iraq (under Saddam Hussein).

1981: President Anwar Sadat is assassinated in Cairo.

1982: Death of King Khalid of Saudi Arabia.

1989: Death of Ayatollah Khomeini.

1991: Second Gulf War. The US and allied troops end Iraqi occupation of Kuwait.

2001: Taliban regime in Afghanistan is overthrown by the US and the Afghan Northern Alliance. The war against the Al-Qaeda terrorist organization is triggered by the September 11 attacks in New York.

2003: Third Gulf War, led by the US and Western allies. Saddam Hussein's regime is overthrown.

Islamic Beliefs and Philosophy
Islam's Understanding of Itself and the Five Pillars of Faith

Perfection in Islam

"Every child is born with a natural predis-position toward the right faith. It is the parents who turn him into a Jew or a Christian or a sorcerer," writes Elias Khoury, born in Beirut in 1948, one of today's leading Arab intellectuals and author of novels and plays with a critical view of social affairs in the Middle East. His opinion reflects the basic Islamic assumption that both the perfect and the original religion of humanity are realized in Islam. To be a non-Muslim, therefore, is to be in a state of imperfection, although the existence of various religious communities is described as a divinely ordained test in the Koran: "Had God willed, He could have made you one congregation. But He thus puts you to the test through the revelations

He has given each of you. You shall compete in righteousness. To God is your final des-tiny—all of you—then He will inform you of everything you had disputed." (sura 5:48).

Confessing Islam and apostasy

Just as there is no formal procedure for ad-mission to Islam (such as baptism or confir-mation in the Catholic Church), there is also no established rite for secession: basically, apostasy from the community is not anti-cipated. Losing faith in Islam, like adultery and murder, is the kind of sin traditionally punished with death. In Europe, this punish-ment was last carried out in 1843 in the Ottoman Empire.

While the Koran does not give any explicit reason for this sanction, it leaves no

Five times a day, at fixed hours, a Muslim faces the direction of Mecca and prays the salat, the ritual prayer. It is left to the believer to decide whether, where, and when they pray in addition to that.

Far left: Believers should face in the direction of Mecca when they pray. Nomads in the desert orient themselves according to the position of the sun.

will unite their beliefs and their actions in everyday life into a unified whole. There is no separation between private beliefs and public actions.

The second pillar: Salat, the act of prayer

Muslims may pray as often as they wish; however, at five times each day—at sunrise, noon, afternoon, sunset, and at night— prayer is mandatory and is called *salat*, the ritual prayer. Apart from that, prayer is a private matter (*du'a*), and largely up to the believer. The following requirements have to be followed when performing *salat*:

1. *Salat* has to be performed in a state of ritual purity, which requires washing the hands, elbows, face, ears, and feet as well as wetting the hair.
2. The times of day (sunrise, noon, etc.) are predetermined.
3. The prayer has to be performed in Arabic.
4. The person praying has to face Mecca.

Left: Islam derives its view of itself solely from the Koran. This 1200-year-old copy is kept in Srinagar.

doubt that disbelief will not be without consequences from God: "Those who disbelieve and repel from the path of God, then die as disbelievers, God will never forgive them." (sura 47:34). Also, Mohammed is reported to have said: "If someone leaves the faith, do not punish them with God's punishment, but kill them with the sword." (2)

The five pillars of Islam

All Muslims are subject to five definite obligations. These five "pillars" are mutually supporting and together shape the ethical nature of the ideal Muslim.

The first pillar: Shahadah, the Islamic profession of faith

"There is no god but Allah, and Mohammed is His messenger." Stating this profession of faith, called the *shahadah*, aloud before two witnesses is enough to make a person a Muslim, also on the formal level—that is, provided the verbal commitment to God is echoed in the person's inner attitude. A Muslim must recognize first and foremost that God is in their thoughts and heart. As a consequence of this religious stance, Muslims

The Friday prayer at the mosque

Once a week, on Fridays, the faithful congregate at noon in a mosque for the public Friday prayer. They pray in long rows alongside one another, regardless of social standing or wealth, as equals among equals—and equals before God. When bowing their heads in prayer, their foreheads touch the floor. The Prophet is reported to have said that one single prayer performed at the mosque is worth twenty-five prayers performed at home. A prayer at the Kaaba is thought to be worth 100,000 prayers.

The third pillar: Sawm, fasting during the month of Ramadan

Above: Evening prayer in the Great Mosque in Mecca. Muslims should undertake a pilgrimage to Mecca at least once in their lives. Visiting Mohammed's grave is part of such a pilgrimage. Every year, hundreds of thousands of Muslims follow this commandment.

Right: The Kaaba, covered with black brocade—here believers can be seen standing in front of it, praying with their arms raised—is supposedly the first site where God was worshipped.

The ninth month in the Islamic lunar calendar is Ramadan, the month of fasting. The Prophet Mohammed received his first revelations in this month. During Ramadan, believers are not supposed to eat or drink during the day, nor are they allowed to indulge in worldly pleasures. At sunset, when the muezzin calls from the nearby mosque, the fast may be broken until sunrise the next morning. The purpose of fasting is to "empty oneself" before God. The tradition of breaking the fast after sunset is a festive occasion during which believers become aware of their fellow people, which is why emphasis is placed on sharing the meal with relatives and friends. Afterward, a Muslim should also give food to the poor.

The fourth pillar: Zakat, charity

In Islam it is a compulsory obligation to help those who are poor and in need, and to support them financially. That some are rich or wealthier than their neighbors is God's doing. In order to show their awareness of this fact, they must share with the poor. Boasting about good deeds invalidates the donation (*sadaqah*), however. Though some Islamic countries levy social contributions (*zakat*), this does not free an individual from the obligation to give voluntary alms. The tax is only intended to support Islam and those whose hearts are yet to be won.

The fifth pillar: Hajj, pilgrimage to Mecca

Once in their lifetime, all who are physically and financially able to do so must visit the city of Mecca. This pilgrimage to the Holy Kaaba in Mecca and other nearby pilgrimage sites traditionally takes place during the last month of the Islamic year. During the Hajj, various rites are performed that Mohammed himself performed. For example, the believer waits at the Plains of Arafat near Mecca, wrapped in a shroud as on the day of resurrection, assuring God: "Here I am at your disposal!" The Kaaba is covered with black brocade embroidered with verses from the Koran in gold. It is believed to be a holy site built by Abraham and his first son, Ishmael, making it the first place in the world where God was worshipped. With millions of people undertaking the pilgrimage, Moslem individuals find themselves part of one great community.

Another part of the Hajj is visiting the tomb of Mohammed in Medina, where tradition has it that prayers and supplications uttered sincerely are never denied.

During the fasting month of Ramadan, fasting is ended by the call of the muezzin at sunset, indicating it is time to break the fast. The ensuing meal with relatives is a festive occasion.

The Koran

The origin of the Koran

The bridge over the main highway connecting Mecca and Jeddah is a representation of an open Koran.

The Koran consists of 114 suras (chapters), sorted by length (with very few exceptions), comprising 6,219 verses in all. Each sura has a unique name: sura 2, for instance, also the longest one, is called The Cow. The names don't necessarily convey anything about the sura's subject matter. Each sura, with the exception of sura 9, The Repentance, starts with the *basmala*, a formula that says "In the name of Allah, most gracious, most merciful," considered an integral part of the original sura form. Suras are loosely strung together statements, not chronologically ordered according to the order of their revelation. The sequences within the suras were compiled at a later stage. The text of the Koran is divided into thirty sections and is written in poetic form (rhyme-prose).

Mohammed's dictation

Originally, the Koran was recited mainly from memory rather than read. Mohammed did not receive his revelations all at once, but gradually over the course of twenty-two years, and every time he received one, he recounted it word for word. His dictations were not only memorized by a great number of Muslims, they were also recorded in writing: on leather, wood, parchment, palm leaves, silk cloths, flat stones, bleached shoulder blades, and more. Even today, the texts of the Koran have entered the memory of a large part of the community through regular liturgical recitation.

Oral tradition

Mohammed received the texts of the Koran in the Hira Cave near Mecca, where the Archangel Gabriel presented him with a cloth bearing the word of God; however, Mohammed, could not read it because he is thought to have been illiterate. The angel therefore recited God's words. Besides the ongoing written recording of the Koran following the Prophet's revelations, another oral tradition emerged during Mohammed's lifetime: the Hadith, sayings by the Prophet that were passed on orally. They were not compiled in their current form until the 9th

and 10th centuries. Along with the Koran, this tradition represents the second most important source of religious instruction.

One Hadith tells of the death of a great number of Koran scholars, about 700, in the Battle of Yamama in 633: "Many sections of the Koran that have been revealed [by Mohammed] were known to those who died on the day of Yamama—but they were not known to those who survived. They had not yet been written down at that time." (3) Thus, parts of the revelation have been irretrievably lost because of the death of those who memorized the Koran. The form of the Koran valid today was only determined by the third caliph, Uthman (644–656), who had all other versions destroyed.

Above: A particularly magnificent copy of the Koran—written in gold on blue parchment—is on view at the Museum for Islamic Art in Kairouan, Tunisia. It is the probably the only Koran of its kind.

Left: The Koran was revealed to Mohammed in the Cave of Hira near Mecca. The Archangel Gabriel handed Mohammed a white cloth bearing the word of Allah, but ended up reading the words out loud, since Mohammed is said to have been illiterate.

Language of the Koran

For Muslims, the Koran is a literal revelation from Allah—and the Arabic language of the Koran is inspired by God. From the Islamic viewpoint, the language of the Koran is Arabic, and is of unsurpassable harmony and perfection because it is the language of Allah. This is why there has frequently been opposition to translations of the Koran into other languages, which can only be regarded at best as "interpretations" of the Arabic original; some reject them entirely. In the Koran, Allah speaks to humankind as "I" or "We". He was not created, but exists in eternity in the Seventh Heaven. Here lies the divine original.

Contents of the Koran

The Book of Allah addresses five main subjects: the Last Judgment, including hell and paradise; biblical themes; legal provisions and theological discourse; ethical and social principles; and religious rules and duties. The Koran refers to the Hebrew Bible several times and mentions Abraham, Moses, King David, and other persons. Compared to the earlier sources, however, the reports are significantly modified, and historical facts are assumed to be known. The Jesus of the New Testament is regarded as an important prophet by the Koran; the idea of him being the Son of God, however, is firmly rejected, as is his death on the cross. According to the Koran, someone else died at the cross in Jesus' place (cf. sura 4:157). The Koran sees itself as a continuation of what Allah revealed to these earlier prophets.

Textual changes in the Koran

Individual statements in the Koran have been altered after their revelation, in the sense that one Koran verse has been made to follow another, thus modifying or qualifying the latter verse. These statements, which sometimes can be interpreted as contradictory, were known as the "interpreted word of Allah." Moreover, it is said that Satan also transmitted false passages to Mohammed, which were later changed. The title of *The Satanic Verses*, a novel published by British writer Salman Rushdie in 1988, is a play on these circumstances.

The Koran after the death of Mohammed

The Koran has the following to say about the alteration of the text after its first revelation: "None of our revelations do we abrogate or cause to be forgotten, but we substitute something better or similar: Knowest thou not that Allah hath power over all things?" (2) In order to interpret the suras properly it is important to date them properly, for, in the event of a contradiction, the younger text overrides the older one. After the death of Mohammed, Zaid-ibn Thabith was commissioned with compiling and writing down the Koran. It is recorded that at least three revelations have been excluded, and therefore, critics doubt the completeness of the Koran, as well as the claim that the Koran is an exact copy of the divine original.

Be that as it may, one principle holds true: any kind of criticism of the Koran is forbidden because no human has the right to do so.

To a Muslim, the Koran is Allah's work, and no human being is therefore entitled to interpret or criticize it. Mohammed was only God's instrument for composing the Koran.

The Koran also recognizes the Jesus of the Christian New Testament; however, he is regarded neither as the most important prophet nor as the son of God. His self-sacrifice on the cross is also denied in Islam.

The divine original of the Koran

Muslims believe that the Koran is an identical copy of the heavenly original—without the punctuation, headings, or ordering of the text into suras. All the parts of any earlier "books"—i. e., the Hebrew scriptures and the New Testament, which partially contradict the Koran—are seen as falsifications. According to the view of most Islamic scholars, the Koran cannot be interpreted without the texts that had been passed on from the Prophet orally (the Hadiths). As rich a source as they are, however, the Hadiths do not present a complete and accurate picture of Mohammed, because these texts were not compiled and recorded until three centuries after his lifetime.

Above: There were vigorous protests against British writer Salman Rushdie and his novel The Satanic Verses. The title of the book refers to a particular circumstance: Legend has it that Mohammed received revelations not only from God, but that Satan also passed on verses to him—flawed passages that were later altered.

Left: Moses (Musa) is an important prophet in Islam. Because of his battle against polytheism and his role as the receiver of divine revelations, his work is sometimes seen as a parallel to that of Mohammed's.

The Sharia

Unity of faith and action

The Sharia is the all-encompassing law of Islam and is based on Mohammed's teachings, both in the Koran and the Hadiths. Apart from cultural and religious obligations, the Sharia also includes criminal and civil law. Literally, *Sharia* means "the way." This refers to the unity of faith and action, whereby God is seen as the only source of law. In some Islamic countries, such as Iran, the Sharia as a religious and political legal concept is equated with state law.

Besides the Sharia, the religious obligations of each Muslim include the five pillars, but also the jihad, or "holy war." The Koran is quite explicit on this; however, as Islamic scholars keep pointing out, this has to be seen against the background of a specific historical situation in which Mohammed's forces were engaged in a desperate fight with the surrounding peoples. The Koran contains such contradictory passages as "Slay the idolaters wherever you find them, and take them captives and besiege them and lie in wait for them in every ambush," and "O you men! Surely We have created you of one male and one female, and made you into nations and tribes that you may know each other." On the one hand, death is demanded for non-believers, while on the other hand our common origin is emphasized and love and understanding demanded. (4)

The Sunnah and the Hadiths

Besides the Koran, which guides Muslims' religious life, the Sunnah is the second most important source for traditions, conventions, and customs stemming from the sayings and actions of the Prophet. As such, the Sunnah is the basis for political, legal, and religious practice. It consists of the body of statements, decisions, and actions attributed to Mohammed, compiled in the Hadiths. However, Muslims differentiate as to whether the

The Koran requires women to dress modestly, but does not specifically mention wearing a veil.

Prophet was expressing himself about theological matters or about affairs of everyday life. In making this distinction, they follow one of Mohammed's sayings: "If I order something in religious matters, obey; however, when I speak of worldly things, I speak as a normal man." (2)

Wearing of the veil

Although there is no explicit commandment in the Koran that women should wear a veil, the Koran does require women to dress modestly in order not to provoke any indecency. Veils came into use around the 9th century and had the effect of socially excluding women. In some Islamic countries, a girl has to wear a veil outside the home as soon as she becomes sexually mature. In Afghanistan during Taliban rule (1996–2001), in Saudi-Arabia, and in Iran, women have had to cloak their entire bodies and wear a veil that partially or completely covers their faces.

Predetermination or free will?

Free will is a controversial subject in Islam, too. There are two prevailing opinions, both of which underpin their arguments with passages from the Koran. Those who want to raise predetermination (*qadar*) to the status of an article of belief assume that Allah, as the creator of the world and humanity, has predetermined the paths of his creation. Sura 54:49 illustrates this fatalistic position: "Surely We have created everything according to a measure." Therefore, human beings do not possess freedom of decision, since God knows all future events in advance. The con-

sequences of predetermination are obvious: a good person is good because that is the will of God; conversely, the same is true of an evil person. Sura 8:17 accordingly states: "So you did not slay them, but it was Allah Who slew them, and you did not smite when you smote (the enemy), but it was Allah Who smote ..." Islamic proponents of free will counter that it is illogical to assume that a merciful and just God would punish anyone who couldn't have acted differently in the first place.

These two camps in Islam have never been reconciled. In practice, Muslims believe in fate (*kismet*), while acting like people in possession of a free will. There is no subject in Islam that is more controversial than the predetermination of an individual's fate and the course of events in life.

Top: While the Koran regulates the religious life of Muslims, in some countries, the Sunnah also provides the basis for political, legal, and religious practice. It consists of Mohammed's personal pronouncements, decisions, and behavioral attitudes.

Above: The Koran expresses contradictory views about people of other faiths and can, according to interpretation, be understood as an encouraging holy war. It is no wonder, therefore, that fundamentalists, such as this Taliban leader, invoke the Koran.

Four schools of law

There are four schools of Sunni Islamic law: Hanafi, Shafi, Hanbali, and Maliki. Each school has compiled their own Sharia; however, these Sharias do not differ significantly from each other.

There are more considerable differences, in contrast, to the Shia school of law. Among other things, Shias allow temporary marriage. On the other hand, all the legal traditions have much in common. For example, there is no provision for adoption of children in Islam.

The Islamic Concept of God and the Last Judgment

Belief in the one and only God

When a Muslim dies, a funerary prayer is said for the deceased. Forgiveness is asked for his or her sins; but the deceased is also asked to intercede with God on behalf of the living.

Muslims worship one single, indivisible God. They decidedly reject polytheism, neither can they accept the Christian concept of God as an entity with three aspects, i.e. the Father, Son, and Holy Spirit. Mohammed introduced monotheism at a time when his countrymen worshipped many gods, spirits, and demons. Allah is seen as a personal God, the creator and sustainer of the world. Sura 112:1–4 explains: "Say: He is Allah, the One and Only. Allah, the Eternal, Absolute. He begets not, neither is He begotten. And there is none like unto Him." The Koran has ninety-nine words for Allah: the Maker, the Creator, the Sustainer, the Wise, the Mighty, the Merciful, the Compassionate, and the Incomparable. Overall, the Koran refers to him 2700 times.

No hundredth name of God

The absence of the hundredth name of God signifies that, ultimately, God cannot be comprehended, no matter how many attributes we use. Muslims pray God's name using the ninety-nine pearls of the Muslim *subha* (or *tasbih*) prayer beads, a kind of rosary. Muslims may have adopted them from Buddhists, and the Crusaders then brought them to the West as an aid for purifying the soul. As in the Christian Bible, Allah created man from clay and breathed His spirit into him. Man thereby became God's representative—*khalifa*—on earth. God has made a pact with humans, which is why the entire creation belongs to him, so it can serve him. At the end of time, God will judge his creation. God is merciful, but he will severely punish sinners

Last Judgment

Just as in Christianity, the Islamic revelations also speak about God's Last Judgment at the end of all time. This heralds the end of the universe, which, like everything else created by God, has a beginning and an end. The Koran does not hold back in its drastic images of this ultimate event. It will be a day that will "turn children gray-headed" (sura 73:17). It is not known where the souls of the dead remain until that day—which will come unexpectedly. All that can be found about this in the Koran is the reference to the so-called Punishment of the Grave (sura 32:11). It is carried out in the name of God by an angel, and according to tradition sinners' graves may be made very narrow and tight, regarded in Islam as being a most uncomfortable experience. (2) The actual hereafter, along with the full splendor of Allah, only enters this world on Judgment Day, finally bringing it to an end forever. The seas will rise, the sun will darken, the stars will fall from heaven, and the sky will disappear (suras 22, 56, 81, and 89 describe

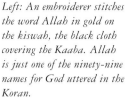

Left: An embroiderer stitches the word Allah in gold on the kiswah, the black cloth covering the Kaaba. Allah is just one of the ninety-nine names for God uttered in the Koran.

Below: The Islamic rosary (tasbih or subha) usually consists of ninety-nine wooden beads symbolizing the ninety-nine names of Allah. There are also variants with thirty-three or eleven pearls that are prayed three or nine times, respectively.

in detail what will happen at the end of the world). Allah is the supreme judge on this final day of judgment and no one except Mohammed will be able to intercede on behalf of sinners. Those to be punished will have to eat the fruit of the tree of Zaqqum, which "like molten brass will boil in the stomachs / like the boiling of scalding water" (sura 44:43–46). Allah is merciful, but never forgives one particular type of sin—the worshipping of other gods in any form, including that god we call luxury.

Who is a believer in the eyes of Allah?

Whoever believes in the following and lives accordingly may call themselves a "Muslim": One must have said the two-fold profession of faith, believe in God, His angels, His prophets, His books and in a life after death. One must also believe that the Koran contains God's unadulterated word; recognize Mohammed and his Sunnah as the last of all the prophets; not question the unambiguous norms of the Sharia (the all-encompassing law); pray the Islamic way; fast; and complete a pilgrimage to Mecca at least once in one's lifetime.

Entering paradise

In some Islamic countries, women are only allowed to visit deceased relatives after the funeral, because, by tradition, only men participate in the burial and the accompanying funeral procession.

"Some faces, on that day, will beam / Looking at their Lord" (sura 75:22f)—the faces of the just. The gate to paradise, described in quite sensual and earthly terms, stands open for all those, men and women, who have had the strongest faith in life, putting God before all else. Paradise is an eternal life in a garden where rivers flow, trees provide shade, and the inhabitants recline on jeweled divans, in pleasant light, eating delicious foods, with a perfect partner—in short, a life in which all the needs and desires of the faithful are met, including many which Muslims are required to carefully control during life on earth.

Many a Christian has been misled by the *houris* (which means "the whites" in Arabic), or beautiful virgins who are said to indulge the men in paradise, and has envisioned scenes of excessive debauchery. In fact, they are mentioned only a few times in the Koran, and those passages are interpreted by many as promises of perfect partners for both women and men in paradise. Sura 2:25 describes paradise, for example, saying, "There for them are pure companions; there for ever they abide."

Gigantic scales and the razor-thin Sirat Bridge

Those who have not sinned need have no fear on God's Day of Judgment, for they will enter his kingdom. Sinners will be weighed on gigantic scales of justice to determine the weight of their sins. All the sins committed are placed on the one side, and on the other lies a minute piece of paper printed with the Islamic profession of faith (*shahada*).

Promises to suicide attackers

In 2005, activist Mohammed Abu Wardeh of Hamas—the Palestinian "Islamic Resistance Movement"—was interviewed and translated as describing how he recruited terrorists for suicide attacks in Israel: "I told them how God compensates martyrs when they sacrifice their lives for their country. God bestows on each of them seventy virgins of paradise, seventy wives, and eternally lasting happiness." The Hamas spokesman deliberately chose the word "martyr" (*shahid*), for suicide is prohibited in Islam, as it is in Christianity. Martyrdom, however, is praised in the Koran.

But the day's most severe trial is considered to be the crossing of the Sirat Bridge, which is described as thinner than a hair and sharper than a sword. Those who fail to complete the crossing fall into the fires of hell, where spirits force red-hot chains into their mouths and pull them out from their buttocks. By contrast, the beauty of eternal life has been formulated by Islamic poets and mystics such as the Indian poet Mohammad Iqbal (1887–1938): "Eternal life is true life, meaning a spiritual experience, ever deepening anew, in the unfathomable depths of the Divine." The Koran describes bliss in paradise in the same amount of detail as it does the agonies of hell.

According to Islamic belief, the sins of the deceased are weighed after their death. One pan of the scale contains the sins committed during their lifetime, while the other holds a piece of paper bearing the Islamic profession of faith, the shahada.

Islamic Mysticism

Sufism

The term Sufism is related both to the Greek word *sophia* ("wisdom") and to the Arabic root *saf* ("purity"). In Sufism, however, wisdom does not refer to reason or the desire to maximize one's knowledge, but more to the wisdom of the heart. Sufis, therefore, not only want to understand the Koran and to live their lives in accordance with it; they also seek to discover its "inner" richness in order to fulfill better their devotion to God. A Sufi is not content with fulfilling the five pillars of Islam and adhering to Sharia (the law). They seek to experience God directly, leading them into a loving union with God, their creator.

This attitude frequently brings Sufis into conflict with orthodox Muslims, since inspired mystics cannot bind themselves to dogmas (doctrines) and conventional beliefs.

Sufis—Islamic mystics— raise their hearts toward God. To get closer to God, they employ meditative techniques, as shown here.

How and what a Sufi believes is often incomprehensible to other Muslims. Even so, the various Sufi schools have exerted a revolutionary and renewing influence on Islam, including, for example, the fact that God is contemplated at all.

The history of Sufism

Sufism has a history of more than 1000 years, during which literally countless orders and brotherhoods have emerged, each of which has developed their own forms of expression. Some also trace the term to the Arabic word *suf*, "wool," referring to the white woolen robe that the first mystics wore as a sign of humility. The first Sufi and founding father of the movement, acknowledged by the later masters, is Hasan al-Basri (640–728), who established a school in Basra (present-day Iraq).

Intoxicated Sufis and identity with God

In addition to representatives of moderate Sufism tolerated by Islamic rulers, a movement emerged that came to be known as the "intoxicated Sufis." These mystics, through their ecstatic and provocative statements, shocked the religious sensibilities of many Muslims. One such Sufi was Al-Hallaj, who was put to death in 922 for blasphemy. Among other things, he taught the following: "I have

become the One I love, and the One I love has become me. We are two spirits infused in one body." This implies that al-Hallaj and God have become one and the same, which represents an unacceptable blasphemy in the eyes of a Muslim. In the 11th century, there were also brotherhoods that misled and exploited the people through magic tricks, further contributing to the bad reputation of the Sufi movement.

Whirling dervishes

It was not until the 13th century that Sufism gained general recognition throughout the Islamic empire—mainly due to the Persian poet and mystic Rumi, who founded the Mevlevi order in Konya (Turkey), an order that to this day primarily cultivates song and dance (samafi) and is therefore also known as the Brotherhood of the Whirling Dervishes.

Sufi techniques of unity with God

To achieve unity with God, the ego, the urge to individuality, has to be fought and overcome. There are many spiritual paths leading to God; however, one of two general directions must be chosen. Some decide upon an emotional path to achieve unity with God. In these orders, the singing of Sufi songs and dancing in the form of rhythmic movements are very important. On the other hand, there are also orders that teach techniques for reaching the highest state of consciousness similar to yoga, addressing more strongly a person's capabilities for perception. At the same time, the students maintain close contact with the master, the head of the order (sheik = Arabic for "the Elder") who gradually passes on the necessary knowledge to the students, and accompanies them as a master, teacher and patron on their life's journey.

Above, left: Whirling Dervishes of the Mevlevi order in Istanbul. The Mevlevi order was founded by the Persian poet Rumi.

Above, right: A Sufi presents hair from the beard of the Islamic mystic Sheik Abdul Qadir Jelani, which is as holy to the Sufis as hair from Mohammed's beard is to other Muslims.

Rumi, the most famous Sufi poet

The Persian poet Jalal ad-Din Rumi (1207–1273) had considerable influence on Sufism through his thoughts and poetry. His quest for God led him to answers such as the following: "God is closer to you than your jugular vein." Asked what Sufism means, Rumi answered: "to find happiness in one's heart when times of sorrow come." Sufism is therefore an attitude toward life with a very deep devotion to a loving God. And so Rumi preached absolute trust in God.

Life in the Islamic Faith
The Mosque

A place of prostration

Mosques are usually centrally-planned buildings topped with multiple cupolas. The mosque (Arabic *masjid*, "place of worship or prostration") is the place of congregation in Islam, and almost always has the same structure: there is an open courtyard in the center of the mosque, especially in Central Asia and India, with a fountain that believers use to perform the ritual washing before prayer. On two sides of the building there are often adjoining rooms for students and scholars. Within the mosque, in the middle of the wall facing Mecca, there is a niche (*mihrab*) that indicates the direction of the Kaaba (*qibla*). To the right of it is the pulpit (*minbar*) for the imam, the prayer leader of the mosque.

Another structural element of the mosque is the minaret, the tower from which the caller (muezzin) calls believers to prayer five times a day (today usually with the help of loudspeakers). In Turkey, Syria, and Egypt, there are also mosques in enclosed buildings, similar to Christian churches.

The mosque in Quba, near Medina, was the first one to be built. It was erected in 632 by Mohammed. He and his followers stayed there briefly before entering Medina.

Conduct of believers

Whenever Moslems enter a mosque, they initially halt at the doorstep that separates the holy section of the mosque from the outside world. This is where Muslims coming for prayer—and visitors—remove their shoes. According to tradition, Mohammed said with regard to mosques: "When you enter the mosque, you should say: 'O Creator! Open the doors of your mercy'." On leaving the mosque, he should say the following: "O Lord! We beg your grace."

If they haven't yet performed the prescribed ablutions, the faithful walk to the fountain in the courtyard to ritually clean their feet. After they have removed their shoes, they carry them, sole to sole, and cross the doorway with their right foot first, entering the area reserved for prayer. Before devoting themselves to pray, they place their shoes in front of them. In former times, men would have done the same with any weapons they might have been carrying. The imam directs the course of prayer.

Women in the mosque

Of course, it is more deserving to perform one's prayer in the mosque instead of at home. Either way, all the ritual prayers must be said in the Arabic language. Mohammed did not forbid women to participate in public prayers at the mosque. In larger mosques, they pray from the gallery.

Above: The joint prayer of the faithful—each year, millions of Muslims come together in Mecca—strengthens the faith of those who pray and gives them a strong sense of community.

The muezzin

The muezzin, the caller, calls believers to prayer; his function is to remind them from the top of the minaret (spires on a mosque) of their obligation to pray: at sunrise, at noon, in the afternoon, at sunset, and at night. In the case of smaller mosques without a minaret, the muezzin may call from the entrance or, as was frequently the case in early Islam, from the roof. All Muslims are obliged to address their God at least five times a day; however, they don't necessarily have to go to a mosque to do this—with the exception of the collective Friday prayer.

Left: From the top of the minaret, the muezzin calls believers to their ritual prayers at sunrise, at noon, in the afternoon, at sunset, and at night.

The four most important mosques

The Dome of the Rock in Jerusalem bears this name because Mohammed is said to have ascended to the heavens to talk to Allah from the rock that lies under the present-day dome.

Mohammed erected the first mosque in 623 AD in Quba, not far from Medina. This mosque did not have a cupola or minaret at the time. In general, mosques are considered holy sites; at the same time, however, they are public places where people can relax, join a conversation, eat and drink, or even sleep. Mosques are often used as rest stops for travelers and strangers. In religious terms, the most important mosques of the Islamic world are those located in Mecca, Medina, Jerusalem, and Quba. According to Mohammed, a prayer in each of these mosques is the equivalent of a small pilgrimage.

Islamic art

There are no figural representations in Islam's sacral art. Pictures showing the face of Mohammed are prohibited. However, the Koran itself does not specify whether God may be represented or not. In the course of history, the opinion that a figurative representation would constitute a provocation of the world's Creator has prevailed; Allah alone is entitled to create representations. The depiction of figures for the purpose of illustration, but without any trace of individuality, is allowed, but only in secular Islamic art.

In place of representational art, a remarkable art of ornamentation and calligraphy has emerged in Islamic countries—it adorns mosques and buildings of Muslims both rich and poor. Over the course of history, this art has experienced several distinct periods: the Umayyad, Abbasid, Fatimid, Seljuq and Moorish styles can be distinguished.

Crowning examples of the Moorish style can be found in southern Spain, particularly the Alhambra in Granada. The Moors were the Muslim conquerors of Spain who, coming from ancient Mauri or Mauritania, invaded Spain around 711 AD and were not expelled until 1492. Their most important works of art and architecture are today part of the world's cultural heritage.

There are no figurative representations in Islamic sacral art.

Birth and Circumcision

Rituals for the newborn

In Moslem families, the *shahadah* (profession of faith) is whispered into the right ear of a newborn, and the call to prayer into the left one. This rite, however, does not establish the child's membership in the Islamic community. The *shahadah* is also the last thing that should be said to a dying person. Names are usually given to children on the sixth or seventh day after birth. Following the example of the Prophet, this day involves making a sacrifice. If possible, the child's father should slaughter one sheep for a daughter and two for a son. Moreover, in some countries, it is also customary to shear the child's hair on this day. The hair is then weighed against silver, which is then donated as alms.

A festive event: circumcision

The circumcision of boys (*hitan*) is considered obligatory by most Muslims; others see it as Sunnah (custom). No mention of the circumcision of girls is found in the Koran. Boys should be circumcised before they reach sexual maturity; it is usually performed between the ages of five and seven. Circumcision is a festive event, a ritual that dates back to the days of Abraham. Festive clothing, presents, and candy compensate for the pain suffered. Turkish boys are often dressed up like little princes—a splendid, ornate suit in bold colors, accompanied by a lined cape, a hat adorned with sequins and feathers, and over everything a sash with the inscription "*maşallah*," the exclamation of joy about "that which God wished." Folk belief ascribes protective power against the "evil eye" to this expression, which is why it is popularly used in connection with children. Talismans (frequently in the shape of an eye made of blue stone or glass) with this inscription are very popular in many parts of the Islamic world.

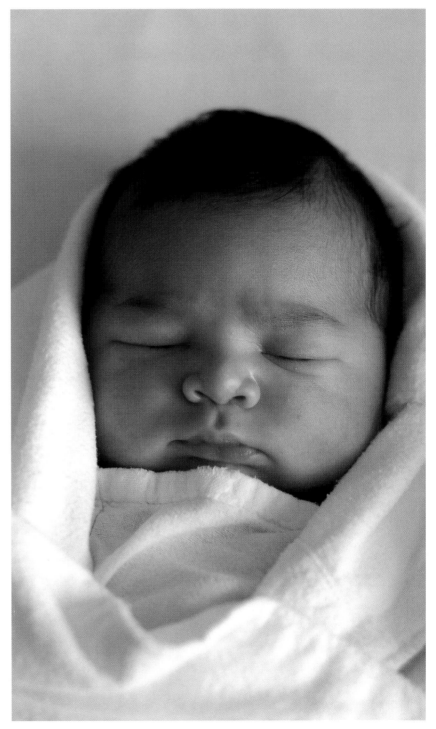

Right after birth, the shahada, the profession of faith, is whispered into the newborn's right ear, and the call to prayer into the left one. However, this does not complete admission to the Islamic community.

Weddings and Marriage

Top: Marriage is considered a duty among Muslims; it is believed to have a stabilizing effect on society.

Above: The night before the wedding is henna night, when henna is applied to the bride's feet, hands, or hair by a happily married woman and a young girl. This custom is supposed to bring good luck.

The wedding ceremony

Marriage is a festive event, and the Hadiths abound with references to the fact that it should be celebrated accordingly. The gift of money to the bride and a feast for relatives and friends are often considered duties in Islamic countries. One Islamic center formulates its concept of an Islamic wedding—typical of Islamic weddings in many parts of the world—as follows: "During the ceremony, participants should be merry, but not transgress the boundaries set by Islam. The only musical instrument allowed is a kind of tambourine. Men and women must sit apart. The drinking of alcohol, mixed dancing, or the dancing of women in front of men is forbidden. It is not the custom to place wedding rings on each other's fingers."

Marriage as a permanent contract

Islam considers matrimony to be the only desirable way of life and the only legitimate setting for sexual relations. Premarital or extramarital sexual relations, in particular those of a homosexual nature, are forbidden. Celibacy and monasticism are also rejected. The priority of matrimony is based on the Koran (24:32): "And marry such of you as are solitary and the pious of your slaves and maidservants. If they be poor, Allah will enrich them of His bounty." Islam ascribes a stabilizing effect on society to marriage, and it bases this notion on the model of the complex, extended family. Matrimony, according to Islamic law, is a contract that is concluded permanently. Sunni Islam does not acknowledge a marriage that is limited in duration from the very beginning.

Islamic marital law

In Shia Islam, on the other hand, divorce is possible, but only under certain circumstances (such as adultery, childlessness, etc.)

A Muslim woman may only choose her husband from within the circle of Muslim men. A Muslim man living in an Islamic country, however, may be married to up to four women at the same time, and furthermore, these women can be of Islamic, Christian, or Jewish faith. In such a relationship, the husband must not impede them in their religious practices—for example attending religious services in their community or eating according to the dietary rules of their own religion.

Problems in mixed marriages

In the case of a Muslim woman marrying a non-Muslim man, it is feared he might prevent her from raising the children in accordance with the Islamic faith or, even worse, turn them away from Islam. Another reason that mixed marriages are not viewed positively is that a Christian or Jewish wife is not obliged to live according to Islamic ideals of ritual purity. In addition, the terms and conditions for choosing a partner state that a valid marriage is to be considered divorced when one of the partners deserts the specified religious framework. Such a marriage is deemed to have failed.

Islam does not prescribe any specific form for a wedding ceremony. Traditionally, however, the ceremony is followed by a celebration with friends and relatives including dance, singing, and a feast.

Polygamy in Islam

Polygamy is permitted by the Koran, but limits the number of wives to four, which was not the case in pre-Islamic times. A marriage contract cannot be made against a woman's wishes; however, the bride does not enter the contract with her groom herself, but requires a male relative or guardian (*wali*) to represent her. Divorced or widowed women who remarry do not require representation, but are allowed to be partners to the contract in their own right.

The contract provides the marriage partners with the possibility of negotiating specific conditions for their marriage. A bride can have the right to remain her husband's only wife set down in writing, thereby restricting the male right to polygamy.

A marriage contract is legally binding when it is concluded in the presence of two respectable witnesses. It is possible to call in an imam or qadi, but not necessary.

Islamic Fundamentalism

The Wahhabis claim to be the only Muslims who interpret the Koran correctly, and to live properly in accordance with Islamic teaching. One of the most famous Wahhabis is Osama bin Laden.

Radical dissociation from the West

The aim of Islamic fundamentalism is to return to the origins of Islam, and its values in life. Islamic fundamentalists strive to establish a social order that implements Islamic law in all areas of life. The civil rights, liberal way of life, and democratic values of the world community do not exist for fundamentalism, because they are not to be found in the Koran. Extreme fundamentalists are ready to die for their convictions and do not consider their deaths to be suicide (a deadly sin in the eyes of Allah), but as martyrdom.

They destroy themselves and others in order to gain the necessary respect and recognition for Islam worldwide through aggression.

The sense of *ummah*, the awareness among Muslims of being a community, has increased as a result of the perceived threat from the West. To Islamists, those who support Islamic political rule, secularism (including the separation of state and religion) is simply unthinkable. Their goal is to fully implement Islam and its legal model on a state level in all Islamic countries, and not to orientate themselves on the Western role model in this respect.

Legitimate use of violence?

The Koran allows resistance against oppression by unjust regimes, as sura 42:41f leaves no doubt: "Certainly, those who stand up for their rights, when injustice befalls them, are not committing any error. The wrong ones are those who treat the people unjustly, and resort to aggression without provocation. These have incurred a painful retribution." During the first centuries of Islam, Muslims separated the world into two spheres: the "sphere of Islam" and the "sphere of war." However, sura 42 also contains the following: "Resorting to patience and forgiveness reflects a true strength of character" (42:43). The Koran remains ambiguous in many of its statements. Sometimes it emphasizes the value of forgiveness, but sometimes it praises armed conflict. And so, an Islamist terrorist who takes his orientation exclusively from the Koran's aggressive passages may claim his stance is completely in accordance with the Koran.

The Wahhabites

The Wahhabites are followers of an ultra-conservative, puritan Islamic movement. On the one hand, this movement emerged as a reaction toward the dominance in Arabia of tribes that had never been fully Islamized and continued to live according to their own tribal and customary laws. On the other hand, it was a counter-reaction to the rule of the Ottomans, who had departed greatly from the teachings of the pious fathers of early Islam. The reformer Mohammed ibn Abd al Wahhab (1703–1792) was a follower of the Sunni Hanbali legal school. He preached the excision of all post-Koran alterations and a return to the true Islam of the predecessors. He allowed only the worship of Allah, and condemned all other form of veneration of saints (including Mohammed), shrines and sepulchres; he also demanded total commitment to Islam (*jihad*).

Effects on extremist fundamentalism

To Abd al-Wahhab, the only true Muslims were those who followed his teachings; all others remained non-believers and had to be fought. The Wahhabites declared jihad on all non-Muslim tribes. In 1773, they conquered Riyadh and established an Islamic state in which everyone could lead a puritanical life of devotion to God according to the laws of the cleansed Sharia. Music, tobacco, and any kind of indulgence were forbidden, and Western modernism was seen as an all-round threat to Islam. Today, the Wahhabites live mainly in Saudi Arabia (where they are the majority of the mainly Sunni population). Osama bin Laden is a Wahhabite, as are the "holy warriors," the Mujahideen.

Above: The Mujahideen also strive to propagate or defend Islam by military means.

Below: Today, the majority of the Wahhabites live in Saudi Arabia. One of their strongholds is Riyadh, the capital city.

Islam in a Modern State

The last ruler of the Ottoman Dynasty was left with religious power only. After relocating the capital to Ankara on October 13, 1923, the Turkish republic was proclaimed on October 29, 1923, thereby sanctioning the constitutional status quo. European civilization had proven superior to the Ottoman Empire. To liberate Turkey from inferiority and dependency, Atatürk deemed a consequential secularization of state and society necessary: "There is no second civilization. Civilization means European civilization. It must be imported with both its roses and its thorns."

Commitment to the Nation

All the people living on Turkish territory were declared Turks. The central maxim was *Ne mutlu Türküm diyene* ("Happy is he who can call himself a Turk"). Only a few years earlier, the elite who felt themselves to be "Ottoman" had despised the "Turks" among their subjects as ignorant farmers and herdsmen. The discovery of "Turkish culture" and the cleansing of the Turkish language were the core elements of the newly-born Turkish state's cultural policy. Islam as a characteristic of people's identity was forced into the background.

Consequential separation of Islam and the state

According to Kemal Atatürk and his reformers, religion stood in the way of the process of modernizing the empire. It should therefore become an individual's private matter.

The abolition of the caliphate amounted to the abolition of Islam as the state religion in the constitution of 1928. In 1937, the principle of laicism, that is, the separation of religion and state, was included in the constitution: "The Turkish state is republican, nationalist, populist, statist, secularist, and revolutionary-reformist."

The reformer Kemal Atatürk

Statues of Atatürk—such as this one in Istanbul—can be found in public spaces and parks in numerous Turkish cities and towns. A great number of public institutions also carry his name.

Mustafa Kemal (1882–1938), the son of a minor official, was raised in the cosmopolitan climate of Salonica (present-day Thessalonica, Greece). He would become the great reformer of the Islamic caliphate state after gathering supporters of a modern Turkish state modeled on Western values around him, and winning free elections with his new ideas. The "Kemalists" subsequently abolished the sultanate on November 1, 1922.

A role-model for other states

"Kemalism" can be regarded as the first attempt of a previously Islamic state to find "its own path of development," and served as a model for later reformers and revolutionaries in Arabic countries and the Middle East, such as Reza Pahlavi (Shah of Iran), President Habib Bourguiba (Tunisia), President Gamal Abdel Nasser (Egypt) and revolutionary leader Muammar al-Gaddafi (Libya). While they all implemented a separation of state and Islam, no reform of a previously Islamic state has had such a lasting impact and was so uncompromisingly carried out as the one in Turkey. All resistance and rebellion was suppressed.

Kemal Atatürk was deeply revered by most Turks during his lifetime, and still is today. The anniversary of his death, on November 10, 1938, was a national day of mourning until 1987. Since 1988, it has been celebrated as Atatürk Memorial Day.

Left: Mustafa Kemal is the founding father of modern Turkey. "Atatürk" is an honorary title meaning "father of the Turks."

Below: Istanbul, one of the oldest cities of the world, is today a modern metropolis with 15 million inhabitants. The city is considered to be the cultural and economic center of Turkey.

HINDUISM

3

The Origins and History of Hinduism
A Religion without a Founder

not suppressed or eradicated, but instead integrated into the existing system.

A "collection of religions"

The religions of Hinduism cannot be traced back to a single common founder. They do not have a common set of teachings or rites and they encompass a wide variety of scriptures. There is no religious center that is common to all of the Hindu faithful. The members of this "collection of religions" do not even share a belief in one or more deities. Monotheistic and polytheistic belief systems are equally possible in Hinduism. A Hindu is familiar with—and frequently also worships—a number of gods; in fact, there are thousands of them. There is no such thing as either/or; rather, there is one thing as well as another.

Hinduism as a term

The term Hinduism as we use it today was not coined in India itself, but rather by European religious scholars of the 19th century. The Indian constitution defines all

Gods and nomads

Beginning around 1800 BC, nomadic tribes migrating from the north gradually came to dominate the previously peaceable Indus civilization. These warlike Aryans also altered the culture of the native people.

Hinduism can in no way be seen as a single religion comparable to Islam, Judaism, or Christianity, but is more a conglomeration of many different religions. Some religious scholars identify Hinduism as a "collection of religions." This has to do with the history of its origins. Approximately 1800 years before the birth of Christ, nomadic tribes migrated to the Indian subcontinent. These warlike Aryan people had been forced to leave their native lands after climatic changes transformed large areas of Central Asia into infertile steppes. The herding tribes that migrated to India brought their deities along with them. Without temples or idols, they worshipped their gods out in the open and glorified their deeds in countless hymns (rhymed ballads).

The Aryan tribes then absorbed the gods of the aboriginal Indian people into their own culture—a practice that characterizes every aspect of Hinduism: old traditions are

> ### The origin of the word Hindu
> The word Hindu is derived from the Sanskrit *sindhu*, meaning "river." Phonetically changed to "hindhu" by the Persians, it initially referred simply to the people who settled along the Indus River. It later came to mean the people of the Indian subcontinent as well as the country itself. When the Arabs reached India around 1200 AD, they began using the term (Arabic: *al-hind*) not only geographically, but also to refer to all Indian people who were not Muslims. In both cases, however, the term was imposed upon the culture from the outside. The Portuguese finally adopted the word Hindu when they arrived in India in the 16th century. They treated Hinduism as the name of a single religion.

religions that originated on Indian soil as Hinduism. According to recent estimates, 800–850 million people practice Hinduism, although the number varies according to which systems of belief are included under the term.

Hinduism is therefore an evolved, multi-faceted collection of various religious currents that share the common ground of professing their belief in Dharma.

A single common ground for all the faithful

The one common belief that is shared by all practicing Hindus is that they are bound by the Sanatana Dharma, or "Eternal Law." This refers to the order that makes life and the universe itself possible, and consequently to behavior that serves to uphold this order. The origins of the Sanatana Dharma are not human; nevertheless, it applies to all people—even the outcastes—for all time.

Left: What we know as Hinduism is a conglomeration of many different religions. Polytheism and monotheism exist peacefully side by side within one religion. No one is excluded because of his or her beliefs.

Below: The Aryan tribes of herdsmen who conquered India brought their own deities with them. Unlike the natives, they worshipped out in the open. Their hymns formed the basis of Hindu scriptures.

The Development of Hinduism

Early culture in the Indus Valley

Today's Hindus practice a religion developed mainly in the first millennium AD. Its origins, however, go back another 2500 years to a culture that blossomed in the Indus Valley for nearly 900 years. Indo-Germanic migrants (Aryans) who conquered this northwestern region of India integrated some of the natives' beliefs and customs into their own religion. From around 1200 BC, the religious hymns—which had been passed on via oral tradition alone—were collected and preserved in priestly circles as Vedas (the word *Veda* means holy knowledge). The Vedas are considered important divine revelations.

The foundations of the modern Hindu faith date back to the high culture of the Indus civilization, which thrived along the Indus River in Pakistan as well as in parts of India and Afghanistan. Its largest known city is Mohenjo-Daro in present-day Pakistan.

Archaeological finds

In the early 1920s, archaeologists from India and England presented the results of their most recent excavations in the Indus Valley. They were able to prove that beginning around 2500 BC, an extremely long-lasting river culture had existed there. Texts written by these Indus people were even discovered on soapstone seals. Up to now, no one has been able to decipher the script, so all our knowledge of the ancient Indus civilization is based on speculation. Although no major settlement of these early inhabitants has yet been discovered along the Indus, illustrations on the seals shed some light on their reli-

gious beliefs. For example, one seal depicts a female figure nursing a baby. She presumably represents an ancient mother goddess, as is found in most primitive cultures. The god Shiva (the destroyer) may have been the model for some of the seals, which depict a deity surrounded by animals. Some of them picture Shiva with a crescent moon above his head, and one shows the god with crossed legs, suggesting that the native people of the Indus Valley were already familiar with yoga techniques.

Downfall and new beginning

The demise of the ancient Indus culture apparently came about with the Aryan migration, which occurred around 1800 BC, though some archaeologists believe the Indus culture was already in decline anyhow. If so, the conquerors from Central Asia actually rejuvenated the Indus culture, thus allowing it to develop further.

One group of migrants settled in northern Greece, and another in Iran (the word Iran is a derivation of Aryan). The group that finally advanced as far as India most likely branched off from that in Iran. Our knowl-

edge of the Aryans stems almost exclusively from the legacy of their sacred literature, the Vedas—particularly the collection of hymns known as the Rig Veda. Upon settling in India, these hunting-herding nomads became farmers, organized themselves into tribes, and worshipped natural deities. They spoke an early form of Sanskrit. Each tribe had a chief, and the family made up the smallest grouping. The Aryans carried out sacrificial rituals. Through their contact—and eventually commingling—with the Indus people, they gradually became acquainted with new deities. In time, their settlements extended as far as the Ganges River valley.

The god Shiva—a first impression

With his frenzied dance, Shiva (Sanskrit, "the Auspicious One"), the dancer, sets the world in motion in order to ultimately destroy it. In one of his many hands he holds a trident. Shiva is the lord of animals and of yoga, the arbiter of demons and spirits. His symbol is the phallus, the power of procreation. His wife is Shakti, who rules over life and death.

The Buddhist Era in Hinduism

The Vedic religion in danger

In the sixth and fifth centuries BC, various cultural movements attempted to undermine the foundations of the Vedic religion. A group of atheist philosophers denied the existence of God and rejected the authority of the Vedic scriptures and the idea of reincarnation. The group also refused to respect the status of the Brahmin priests. In addition, the followers of Gautama Buddha also broke ranks with the Vedic tradition and pursued their own religious path. According to Hindu belief, Buddha is the incarnation of the god Vishnu. The Vedic scriptures provide the basis for this idea. There it is written, "At the beginning of the Kali Yuga (in Hinduism, the last of the four ages into which the cycle of the earth is divided), the Lord will appear as Buddha, the son of Anjana, in the province of Gaya, to mislead those who envy the faithful." (1)

Buddha's rejection of the holy scriptures

Above all else, Buddha preached non-violence and taught fundamental moral laws with the aim of purifying the people. Buddha himself rejected the Vedic scriptures. Many Hindu scholars interpreted this rejection as "feigned," arguing that the people were too sinful to recognize the real meaning of the Vedas. When King Ashoka converted to Buddhism in the third century BC and became a champion of the religion, the authority of the Brahmins was undermined for some time to come. After Ashoka's death (232 BC), the empire broke apart. The new kingdoms of northern India continued to follow Ashoka's example and supported Buddhism. Through the end of the third century AD, invading armies repeatedly attacked northwestern India, and it was during this period of crisis that the Brahmins reinterpreted the Vedic religion in order to revive it.

Below, left: This Gupta sculpture in Mamallapuram, dating from the years 630–668 AD, depicts the punishment of the hero Arjuna. The two-part relief, nearly 33 feet (10 m) high, includes among other things a war elephant used during this period.

Below, right: After converting to Buddhism in the third century BC, King Ashoka commissioned many Buddhist works of art. His avowal of the Buddhist faith undermined the authority of the Brahmins for quite some time to come.

The coexistence of Buddhism and Hinduism

Animal sacrifices, of which Buddha strongly disapproved, were discontinued in the first century BC. The vast number of ceremonies was significantly reduced and a unique philosophical tradition was developed. The great Indian hero epics such as the Ramayana and the Mahabharata were also rewritten in this period. Both epics assumed the status of holy scripture, and their heroes were transformed into incarnations of Vishnu.

After 100 AD, Brahmanic law took on more significance and was set down in writing. This set of guidelines, still highly influential for broad sections of Hinduism, contains extensive information on subjects such as the caste system, marriage, burial rituals, kings' duties, Brahmin authority, the concept of Karma and the nature of the soul. Following the Gupta Dynasty's rise to power in the fourth century AD, the political situation in northern and central India became more stable. Ancient India reached its cultural zenith under Chandragupta II (ca. 380–415 AD): scholars, poets and philosophers found patronage, Hindu priests were granted imperial protection, and Buddhist monasteries blossomed. A long period of peace and prosperity ensued.

The Gupta kings

In the fifth century, the first Bhakti movements emerged. Near the end of the fifth century, the Huns attacked the Gupta Empire but were defeated. Following the death of the last Gupta king, the country broke up into a number of small kingdoms. Although the Gupta kings had generously supported Buddhist monasteries and had Buddhist advisors at their courts, it was during this period that Brahmanic Hinduism developed in the form we know today.

According to Hindu belief, Buddha is the incarnation of the god Vishnu. Hindu scriptures state that Buddha will appear at the beginning of the Kali Yuga in order to delude the people.

Hinduism and the West

Calcutta—shown here, the monument in honor of Queen Victoria—was the gateway to India for the Western world. Great Britain colonized and governed India until 1947, and Calcutta became the center of British power.

The start of an exchange with the West

On May 20, 1498, the Portuguese explorer Vasco da Gama dropped anchor in the harbor of Calicut for the first time. From that time on, this city on the southwest coast of India would evolve into an important center of trade. Vasco da Gama had opened up a new European trade route to the Far East, one that would free traders from their previous dependence on Muslim countries. Now Europeans could use the sea route, and they began establishing trading posts in India. The British Empire colonized India and governed it until 1947. During this period, Calcutta rose to become the center of British power in India, and beginning in the 18th century, a lively exchange developed be-

tween Hinduism and Christianity. Western ideas and technology led to reforms within Hinduism—not least due to the influence of charismatic personalities including Ram Mohan Roy, Dayananda Saraswati, Sri Ramakrishna, and especially Rabindranath Tagore.

The reformers

Ram Mohan Roy (1772–1833), a Bengali Brahmin, was impressed by Christianity, particularly in regard to human rights. Roy spoke out against child marriages and opposed the practice by which widows sacrificed themselves on their husband's funeral pyres. He also rejected the use of images (*murtis*) in worship. In 1828, Roy founded the Brahma Samaj (Brahma Society), which taught strict monotheism. Another great Hindu reformer was Dayananda Saraswati (1824–1883). A Brahmin, he dedicated his life to returning Hinduism to the pure teachings of the Vedas; for him, they represented the source of all knowledge.

God can be found through every religion

Dayananda Saraswati rejected religious icons, condemned the caste system and strictly opposed the belief that gods could incarnate themselves into human beings. He founded the Arja Samaj, a society that still continues

interest that Vivekananda had awakened—as well as, perhaps, Queen Victoria's fascination with Indian culture (she even learned the language)—well-known Hindus and Hindu organizations now began traveling to the West. This cultural enrichment was not only one-sided. Many Hindus, including Mahatma Gandhi, were influenced by 19th-century Western thinkers such as John Ruskin and Leo Tolstoy, as well as by the teachings of Jesus. In addition, the Irish activist Annie Besant (1847–1933), traveled to India in 1893 and founded the Central Hindu College in Varanasi (Benares), a site of pilgrimages. Annie Besant campaigned determinedly for the education of Hindu women as well as for the advancement of Theosophy, an esoteric-religious system that was strongly influenced by Hindu beliefs.

Left: The poet and Nobel Laureate in literature Rabindranath Tagore was a native of Bengal. He became known in the West for his emphasis on divine love, a belief he also expounded on in his most famous volume of poetry, "Gitanjali."

Below: On May 20, 1498, the Portuguese explorer Vasco da Gama dropped anchor in Calicut harbor for the first time. From that day onward, the city on India's southwest coast began to develop into an important center of trade.

to spread Saraswati's teachings among people of all castes with missionary zeal. One of Saraswati's contemporaries was Sri Rama-krishna (1836–1886), a poor Bengali Brahmin who, as a result of the mystical visions he experienced, concluded that God could be reached through every religion. This also brought him fame in the West. The Rama-krishna Mission was founded in 1897 under the leadership of his pupil, Swami Vive-kananda (1863–1902). His diligent work increased awareness of Hinduism in the Western world. The poet and Nobel laureate in literature, Rabindranath Tagore (1861–1941), also came from Bengal. He, too, became known in the West for his emphasis on divine love and his denunciation of nationalism as "organized egoism."

Hindu influences in the West

The beginnings of Hinduism's cultural influence on the Western world date back to 1893, when the Hindu aesthete Swami Vive-kananda took part in the World Parliament of Religions in Chicago. His reserved manner and deep spirituality made a strong impression on the participants. Vivekananda presented his vision of Hinduism as a great, all-encompassing faith. At the end of the conference, some of the Western participants even questioned the logic in continuing to send Christian missionaries to India. Encouraged by the

India after independence

Since the Second World War and India's independence in 1947, Hinduism has evolved still further. Despite the existence of a conservative and orthodox branch, new forms of Hinduism have developed—for example, in the Santoshi Mata Cult. Santoshi Mata is the daughter of the elephant-headed god Ganesha; she was originally a little-known deity.

However, a remarkable film portrait of the goddess released in India led to a substantial rise in her popularity within the country. Mahatma Gandhi also contributed greatly to Hinduism's reputation in the rest of the world, as did the Hare Krishna movement and the popularity of Transcendental Meditation. All of these things have helped keep Western interest in the world's oldest living religion alive.

Can Dharma exist outside of India?

A large number of Hindus believe that their Divine Law (Dharma) can only be practiced within India, convinced that crossing the Kala Pani—the "Black Ocean"—would make them impure and unable to continue their lives as Hindus. Others do not agree with this view. It is only in the last 120 years that many Hindus have moved to other parts of the world—especially to Great Britain, the Caribbean, Canada, and East Africa, as well as the United States and Europe.

For many years, disciples of the Hare Krishna movement could be seen in their saffron-colored robes, singing and playing music on the streets of numerous Western cities. Many Europeans expressed irritation at the flamboyant Krishnas.

The Hare Krishna movement

Devotees of the Hare Krishna movement—founded in the United States in 1966 by Swami Pabhupada (1896–1977)—were seen on the streets of many Western cities in the 1960s and 1980s. Disciples of the movement, in their saffron yellow robes, achieved a high level of recognition from their association with the British star and former Beatle, George Harrison. Following the death of their founder—whose wish was to spread Vedic culture and religion in the West—eleven successor gurus (spiritual leaders and initiators) were appointed, forming the movement's highest governing body. However, many were forced to resign owing to misconduct (one was even sentenced to 30 years in prison). Krishna (Krsna) is the highest personal god in the religion; he demands that his disciples abstain from eating meat, using drugs or intoxicants, gambling or sex outside marriage. Life in the temples and farming communities (particularly in the USA) revolves around ecstatic worship before images of Krishna and other deities of the Krishna Bhakti. "Bhakti" means devotion to God, who in turn redeems human beings through love; in Hinduism, it represents one of the main paths of religious life. Members of the Hare Krishna movement ask for donations and distribute religious literature on city streets.

A Christian ashram

In 1968, the British Benedictine monk Bede Griffiths (1906–1993) began developing a religious center in southern India—an ashram—that was founded on Indian principles. In this community he attempted to realize his vision of *The Marriage of East and West* (which is also the title of one of his books). His teachings and meditation techniques integrate aspects of both Hindu and Christian spirituality.

Opposite page: Varanasi, on the banks of the Ganges, is the holiest city in Hinduism and a pilgrimage destination.

Left: After 1877, Queen Victoria of Great Britain bore the title "Empress of India," establishing that India had become a major pillar of the British Empire.

Religious Currents in Hinduism

A Sikh immerses himself in the holy scriptures of Guru Granth Sahib at the temple of Amritsar. However, no pope, no temple, nor any law or book determines the direction of religious belief in Hinduism.

Well-known belief systems in Hinduism

Hinduism is characterized by a great number of religious currents that express the central metaphysical questions of life. Unlike the monotheistic religions (such as Christianity or Judaism), the various currents do not aim for uniformity. Rather, monotheism and polytheism exist side by side, and it seems to be up to the faithful themselves to decide what they do or do not wish to believe. No pope, no dogma, no temple, nor any law or book determines the belief system in Hinduism. Even the question of the means to human salvation—which in Christianity, for example, is answered unequivocally, namely through Christ alone—is answered in a variety of creative ways in Hinduism.

Vishnuism and Shaivism

These two belief systems differ widely, since they make use of different holy texts and envision different paths to redemption. Some authors consider the differences to be so great that they speak of two religions under one roof—that is, Hinduism. The followers of both systems live ascetically in cloisters and can be identified by the different symbols on their foreheads. Shaivists wear horizontal lines; Vishnuists wear vertical ones. Their daily lives are shaped by worship and rituals. In contrast to the Vishnuists, Shaivists do not believe in avatars (incarnations) of their god. Their symbol for Shiva is the lingam (phallus). The different religious groups respect one another, since the idea of a single sanctifying religion is foreign to them. No one has a monopoly on the truth, because the divine reveals itself in countless different forms.

Shaktism

Shakti is Parvati, wife of the god Shiva. At the same time, Shakti is also an aspect of this goddess—namely female energy—and is highly revered as the mother goddess. Shaktism is the practice of ritual sexuality with the aim of stimulating creative energy in human beings. This occurs during the sexual act, which is performed using special techniques. Shaktism is at once hedonism, sensuality, and adoration of the feminine as well as a quest for salvation. Shaktist cults probably first developed in the first millennium AD in the Indus Valley culture. Here, the earth is seen as a fertile goddess: she causes everything to come into being and die away again in an endless cycle. Shakti alone preserves and destroys the world; she fulfills wishes, bestows mercy, and brings salvation. Until the beginning of the 20th century, human sacrifice was also practiced in the cult surrounding Shakti/Kali.

Tantrism

Tantrism is concerned with the quest for divine unity by means of magical practices. Here, too, a great mother goddess plays a primary role. All of her manifestations are images of eternal becoming and passing away: salvation is sought in the unification of opposites. Through sexual acts, practitioners seek the redeeming power of the goddess in the union of a man and a woman. The central focus is always on the magical ritual, which follows closely on the esoteric concept of micro- and macrocosms. These teachings—which have also been familiar in the West since ancient times—are based on the assumption that there is a correlation between the largest and the smallest elements of both the universe and human beings themselves. Every material form is simply a visible expression of the hidden power that flows through everything. A human being is formed in a way that corresponds exactly to the universe.

Sikhs: only one god and the Golden Temple

Nearly three-quarters of the world's 23 million Sikhs live in the border region between India and Pakistan. Their belief in a single god and a single human race and their rejection of the caste system was founded by Guru Nanak (1469–1539), who recommended that his followers lead a life focused on God. The Sikhs' most important commandments are to practice meditation, virtue, and charity to beggars and the poor. Sikhs also

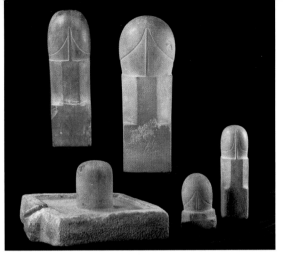

Left: In Shaivism, the symbol for Shiva is a lingam or phallus, a male sexual organ. On the one hand, it is a symbol of fertility; on the other, a symbol of the unity of life and death.

believe in reincarnation, although people who are completely devoted to God can achieve redemption.

Although Sikhs reject Islam, they are fairly tolerant toward other religions. Nanak's tenth successor, Gobind Sing (1675–1708), restructured Sikhism into a strict and militaristic society. Male Sikhs have been recognized ever since by their beards, long hair and green turbans; many still carry sabers. Their sanctuary, the Golden Temple, is in Amritsar in Punjab, north of Delhi. Their sacred texts consist of the written legacies of the ten gurus and the book of Adi Granth (although named for a particular guru, this book also contains texts by other Sikh holy men).

Below: The awe-inspiring Golden Temple, the sanctuary of the Sikhs, is in Amritsar in Punjab, north of Delhi.

Reformers

Opposite page, top: In 1914, Gandhi returned to India, where he subsequently committed himself to the struggle against British colonial rule. He initiated numerous protest marches, such as the "Salt March" of 1930 (pictured here), whiched aimed to break the British monopoly on salt.

A great Hindu—Mahatma Gandhi

Mohandas Karamchand Gandhi (1869–1948), called Mahatma—"Great Soul," a title that Indians bestow only on people of extraordinary spirit and heart—was the father of, and fighter for, Indian independence from British colonial rule. Today, his name is a symbol for non-violent protest and respect for human rights. He was born into the third Hindu caste of the Vaishyas—the merchants—and campaigned for the abolition of the caste system.

Gandhi's political and religious influence

The son of a chief minister in the principality of Probandar (then under British rule), Gandhi grew up in a prosperous and deeply religious family. In 1888, he began studying law in England, where he became familiar

Opposite page, bottom: Integral yoga is fundamentally different from traditional yoga. Its purpose is not to lead the practitioner outside of the world, but rather deeper into it. Sri Aurobindo developed this technique and popularized it throughout India.

Right: Mohandas Karamchand Gandhi, called Mahatma, was the father of India's independence from British colonial rule. Mahatma means "Great Soul," and is a title that Indians bestow only on people with extraordinary spirits and hearts.

with Christ's Sermon on the Mount as well as the books of Russian author Leo Tolstoy. These works inspired his later ideas of non-violent protest. In 1891, he was accredited as an attorney in Rajkot. In 1893, Gandhi settled in South Africa as an attorney and political leader for Indian immigrants. Here, he founded the Natal Indian Congress for organized resistance to state-sponsored discrimination. In 1914, Gandhi returned to India, where he subsequently committed himself to the struggle against British colonial rule and the ostracism of the Pariahs, the lowest caste of Untouchables.

Gandhi initiated numerous protest activities and marches—even calling for a general strike—and was repeatedly arrested during this period. More than once, he continued to protest while in prison by fasting. During World War II he campaigned for British withdrawal ("Quit India!") and Indian independence, and was imprisoned again. On January 30, 1948, Gandhi was shot and killed in Delhi by a Hindu fanatic. After his cremation, his ashes were scattered onto the Ganges.

A modernizer of yoga: Sri Aurobindo

Sri Aurobindo (1872–1950), a Bengali Brahmin, philosopher and yoga teacher, helped guide traditional yoga onto a new path. He lived in England for nearly fourteen years, where he became familiar with Western thought and combined it with the religion of his own country. After returning to India, he worked in the civil service and was imprisoned for allegedly masterminding a bombing plot. During his imprisonment, Aurobindo read the Bhagavad Gita, and in the process, a new, fundamental insight took root in the learned man. From then on, he devoted himself to yoga, and following his release from prison in 1910, he opened a yoga school in Pondicherry. After Aurobindo's death, the school continued to be run by a Frenchwoman known as "The

Mother." Since that time, Sri Aurobindo's followers have been working to build a city that will eventually be able to host 50,000 people in search of spiritual healing.

Integral yoga

According to Aurobindo, people can expand their consciousness beyond its normal limits, opening it to the light so that God can enter. This leads to overall spiritualization not only of the individual, but of the entire world. "The first imperative is that a person discovers the spirit, the divine reality in him or herself and then expresses it in every aspect of his life and being. Divine life is inner life. Godliness does not exist in a person's external life until an apotheosis has taken place inside the self." (5) This "integral yoga" differs from traditional yoga, leading practitioners not outside the world, but rather into it, which makes their actions within the world an expression of their connection with God.

Hindu Beliefs and Philosophy
The Vedas

Ritual impurity shapes every aspect of the Hindu faith. According to Hindu belief, a bath in the Ganges is one way to achieve purification.

The Vedas point out the "path of hearing"

The Vedas are holy revelations that Hindus believe are not of human origin. Western scholars and seekers, in particular, also speak of the "Vedic literature." These texts originated between 1500 and 500 BC, and are divided into three categories. For a faithful Hindu—today as in the past—the revelatory wisdom of the Vedas follows the "path of hearing." This hearing extends beyond what the human ear can hear and also refers to the act of hearing from within. The sacred revelation in word form of the Vedas is eternal and has no beginning in time. It reveals its true meaning only when someone speaks it or listens to it—and when the listener grasps it. Hindus believe this knowledge emanates from divine breath: "Just as

Ritual impurity

The concept of ritual impurity as a state of constant peril, comparable to sin, permeates every aspect of the Hindu faith. Hindus may become permanently or temporarily impure through objects, animals or people; this ritual—not physical—impurity can be transferred to anyone who comes into contact with it. It can be expunged by means of cleansing ceremonies (baths) or—in extreme cases such as the murder of a Brahmin, consumption of spirits, or the killing of a cow—through an atonement ceremony carried out by a council of Brahmins (Parishad). Atonement ceremonies may extend over a long period. They consist of performing special tasks such as fasting or drinking hot cow's urine. Presenting gifts to Brahmins or making long pilgrimages can also bring atonement.

our own breath flows easily, these writings emanate from the highest Brahmin with no effort on his part." (2) However, in order for this to occur, a person must be ritually pure.

Attempts at systematization

The Vedas are classified into three categories that make up the *shruti* (that which is heard or revealed), and are binding for all Hindus:

1. Samhita: This includes the Rig Veda, the Sama Veda (melodies sung during sacrifices), the Yajur Veda (sacrificial formulas), and the Atharva Veda (magical formulas). The Rig Veda originated ca. 1200 BC and consists of 1,028 hymns compiled in ten books—the so-called Mandalas (circles or schools)—focused on the various gods of the holy Indian firmament. The tenth book also contains speculation about the origins of humankind and the world. The study of the Rig Veda was previously limited to the Brahmins (the priest caste), as the hymns were thought to be divine revelations communicated through prophets (Rishis).
2. Brahmanas: These are explanations and instructions for sacrificial rituals that are intended exclusively for priests.
3. Aranyakas and Upanishads: The Upanishads consist of 108 instructional religious poems that follow from the Vedas and are thus also known as the Vedanta (end of the Vedas). The Upanishads are also held to be secret teachings. The central concept of these writings is the unity of Atman (the unchanging essence of a person, also life force or breath) and Brahman (world soul,

the absolute, which also forms the foundation of the soul). Aranyakas are the forest books, whose teachings were not passed on in the villages, but rather in the forests. Using the spiritual background of Western spiritual understanding, many Indologists and religious scholars of the last two centuries have attempted to classify Indian literature. However, they have not been terribly successful: the literature is too extensive, the texts too cryptic, and the Sanskrit language too multi-layered. Vedic literature is grouped together under the general term "Shastra" ("that which directs, reprimands, and keeps on the right path").

Above: The Vedas are holy revelations in word form that only reveal their true meaning when they are listened to or spoken.

Below: Beginning in very early times, the cow was honored as a symbol of the sanctity of the earth. Therefore, according to Hindu belief, killing a cow will make a person impure.

The sacred cow

Beginning very early on—ca. 1000 BC—the people of India revered the cow as a symbol for the sanctity of the earth. The law against killing cows stems from approximately the same era. Just as a cow nourishes her young, so Mother Earth cares for every living creature. Hindus consider products made from cow's milk to have magical powers. The religious symbol became a national one when British occupiers and Muslim enemies permitted and openly demonstrated consumption of beef.

Shruti and smriti

The Vedic texts are divided into *shruti* and *smriti*. The shruti consist of the three classes of Vedas as well as the Upanishads. The name stems from the Sanskrit root *sru* (to hear), meaning "that which is heard." They were originally heard and passed on by "Rishis" (seers or holy men). According to Hindu belief, their origins were not the result of any human deed. The *smriti* ("that which is remembered") are the revelations, instructional books, books of law, poetry books such as the Bhagavad Gita, as well as works by the founders of the six classical schools of Indian philosophy. An allegory compares shruti with a mother, and smriti with a sister. A child listens first to its mother, and later learns further from his or her sister.

The Vedas continue to be written today

Depending upon their understanding, different philosophers place greater emphasis on certain texts of the Vedic revelation and pay

A museum in New Delhi displays a long, illustrated poem, written in Sanskrit in 1730, which deals with the love affair between Rhada and the god Krishna, who had a great weakness for women.

Vedic knowledge is eternal
Vedic knowledge is eternal. Because the cosmos is in a state of continual flux, the knowledge of the Vedas is constantly being interpreted anew. Thus, for a Hindu, it is taken for granted that human individuality and self is expressed in a variety of philosophical perspectives. For some of the faithful, the myriad paths to healing and Yoga disciplines that are contained in the Vedic writings are like an enormous, timeless plan for religious education, in which human individuality is embedded.

relatively little attention to others. Thus, there are some scholars who only count shruti among the Vedas, because they believe these contain the original revelation. Even the Bhagavad Gita's inclusion in the Vedas then becomes a subject of debate. On the other hand, Rupa Gosvami, a 16th-century Vedic philosopher, assumed that a person who simply followed the shrutis was doing nothing more than putting the words

The family is important in Hinduism. An allegory compares shruti with a mother and smriti with a sister. A child first hears information from its mother and later learns further from its sister.

of the texts into his or her mouth without understanding them or living them. According to this view, a more recent text that is oriented on the original Vedic writings and expands upon their meanings and objectives can also be recognized as a genuine Vedic text, even if it does not belong to the original collection of writings. This practice of constantly adding to the canon of holy scriptures is unique among all religions.

No pre-described path

The Vedas do not offer a predetermined path; rather, they present believers with an unlimited spectrum of varying paths and philosophical approaches. A person should feel addressed at their personal level of conscious development and according to their own affinities. The Vedas aim to give people courage to develop further—particularly in their spiritual existence. Above all, however, the Vedic texts—the Shastras—aim to achieve a harmonious whole, namely the unity of the human being and the cosmos.

A tolerant religion

The German Indologist Helmuth von Glasenapp (1891–1963) was deeply impressed by this religion that is able to exist without dogma, and recognized in it a core of tolerance: "The coexistence of such fundamentally different perspectives—as well as the fact that the representatives of these perspectives have never used their differences as a provocation for any significant religious war—stems from the fact that most Indians do not believe that metaphysical truths can be exhaustively embodied according to any logical system." (3)

Vedic knowledge is eternal. Because the cosmos is in a constant state of change, a Sadhu—a holy man—devotes himself to the continual reinterpretation of Vedic teachings.

No claims of absoluteness

For Hindus, there are no texts that do not contain mistakes. God's revelation, here written on a Hindu prayer flag, is the absolute truth; however, it is seldom received in its original state of purity.

According to the views of Hindu scholars, the Indian Shastras (holy books) contain nowhere near the amount of information that it would be possible to receive from their eternal father. There is no book without a mistake. God's revelation is the absolute truth, but it is rarely received and preserved in its original purity. For this reason, Hindus believe that new revelations are constantly necessary in order to obtain the truth in its pure state. Hindu scholars proceed very carefully when studying old authors—no matter how wise these ancients are thought to have been. Thus, they are completely free to reject false interpretations that they find unacceptable for their personal peace of mind.

The great Hindu philosopher and saint Maharshi Vyasa, who lived more than two thousand years ago, was not satisfied with the information he found compiled in the Vedas. He was not content to accept the incomplete version of the truth that had been passed down to him from a long-forgotten era. He therefore decided that he himself would have to knock on the door of this inexhaustible treasure chamber of truth, from which the scholars of old had also drawn their wisdom.

Forming one's own opinion about the sacred Vedas

The philosopher Vyasa felt everyone had the fundamental freedom to form their own opinion about the Vedas and their content. No statement made in Hinduism is considered absolute. No wise person has ever been able to think through to the end and speak perfect truth. Vyasa recognized that no believer should simply allow him or herself to be led by those who lived and thought centuries previously. All must learn to think for themselves and try to discover truths that still lie hidden. What is essential is the spirit of the Shastras, the holy texts, and not simply the words.

The Hindu Deities

Many manifestations of a single god

The world of Hindu gods and demigods is bewildering in its variety and complexity. In contrast to Western interpretations, which tend all too quickly to equate this divine world with the polytheism of the ancient Greeks or Romans, Vedic monotheism considers these godly figures to be various aspects of a single god, one god who makes itself known in a plethora of divine manifestations. However, the Vedas also speak of the many different forms of the one divine force, Brahman. The three demigods—Brahma, Vishnu, and Shiva—represent creation, its preservation, and its destruction, respectively.

Left: In Indian iconography, Krishna can be recognized by his blue skin. His divinity is also apparent from his size in comparison to the woman at his side.

Below: This priest of Shiva has adorned himself with a multitude of religious insignia—among them, the trident, the symbol of Shiva, Lord of the Universe.

The god Krishna

Krishna is considered the origin of all other gods and their aspects. Hindus tell of a man who visited various temples to discover their common source. When he came to Brahma, he observed the god in the act of creating the world. He saw Shiva perform his dance of the world's destruction and he saw Vishnu carrying out his role, protecting the world. When the man visited Krishna's temple he had a surprise: he saw a cowherd boy frolicking with friends. Another time, he saw Krishna in a cozy gathering with the maidens of Vraja. The man concluded that the blithe and happy Krishna could only be the source of all things. In Indian iconography, Krishna with his magic flute can be recognized by his bluish-black skin—a joyful god who is not averse to sensuality. In the most important Hindu instructional text, the Bhagavad Gita—which covers subjects like ethics, aesthetics, and the struggle against evil—it is the god Krishna, in the role of charioteer, who narrates the text.

Pl. 33.   Voyage aux Indes et à la Chine, Tom. I. Pag. 155.

P. Sonnerat pinx.   Poisson Sc.

BROUMA

The unfathomable principle of Brahman

As the four-headed god of creation, Brahma keeps all points of the compass in his sight at all times. He is considered to be the oldest god in Hinduism and the primary god of the Brahmins. His origins are assumed to date back to Aryan migrants to India.

There is one principle governing everything, so incomprehensible to human understanding that it cannot be reached—let alone invoked—by humans: Brahman. Brahman is the all-pervading world soul that cannot be divided. Everything we perceive, in contrast, is subject to and part of an illusory world. It is the task of all faithful Hindus to recognize this, to see through the illusion. Since Brahman cannot be imagined, Hindus seek out an intermediary with whom they can communicate, an Ishta-deva, which reflects an aspect of Brahman that each believer selects, for example, eternity. In this respect, an Ishta-deva is always a product of illusion, but believers are entirely conscious of this fact. For them, the Ishta-deva represents a bridge that can bring them closer to the absolute.

Brahma, Vishnu, and Shiva

Three great gods dominate the world of Indian deities. The god Brahma, the four-headed god of creation, is the oldest god in Hinduism and the primary god of the Brahmins. He created the universe, and each of his four heads faces in one of the four directions of the compass. In his four hands, he holds the four Vedas—the sacred texts of revelation. Together, Brahma, Vishnu and Shiva form a Trimurti—a trinity—in which each god plays a specific role: Brahma is the creator, Vishnu the preserver, and Shiva the destroyer.

All three gods court the favor of human beings and compete with one another for followers. Generally, a faithful Hindu will select one of the three as his or her favorite god—without renouncing or rejecting the other two. The German religious historian and pioneer of comparative religious studies Max Müller (1823–1900) coined the term "henotheism" to describe this type of devotion to a single god even though three primary gods exist. This form of worship is only found in polytheistic religions such as Hinduism. At the same time, a form of pure monotheism also exists in Hinduism, as demonstrated by the worshippers of Krishna. They pray exclusively to Krishna, who is a complete incarnation of Vishnu (comparable to Christ, the human incarnation of God). Each of the three gods has a wife at his side, since without a female counterpart they would be incomplete. On this subject, a Hindu proverb states: "It is not possible for a bird to fly with only one wing." Brahma's consort is Saraswati, the goddess of knowledge. Vishnu's wife is Lakshmi, the goddess of beauty and good fortune, and Shiva's wife is called

Maya

Whereas Brahman is unattainable and unfathomable, the visible world is subject to the power of Maya—"that which is not." In other words, the world is only a false front, a sham—that is, pure illusion. The one and only thing that truly exists, the absolute truth, is the eternal Brahman. The goal for achieving salvation—in Buddhism as well as in Hinduism—is to see through the illusion. In this way, Maya can be compared to a veil that humans have to rent.

Parvati (or Shakti) and represents inner strength and energy on the one hand and maternal goodness and beneficence on the other. In the guise of the goddess Kali, however, she embodies the destruction of life.

Vishnu the preserver

Vishnu is a protector. He ensures that no damage is done to creation. In order to do so, he comes to earth in the form of numerous avatars to fight against evil forces. He can do this in the form of either an animal or a person. Up to now, there have been nine incarnations of Vishnu; the first of these was a fish, who assisted the people during the great flood. The most beloved avatar is the eighth, the shepherd god Krishna with his flute, who loves everything that tastes good. Buddha is Vishnu's most recent incarnation. His tenth avatar will be Kalki, who, as a rider of the Apocalypse, will obliterate all evil from the face of the earth.

Below: Shiva is the great yoga master and lord over spirits and demons. Along with his wife Parvati and his two sons, Ganesha and Skanda, he lives on the holy mountain of Kailash in the Himalayas.

Right: Vishnu, the preserver, ensures that no damage is done to creation. He comes to the earth in both human and animal forms. |

Shiva, the destroyer

Opposite page, top: Ganesha was created by his mother, Parvati, out of her bath water. He is known as the god of wisdom and worldly success.

Vishnu is beloved because he can take on any nature or form, appearing sometimes in female form and sometimes as a male; but Shiva also has a large following. Shiva is a multi-faceted, benevolent and terrible god. In a frenzied dance, he sets the course of the world in motion only to impassively destroy it in the end. He is pictured with a trident in his hands, like that of the ocean god Neptune in classical mythology. Shiva's trident is a symbol for the Lord of the Universe: the great yoga master, the dancer who rules over spirits and demons. Shiva lives with his wife,

Parvati, the many-sided mother goddess

Shiva's consort, Parvati, is revered under many different names. As Aba or Ambika, she is a loving goddess with motherly instincts. As Kali, she is brutal, wild and terrifying. Kali is black and many-armed; in earlier times, she demanded blood and human sacrifices. Kali eats her children, thereby producing new life. In the role of Durga, Kali/Parvati is a war goddess who fights against demons. As Shakti, she represents female power. A creator and mistress over death, she has won over many followers over the course of time.

Right: Indra is the highest-ranking god in the Vedic scriptures, the lord of war and ruler over thunder and storms. As a champion of goodness, he fights against evil. Here, he is seen riding a war elephant into battle.

Indra ou Devendren,

S. इंद्र: T. ᢕᡢᢉᢐᢧᡊᢥᢛᢙ

Parvati (Shakti), and his two sons, Ganesha and Skanda, on the sacred Mount Kailash in the Himalayas. The pyramid-shaped Mound Kailash is also revered in Tibetan Buddhism. Shiva's external characteristics include a braided crown of hair in which rest a crescent moon, snakes, and the river goddess Ganga. The eye of insight appears vertically on his forehead. His body is wrapped in the skin of a beast of prey; a cobra winds itself around his neck. Shiva is a dancer. In this function, he is depicted with bells around his ankles as Nataraja, the god of the dance.

Ganesha, the elephant god

Ganesha is the elephant-headed, pot-bellied son of Shiva. Shiva, however, did not beget him. His wife Parvati created Ganesha out of her own bath water. Ganesha is seen as the god of wisdom and worldly success. He has a sweet tooth and is often depicted with a bowl of candies. His relationship to his father, Shiva, is ambivalent, since the latter once cut off his son's human head when Ganesha was standing in his way. Ganesha did not recognize Shiva. When Parvati begged her husband to bring her son back to life, Shiva did not refuse—but he selected a new head for Ganesha from the first animal that walked by them, which was an elephant. Ganesha is revered by scholars, students and academics. In southern India, a festival bearing his name is held in his honor from late August to early September. Ganesha enjoys removing obstacles for his followers.

Gods as protectors of the world, a monkey as rescuer

Among the other gods in the Hindu firmament, several emerge as "protectors of the world." For example, they are rulers of the points of the compass-such as Indra, Yama, Varuna and Kubera. Surya, the sun god, and Soma, the moon god, can also serve as rulers of the south and north. Individually, Indra is worshipped as the god of rain and thunderstorms and Varuna as the god of water. Yet another god, the monkey king Hanuman, helped the hero Rama rescue his kidnapped wife from the demon god Ravana—a story recounted in the much-loved Ramayana, an epic poem told in 24,000 two-line verses. Rama, the seventh incarnation of Vishnu, reigned for 10,000 years afterwards.

The monkey king Hanuman—depicted here as a statue at the Kali Amman Temple in Singapore—enjoys immense popularity in India. He was elevated by Rama to divine status and is considered to be unsurpassed in strength, gentleness, and cleverness.

The Hindu Calendar

We are living in the final age

The god Vishnu sends ten avatars—gods in human form—to rescue the world. One of these ten avatars is Buddha.

The entire history of the world proceeds in a cyclical time span, which, from a philosophical and theological point of view, means first of all that every time the world is destroyed, it is created again anew. One age of the world consists of four periods that flow into one another. We are living in the darkest and final period, the Kali Yuga, which lasts for 432,000 years. It began with the death of Krishna in the year 3102 BC and will end with Vishnu's arrival in the form of his tenth incarnation, Kali, who will herald in a new age of peace and harmony. This new, first age of the next cycle is called Satya Yuga, and will last 1,728,000 years. It will be followed by Treta Yuga (1,296,000 years), Dvapara Yuga (864,000 years), and finally Kali Yuga once more. These four Yugas combine to make up a cycle of the world, called a Maha Yuga. 1000 Maha Yugas make up a Kalpa, a phase as long as "one day and one night of Brahma."

Avatars, primal matter, and the cosmic egg

Each cycle of the world begins with peace and harmony which, from a human point of view, seems never-ending. Later, however, the world begins to deteriorate in all of its moral aspects. The god Vishnu sends ten avatars, or gods in human form, as saviors of the world. The ten avatars of Vishnu appear as animals, a man-lion, a hero, a wise man, Krishna and Buddha. Finally, when 100 Brahma years have passed, the world egg dissolves and becomes primal matter; after a long pause it comes into being once again in a new period of creation.

This vision contains clear parallels to modern cosmology, which assumes that the universe begins with a Big Bang and then keeps expanding—until a countermovement finally draws it all together again at one minuscule point. Some astronomers also believe that the universe is constantly being created anew by a Big Bang.

Karma, Death, and Reincarnation

Endless cycles and transmigration

Transmigration and Karma are central themes in all the religions of Hinduism. Whereas Atman dissolves away with death, Karma remains. Hindus believe that the world proceeds on a cyclical course that has no beginning and no end. In this way, the cycle of the world is like a snake that bites its own tail. The driving force of this endless cycle is Karma—the principle of cause and effect. The result is reincarnation, because the deeds from a person's previous life trigger a mechanism of retribution. Actions must be thought of as a collection of energies that try to counterbalance each other and dissolve harmoniously, but are unable to do so because there are too few positive deeds. If a person has amassed good deeds in his last life, his reward will be an afterlife in a state like paradise until he is reborn. The next life assigned to him depends upon his Karma. Nevertheless, it is possible to dismantle all of one's Karma and break through the cycle of rebirth. When this occurs, a person enters the Brahman Nirvana, an indescribable state of absoluteness that human beings are incapable of imagining.

What is Nirvana?

Western people fear the nothingness associated with destruction as a bottomless black hole. Nirvana is different. A person can reach Nirvana in this life through *moksha* (release), in which all striving for action and life is extinguished. Nirvana is a condition free of suffering, a state of complete release, where the consciousness is no longer aware of itself. In Hinduism, the individual soul dissolves into the absolute such that it becomes identical to it.

The life to which a person is assigned depends upon his or her Karma. Sadhus like this man renounce all earthly comforts in order to achieve moksha (release) in this life.

The soul, heaven, and hell

The Hindu concept of heaven and hell has nothing in common with Christian concepts. Rising above the surface of the earth is the mystical, golden Mount Meru (the temple of Angkor Wat in Cambodia is modeled after it). Beneath Mount Meru lie the hellish kingdoms of evil spirits and demons. Above the earth soar the upper worlds, which are populated by the gods and good spirits. A shell like that of an egg surrounds and protects the world. Many "world eggs" of this kind exist alongside each other in never-ending space. Every living creature possesses a soul—jiva or atman—that is a part of Brahman and returns there after death. It is not preserved in the Christian sense of an individual; rather, it dissolves itself within Brahman. What remains are the Karmic energies. This means, in other words, that human beings do not possess historical individuality. Our good and bad deeds remain in the cycle of the world as a "personal energy template." After death, the physical body dissolves—ideally, it should be burned. What remains is to live according to the Dharma, in order to free oneself from the eternal cycle. But this is only possible within the boundaries of human existence. Nevertheless, Hinduism also includes the concept that human beings possess, in addition to the physical body, other bodies of finer matter.

Hindu concepts of the afterlife

When Indo-Germanic nomads (Aryans) migrated to the Indus Valley in the second millennium BC, they brought with them their ideas of a life after death. However, their oldest document, the Rig Veda, contains sparse information on this subject. We can, nevertheless, draw the following from it: after a corpse is burned, the soul enters into a temporary state, called "preta." In this state, it remains on earth as a ghost and waits to enter the ancestral world. When the spirit enters the realm of the dead, it must cross dangerous waters and pass by the dogs of the god of death, Yama. In the world of the ancestors, the new arrival is greeted with eternal life, restoration of the body, delicious food and musical entertainment in pleasant company.

Description from the Rig Veda

"Where the eternal light is found, in the world where the sun rests, bring me to this place. In the undying, everlasting world, where these last waters lie, make me immortal there! Where wishes and appetites are fulfilled, where the sun is at its highest point, where the spirits dine and are satisfied, make me immortal there!" (4) The 1,028 hymns of the Rig Veda are addressed to the various gods (such as Indra, the patron of warriors). According to the Rig Veda, pleasures in the afterlife will only come to those who have led a good life. Evildoers will be throne into a hell, characterized by a deep, black darkness. Nothing is known, however, about any eventual punishment.

Life in the Hindu Faith
The Castes

A clearly defined caste system

There is no specific statement of faith in Hinduism; it defies clear definition and enjoys a wide variety of customs, ceremonies and religious ideas. The house of every faithful Hindu contains a small altar with an image of a deity. Many people spend at least half an hour twice a day in front of the altar, in prayerful concentration. Common to all Hindus is an understanding that the world functions according to a strict organizational principle. All living creatures are subject to a clearly defined class system: at the bottom are the plants, at the top are those people who lead a pure, moral life. Between these two poles lie animals, bad people, and the less virtuous.

The allocation of castes

The hierarchy of human beings is clearly established in Hinduism. Even though the government denounces the caste system, the majority of Indians believe that every living

Farm laborers belong to the lowest caste and thus—with the exception of the Untouchables—make up the lowest stratum of society.

The caste system
Priests or Brahmins are placed on the top rung of the ladder in the caste system und strive to be near the gods. All of them share the goal of release (moksha) from the cycle of life. They avoid impurity through adherence to rituals and commandments. Pure and impure objects are strictly classified, and the most significant expression of this is the caste system. The entire purpose of the caste system is to remind individuals of the duties and responsibilities that they learn within their caste. If the system were to be abolished, the duties assigned each person at birth would be pushed into the background due to human indolence. Although the Indian constitution has nominally done away with the caste system, it still lives on among the people.

Left: The priests and scholars, or Brahmins, form the top rung of the caste system hierarchy. They wish to be close to the gods and aim to achieve release (moksha) from the cycle of life.

What is second birth?

According to the beliefs of the Brahmins, Kshatriyas (warriors and aristocrats) and Vaishyas (merchants and cattle breeders), children do not attain full membership in their respective castes until they are twelve years old. They are then welcomed into the caste in a solemn ceremony. From this time on, they are allowed to study the Vedas and to wear a holy cord—which is laid over their shoulders—as a sign of being twice-born in the caste.

creature is assigned his or her place at birth according to the law of the world (Dharma). The belief in the spirit and purpose of this religious institution—which aims to dismantle Karma—is still so deeply rooted among the people that politicians are incapable of overcoming or forbidding it. Even today, in India, to be born into a caste is taken for granted by many people. After all, the system also has its advantages, namely security and a foothold in society.

The Brahmin caste

The caste system has four major castes. The highest of these are the *Brahmins*, because they fully subordinate their lives to religion and live according to guidelines that protect them from ritual impurity. Brahmins have an exceptional position in society and are considered "pure" in both a physical and spiritual sense. A further distinction is made within the Brahmin caste itself: here, the highest-ranking group is that of the Pandits, or scholars.

The warrior, merchant, and laborer castes

The second highest caste is that of the *Kshatriyas*, the warriors and aristocrats who protect society and ensure that order is maintained. Third in ranking are the *Vaishyas*, the caste of merchants, as well as farmers and cattle breeders. In fourth place are the

Sudras, laborers and farm workers. In addition, classification of various occupations as well as marriage has produced many intermediate castes—for example, the *Dhobi* (launderers) or the goldsmiths. Elevated above all the castes are the monks and all those who choose a truly spiritual path in life.

Below: Merchants belong to the third caste, the Vaishyas. Since merchants control all of the trade in India, the wealthy upper class of citizens in Indian cities is now largely made up of members of this caste.

The caste of Untouchables

The so-called Untouchables now refer to themselves as Harijans, a title of honor bestowed on them by Mahatma Gandhi. To this day, they are only permitted to hold the most menial jobs; however, they have begun to protest against the system.

Compulsory membership in the caste system was abolished at the time of India's independence. It is against the law to discrimi-

More flexible caste rules

For fear of becoming impure, caste members pay special attention to three critical activities: eating, work, and marriage. Holding a particular occupation and where one lives are important indicators of a person's caste. Nowadays, members of a lower caste are allowed to eat with people from a higher caste; rules governing marriage have also become less strict. Nevertheless, people are still afraid of being made unclean. Violation of certain rules can result in a demotion in social standing.

nate against the so-called outcastes (as the lowest caste, or Pariahs are also called). Nevertheless, these so-called "Untouchables" still face great injustice, since even the law cannot prevent other groups from despising and physically avoiding them. It was long forbidden for an Untouchable to enter a temple. Thus, one can still read reports in Indian newspapers about protests held when a certain quota of university admissions are made available to Pariahs. On the other hand, no one is outraged when members of the upper castes burn down the huts of the Untouchables. Nowadays, they refer to themselves as Harijans (children of God), a title of honor bestowed on them by Mahatma Gandhi, who lived in their midst for some period of time.

Today, the Harijans are fighting back against their oppression, and in rural areas, farm laborers' meetings are repeatedly held

The fate of girls and women

In Indian society, girls are considered less valuable than male offspring. Baby girls are more frequently aborted or killed after birth; their mortality rate in the first five years of life is 43 percent higher than that of boys. Girls are breastfed for shorter periods and are given less and lower-quality food than boys. In case of illness, the chances of a girl receiving medical treatment are slim. According to law, a man has the status of a god as far as his wife is concerned: she is not allowed to leave him, but he may drive her away if she is disobedient. The Hindu code of behavior—called the laws of Manu—states that a woman should not lose her patience if her husband abuses her. In addition, up until 1829, it was customary for a wife to allow herself to be burned alive along with the body of her dead husband.

Particularly in rural areas, girls are in constant danger of being maimed or even killed by their own families.

Below: Men choose their wives primarily for their dowries. Love in the Western sense of the word is seldom the reason for marriage. Normally, people may only marry within their own caste. However, if the bride offers enough money, she can change this rule.

at which the participants demand higher wages and resolve to refuse unclean and unpaid work for Harijan women. The landowners' reactions vary widely—from hiring outside laborers who receive higher wages to burning down the houses of those who demand their rights.

Marriage into other castes

Membership in a certain caste, relatives and astrological factors all determine the planning of an Indian wedding. Men may also marry women because of their dowries. Normally, people are only allowed to marry within their own caste; however it is highly desirable for a woman to marry into a higher caste. A man does not lose his social status through such a marriage, but the parents of a bride from a lower caste are required to pay a very high dowry, which not infrequently exhausts their life's savings and may even push them into debt. The reasons for a marriage between two different castes are much more likely to be financial than romantic. Men of higher castes wish to achieve monetary gain through the marriage, and even today, it is not unheard of for the young woman to be burned to death in the kitchen by her husband's family soon after the marriage—namely, when the dowry has been spent.

Hindu Practices

Chakras and tantras

According to the teachings of Tantrism, a religious movement in existence since the fifth century that strongly influenced both Hinduism and Buddhism, the body requires cosmic energy in order to live. Within the body's primary energy channel, which runs along the spine, are six main chakras that collect and distribute cosmic energy. A seventh chakra is located outside the body, slightly above the head (still within the aura.) The highest energy—the "Kundalini"—rests like a snake in the lowest chakra. When it is awakened, it uncoils and rises, serpent-like, activating one chakra after another along its way. In addition to an incomparable feeling of happiness, the activation of the chakras through the rising Kundalini supposedly awakens supernatural powers.

The Tantric scriptures are texts that are classified among the Vedas but which do not have any general binding relevance. Tantras take the form of conversations between Shiva and his wife Shakti, dealing with the creation and destruction of the world, the worship of gods and the attainment of supernatural powers, culminating in a union with the most high.

Asceticism and Yoga

Hindus search for ways and means to attain redemption. In asceticism, the practitioner renounces all material possessions, goes without sleep, nourishment or comfort, and

A Sadhu tries to achieve redemption at any cost. In asceticism, he renounces all worldly pleasures, goes without sleep or sex, and often makes incredible demands on his body, like the man seen here.

Hevajra is one of the highest deities in Tantra Yoga. This god is pictured as dark blue, with eight faces, two or sixteen arms, and four legs. His head is adorned with a tiara made of five skulls.

abstains from sex. He also avoids other people, since he does not wish to speak. Asceticism is a small but important step on the way to redemption. Its purpose is to elevate and sanctify a person's spiritual energy. Yoga (Sanskrit, "to yoke; to join or unite") is directed toward the divine.

Through yoga, the practitioner is freed from fear and gains power over his or her body, as in Hatha Yoga. Bhakti Yoga strengthens loving devotion to god, while Kundalini Yoga leads to higher levels of consciousness.

The sacred syllable of Hinduism

"Om" or "Aum" is the symbol of the absolute and the holy syllable of Hinduism. The symbol Om stands for the division of the world into three parts: body, spirit, and unconscious. Om, the primal syllable, encompasses the entire cosmos and is an essential element of the essential mantras. Om is the symbol of the unrecognizable Brahman; it contains the past, present, and future. A person who uses Om in meditation aims to advance to absolute truth. For students of

The syllable Om or Aum stands for the division of the world into three parts: body, spirit, and unconscious. Here, it is written in red on a white wall; it is an essential part of the most important mantras.

In Advaita Yoga, the earth is nothing more than an illusion. In this highly specialized form of yoga, the practitioner seeks to achieve a complete absence of thought. The yogi is left with only a shapeless image of his or her self which, in the end, must dissolve as well.

yoga, Om is the sound that is the origin of creation and through which human beings can find their way back to their origins.

Bhakti: absolute devotion

Bhakti signifies absolute devotion to a single god. Krishna, in particular—the blue-skinned incarnation of Vishnu—is worshipped in this way by his followers. Bhakti is interpreted in a very emotional way: it has its origins in emotions and visibly expresses that the believer experiences any separation from God as painful. In this way, he or she hopes to overcome the separation. Bhakti cannot be used for the purpose of fulfilling a particular wish, because this type of love to God intrinsically keeps all wishes at bay. Rather, Bhakti is associated with self-abandonment, since the believer wants nothing other than God. According to Bhakti Yoga, a person lives in bliss when he or she knows and loves God. As an allegory for this state, the practitioner imagines herself as Rhada, Krishna's beloved: the love between the god and his beloved represents a mystical connection. However, Bhakti also means mercy and empathy, a spiritual power that is supported by atman.

The usage and meaning of mantras

Mantras, or sound words, are magical phrases—usually letters of the Sanskrit alphabet or incomplete sentences—associated with certain rituals or gods and used in order to bring about a reaction. Mantras ("songs of deliverance") such as the syllable Om are sacred sounds and, in the minds of the faithful, carriers of energy. Some mantras are the names of deities or cosmic beings whose energy can be captured through the repetition of their names. The mantra "Hare Krishna," for example is very well known in the Western world. The magical idea behind the repeated recitation of the words is that, as mental and acoustic patterns of vibration, they can create new realities. Mantras are thought to be full of energy and power. Therefore, anyone who wishes to use them properly and responsibly should know the meaning of a particular mantra, so as not to send messages into the universe or create things that are not intended.

Advaita Yoga

In Advaita Yoga, creation is considered an illusion. This yoga technique consists of silencing one's thoughts to the point of achieving a deep inner stillness. Silence can be cultivated to the point where the surrounding world is completely forgotten, and the yogi is left with only a formless awareness of his or herself. To do this, the yogi labels any thoughts that arise with "neti, neti," meaning, more or less, "not this, not that." A Hindu sage has explained the practice and compared the created world to the play of light and shadow made by a film projected onto a screen. Someone watching the film doesn't see the screen; nevertheless, the screen is the only thing that is solid and enduring, and, unlike the film flickering across it, is the only thing that is constant. Advaita has also become known in the Western world. Its followers are mainly those who wish to examine the intellectual and philosophical aspects of yoga.

Gurus

Teachers to whom one owes obedience

Gurus have existed in every era of Hinduism. They are usually considered to be partial incarnations of some deity. A partial incarnation means that they do not represent the god himself—in the way that Krishna represents the god Vishnu—but always remain human (comparable to the demigods in the ancient Greek Pantheon). In Hinduism, Gurus are classified according to the following hierarchy: parents are at the bottom, since they are responsible for early education; they are followed by the teachers that accompany one into the world; after this, a chosen deity can take on the role of a guru, or, alternatively, one can choose a spiritual leader with a wide reputation.

Sai Baba, guru and magician

Sai Baba (whose real name is Sathyanarayana Raju, born in 1926) considers himself to be the reincarnation of an Indian guru who died in 1918—Sai Baba of Shirdi—and who was revered even by Indian Muslims as a spreader of wisdom. Sai Baba became known far beyond India in the 1950s, in part because of the spiritual healings he is said to have performed. He is sometimes honored as a partial incarnation of the god Vishnu. He is reported to have made objects materialize out of nowhere. Sai Baba claims to be—and was proclaimed by the Sai religion in 1976—the incarnation of absolute love and thus of the one god who is worshipped in many religions under many different names.

In this way, no one must abandon their previous faith in order to become a follower of Sai Baba. Veneration of the image of the guru or personal experience of his presence in an Ashram also plays a major role in the religion. For Western followers, Christmas celebration at the Ashram is particularly significant: Sai Baba is repeatedly identified with Christ and is revered accordingly.

Left: Sai Baba is India's most famous spiritual healer to date, and is well known far beyond his own country. A Western film team has attempted—without success—to determine whether or not he could actually cause objects to materialize out of thin air.

Below: Gurus such as Sri Ganapathi have existed in every era of Hinduism. They are generally considered to be partial incarnations of some deity. Partial incarnation means that they do not represent the god himself, but always remain human beings.

The Hindu Temple as a Residence of the Gods

Bridges between humans and gods

In artistically designed Hindu temples, the "focal point of social as well as spiritual life in the community of the faithful" can be found. "Temples were built in every part of India at different times. The temple reflects the ideals and the way of life of the people who built it, and for whom it is a bridge between the human world and the world of the gods." (7) The site of a temple is always located near a recognized holy place. It is ritually purified before planning and construction take place. The floor plan of a

The site of a temple, like that in Baijnath, is always located near a recognized holy place. Here, a Hindu woman sprinkles the bull Nandi—honored as Shiva's mount—with water.

temple is a sacred geometric mandala—a concentric pattern of shapes (for example, a square). The square is "divided into several sub-squares by a grid of intersecting lines [...] This configuration of central squares with other, surrounding squares is seen as a microscopic image of the universe in its concentric structure." (8)

The image of the deity as an aide to communication

In this way, the world of the gods—the universe—is connected to the human structure

of the temple. It is a miniature reconstruction of the universe. This identification of the universe with its model is based on the idea of a visual correlation between the world of the gods and that of human beings. At the same time, the temple structure is an expression of the financial strength of the local ruler. Daily visits to the temple are not a necessity for Hindus. Normally, people only go there when they are seeking help or a blessing from a particular god. In the sanctuary of every temple is a statue made of stone or metal, or a symbol corresponding to the god in question. The image of the deity serves as a means of communication. The believers temporarily experience the presence of the god within the image.

In the inner sanctuary

A small sanctuary in the interior of the temple contains images and symbols of the deity to whom the temple is dedicated. The image of the god represents a means of attaining unity with the deity; in general, however, it is not identified with the deity itself. The god or goddess resides only temporarily inside the image. A person who wishes to worship the gods must, of course, be pure; thus, worship always takes place after the daily bath and before the meal. Visitors to the temple ring the bell at the entrance (to announce their arrival as well as to drive away any evil

influences). There is a constant coming and going of people at the temple; there are no set times for prayer. One of the most important Hindu rituals is circling the inner sanctum in a clockwise direction. In this way, the believer symbolically follows the path of the sun toward eternal world order. The goal is only reached when the circling is completed.

Above: The columns of the Jain temple in Ranakpur are decorated with intricate designs. A statue made of stone or metal can be found in the sanctuary of this temple, as well. It represents the god who resides here.

Gorgeous images of the deities

Sacred images of Hindu gods and goddesses are always beautifully designed in order to coax the deities into "settling" in the respective sculpture or picture. Hindu artistic tradition has developed special body types for sacred images. Gods are pictured with broad shoulders and chests, a narrow waist with a belly that swells slightly over the waist, and strong, cylindrical limbs. The major characteristics of female deities are an elaborate headdress, jewelry, ample, round breasts, a small waist, wide hips, and a graceful posture. The aura of many goddesses projects happiness, prosperity, and mental and spiritual contentment. The images tend to be extremely colorful, containing many shades of pink, blue, and violet.

Left: The sacred image—in this case a mandala—serves as a means of communication with the deity. Generally, however, it is not identified with the deity itself. Priests pray to the deity as it temporarily resides in the center of the image.

A priest's duty is to arouse the attention of the god. This woman standing in front of the sacred image of the elephant god Ganesha is awaiting the god's arrival with her child, whose head has been ritually shaved.

touched the sacred image or as food that has been offered to the god. In a gesture of the deity's mercy, the food is returned to the suppliants, who then partake of it. The priest marks the temple visitors' foreheads with a dot of red powder, indicating that they are under the protection of the temple deity.

Sacrificial priests

Almost all of the pujaris—the priests who perform religious ceremonies—are simple men, usually without a theological education. They are regarded as workmen in the services of worship, and the Brahmins look down on these poorer fellow caste members with pity.

The Arathi ceremony

Worship of the deity in a temple culminates in the Arathi ceremony. First, the priest rings a bell "to arouse the god's attention, who then makes his presence known to the faithful as he appears in his sacred image. The priest circles an oil lamp three times in front of the deity and then presents it to the worshippers. They hold their hands above the flame, then touch their foreheads, in order to receive the divine within themselves." (9) Sacred statues are ceremonially awakened each day with temple music; they are washed, dressed, and adorned with jewels, and given food several times each day. In the evening, they are carried into a bedchamber to join their consorts. Once a year the statues are placed in huge wooden wagons and carried through the town to bless all the faithful from an exalted height.

Duties of the temple priests

In every religion, priests serve as intermediaries between people and their God or gods. Their knowledge of the scriptures, secret texts, specific formulas and magical spells, and their meanings make them indispensable to the faithful in rituals and sacrificial ceremonies. Only the priests are able to summon the deity into the statue in which—according to Hindu understanding—it is not always present. The priest also accepts offerings that people bring and issues the blessings of the deity, either in the form of water that has

In Hinduism, there are no examinations in matters of faith; there is no organization that appoints or oversees priests. A pujari acquires his position in a temple because he belongs to a Brahmin family that has performed the same service for generations. A temple's primary source of income consists of donations from the faithful. In order to convince the deity to enter the statue, the priest thoroughly purifies himself, as well as his surroundings. He courts the deity with words of welcome, foot washings, sweet morsels, anointments, incense, food, and the holy cord.

Left: The large man-made
lake of Gadi Sagar at the
temple of Jaisalmer is
surrounded by beautifully
constructed shrines and
smaller temples. In the past,
it served as a water reservoir
for the nearby city.

Below: A priest in Varanasi
accepts a woman's gifts. She
lays the offering on a huge
lingam of the god Shiva. The
priest reads from the holy
scriptures and dispenses the
deity's blessing.

Sacrificial offerings

Favorite oblations include food such as rice,
fruit or coconuts, which are offered to the
gods along with flowers and incense. The
coconut symbolizes the "fruit of past deeds."
Rice represents fertility; flowers are symbols
of purity and reincarnation, thereby making
them appropriate adornments for the deity.
Perfume, incense and light (burning candles)
are also standard sacrificial offerings. The
shell of the coconut symbolizes the crude
body; the coconut meat represents the soul
with all of its desires and attachments. When
the priest breaks the shell apart, he shows
the worshippers the white inner core. This
action stands for the breaking open of the
intellect and the release of all the highest
qualities. At the same time, the coconut milk
flows down at the feet of the deity, symbolizing the merging of the individual spirit with
the cosmic.

Pilgrimages and Sacred Festivals

The holy city of Varanasi

For Hindus, like Muslims, pilgrimages are a very important aspect of religious practice. However, in contrast to the importance of Mecca for Islam, nearly every place in India can be a center of holy pilgrimage. Thus, statistics about the number of Hindu pilgrimage sites (Tirthas) vary, "between 58 and 64,000 [...] depending on whether one counts only the main cities such as Varanasi (Benares) and Haridwar or includes local, lesser known sites." (10) Varanasi, on the Ganges, is the holy city where Shiva once appeared and lived as an ascetic (though Varanasi is also associated with Rama, an incarnation of Vishnu), and has remained famous because—according to the beliefs of

Many Hindus, like the people here in Haridwar, spend long periods of time on pilgrimages, traveling from one holy site to the next. In the foreground we see Naga Baba Sadhu, a warrior of Shiva, adorned with garlands of flowers.

his followers—Shiva never left the city. For Hindus living abroad, simply making a visit to India could amount to a Tirthayatra, or pilgrimage. Hindu holy sites are usually located on riverbanks, coasts, beaches or on mountains. Intersections between land and water or between two—or better still, three—rivers often have a sacred significance. A location can also take on greater importance though a historical or legendary event.

Sacred festivals

Hindu pilgrims highly value festivals. The date of the huge Kumbhamela Festival, held every three years in four different locations, is determined astrologically, and it attracts millions of pilgrims each time. During the

Left: Every year, hundreds of thousands of Hindus make the pilgrimage to Pushkar in order to cleanse themselves of impurities in the sacred lake and to pray in the only remaining temple honoring the god Brahma.

Dassera Festival, held each year in October and November, the story of Ramayana is performed in a 30-day cycle. Particularly on Krishna's birthday or at the Holi Festival of the spring equinox, visitors from Vrindavan and its surrounding area—which are associated with the god—hope to see a vision of Krishna cavorting with his female friends, the Gopis (cowherd girls).

A last temple for Brahma

Many Hindus make a pilgrimage by train to numerous locations throughout India. The journey takes approximately ten weeks, depending on how long the pilgrims remain in each place. A highlight of such a trip is the lake near Pushkara-kshetra (blue lotus flower) in western India, site of the only remaining temple of Brahma, the creator. There are also modern Tirthas, such as the site along the Yamuna in Delhi where Mahatma Gandhi was cremated. Heads of state are brought here, and hundreds of Hindus leave garlands of flowers at the site every day. On a pilgrimage, all participants are made equal through a common goal. In the Ganges, the pure are made even purer, and the impurities of the unclean are washed away, at least for a time. In the sacred water—and in all places in the holy cities of Varanasi and Haridwar—caste differences are theoretically abolished. Hindus may consider the caste system to be a divine statute, but it has no meaning in eternity; Hindus believe that, at least for the

period of the pilgrimage, a sincere pilgrim enters eternity.

The value of pilgrimage

Some Hindus evaluate pilgrimage by the distance covered—ideally on foot—the site's holiness, and the pilgrim's purpose. Others insist that true pilgrimage is an inner journey of the soul: anyone embarking on such a journey need make no physical pilgrimage. Ramprasad Sen, an 18th century devotee of the goddess Kali, said: "What do I want with Varanasi? Kali's feet are shrines enough for me. When I meditate on her, deep in the lotus of my heart, I float on an ocean of well-being."

Below: These three devout pilgrims have painted their faces with ashes as a sign of repentance. For them, true pilgrimage is the inner journey of the soul, and anyone who embarks on such a journey does not need to make a physical pilgrimage.

BUDDHISM

The Origins and History of Buddhism
Siddhartha Gautama

The birth and life of the Buddha

Buddha—"the Enlightened One" (ca. 560–ca. 480 BC)—was born Prince Siddhartha Gautama in the house of King Suddhodana in Lumbini, in the border area between India and Nepal. His life is recounted in numerous Sanskrit texts (the Vedas and other Indian texts), but none of these were written until several centuries after his death. Yet Buddha certainly existed, since several of his life details have been confirmed. His father, King Suddhodana, was the ruler of a small nation. Siddhartha's mother is said to have died seven days after her son's birth. His father provided him with a good education and arranged a marriage for him while he was still very young. Siddhartha Gautama left his family when he was 29 years old, having been seized by a deep identity crisis. He sought wisdom from wandering teachers. At the age of 35 he became enlightened. After this, he traveled across the country as a teacher, accompanied by an ever-growing throng of pupils, and died aged about 80.

Political conditions in India

During Buddha's lifetime, life in India was marked by exploitation, human rights violations, widespread bondage and serfdom and bitter poverty, causing deep-seated tensions among the population. People longed for a change in social conditions. Due to the corruption and tyranny of the rulers, the country experienced nothing but constant war. The lower levels of society were terribly exploited and oppressed, and the established religion helped solidify the unjust conditions. The people yearned for liberation. The word for release, *moksha* (freedom from servitude) had, on the one hand, a fundamental political significance; on the other, it was an important element in the doctrine of incarnation.

Legends about Buddha, the Enlightened One

Historical facts

We have no firm knowledge about Buddha's life. Many biographies, including those held to be true accounts of his life, were written long after Buddha's death; nevertheless, they confirm a number of historical events.

Supernatural conception

Like Jesus, Buddha was also fathered by a god. The God of the Three Worlds came down from heaven and entered a woman's body on the right side in the form of a young white elephant with six tusks. Queen Maya, Siddhartha's mother, recounted that "it was a feeling of physical bliss and utter joy of the spirit such that I was transported into the deepest state of rapture." (1)

The birth and education of Prince Siddhartha

Upon the birth of his son, wise men from every part of the country prophesied to King Suddhodana: "The prince will become a great man, a king who rules over the world, in whose kingdom justice shall reside. He will present the world with a new law, a better law. He will establish a peaceful kingdom which extends to the edges of the ocean. All nations will be happy under his rule." (1) The king did not wish for Siddhartha ever to see anything sad, ugly, or unpleasant. He spoiled him and granted all his wishes. On his eleventh birthday, the boy was presented with the holy cord and from then on became a full-fledged Hindu. The Brahmins said: "A person must be born twice over, once from his mother's womb, and a second time through upbringing and learning." (1)

The four excursions

According to legend, Buddha decided to leave the protected world of his father's home after venturing out of it on four occasions. In his first excursion, Siddhartha went out through the eastern gate of the city and met an elderly man. He was overcome by the sight of old age: strength and energy were gone, the senses waning. Siddhartha was surprised when the old man told him it is everyone's fate to become old and frail: a healthy body does not endure, but begins to decay as soon as it enters the world. On his second excursion, Siddhartha left the city through the south gate. There he met a sick and suffering man. The prince realized that all happiness is illusory and that the world is ruled by suffering. Siddhartha's third excursion led him through the western gate of the city, where he saw a funeral procession. The prince was surrounded by weeping and mourning people. He then recognized that life is not everlasting. On his fourth and last excursion, Siddhartha left the city through the northern gate. An itinerant monk with a serene disposition crossed his path: he had given up everything and now sought inner peace in homelessness.

Below, left: Siddhartha Gautama was a prince for whom sages across the country prophesied a great future. At initiation, young monks are partly dressed as he was.

Below, right: The old man that Buddha met on his first excursion explained to him that growing old and weak is part of human destiny.

Above: Sitting under a fig tree, Buddha became enlightened after the devil first attempted to tempt him. The fig tree is known by today's Buddhists as the "tree of wisdom."

Opposite page, top: Siddhartha apprenticed himself to two ascetics, but ultimately recognized the senselessness of the practice. It is therefore not surprising that Buddhism rejects extreme forms of asceticism.

Opposite page, bottom: According to legend, Buddha made the decision to die at the age of 80. After preaching a sermon at what is now Varanasi, he settled down to meditate between two trees, and entered Nirvana while doing so.

Siddhartha's departure from his wife and family

As a young prince, Siddhartha enjoyed the comforts of his family home, but after having seen old age, sickness, suffering, and death in others, he began to question his previous life: "What would happen if I, who have recognized the horrors of old age, sickness, and death, were to seek a state that is free of those things, a state of ultimate peace, of Nirvana? I shaved my hair and beard, put on the robes of an ascetic, and moved out of my house into homelessness." (1) The prince thus left his palace, wife, and child and traveled as an ascetic for six years.

The ascetic

Siddhartha had two ascetics as teachers and models. He castigated himself as they did, refused food and drink, and denied himself every comfort. In fact, he nearly starved himself to death. But after a dream he decided to reject extreme asceticism and began eating again, realizing the futility of all types of mortification. He now saw that he could not find the truth in a hard ascetic life; rather, he must seek it within himself. He meditated and freed his soul through a form of moderate asceticism. He knew that enlightenment was to be found on a middle path rather than on an extreme one.

Buddha's death

After his enlightenment, Buddha traveled to the Indian city of Benares (now Varanasi) and delivered an important sermon, now a major Buddhist text known as the "Discourse on Setting in Motion the Wheel of Dharma."

Buddha's enlightenment

Siddhartha spent many years as an itinerant monk. One night, when he was deep in meditation under a fig tree, the devil appeared. He showed Siddhartha images of his life in his father's court, where he had lacked for nothing, in an attempt to entice him. Siddhartha resisted every temptation, and after forty-nine days, as a new day dawned, he achieved complete enlightenment. The path out of suffering and the "Four Noble Truths" were revealed to him. The prince and wandering monk had become an Enlightened One—a Buddha.

The path to perfection

When a person can abandon greed, hate, and delusion, he or she can, like Buddha, become enlightened. However, few people can achieve this because the amount of Karma they need to dissolve—which they have collected in previous lives through good and bad deeds as well as lack of recognition of the real world—is simply too great, making the achievement of enlightenment too long and tedious. Buddha taught people how to follow this difficult path to perfection over the course of their many existences.

Buddha continued to teach for forty more years, and founded monasteries and a community (the Sangha) with the aid of his noble friends. At 80, Buddha decided to die in Kushinagar. He prepared a place between two trees, and his soul entered Nirvana as he meditated. Today, many Tibetan monks practice the same ritual at the end of their lives.

Buddha's teachings

Buddha preached: "Recognize that the source of suffering in the world is the thirst for reincarnation, the thirst for satisfaction of the five external and internal senses, the thirst for death." This is overcome by the "Eightfold Path": right understanding, right thought, right speech, right action, right livelihood, right effort, right mindfulness, and right meditation. He also taught the Five Precepts for daily life: "Have sympathy and respect for even the lowest living creatures. Give and receive freely, but do not take anything that is not yours to take. Never tell a lie, even when the situation seems to excuse it. Avoid intoxicants; respect your wives and do not engage in sexual misconduct." (1)

Yana

Buddha calls for the self's continual release from physical feelings, property, images, and ideas. In Sanskrit, Buddhism is called *Yana*, which means "vehicle" or "ferry." Buddhist deciples are led to escape, let go, forsake the world—not to hold on. They must follow the path unaided. There is no God, and the reward is eternal release.

Hinayana and Mahayana Buddhism

Above: A Buddhist temple in Sri Lanka, today the stronghold of Hinayana, or so-called monastic Buddhism.

Right: After the savage, warlike King Ashoka became familiar with the teachings of Buddha, he transformed himself and wished to become enlightened as well. He had many buildings constructed in Buddha's honor, such as this one decorated with "Buddha's eyes."

Hinayana Buddhism

The followers of the historical Buddha were, without exception, monks. Aristocratic benefactors quickly helped them found the first monasteries, where an elite consciousness and strict rules for monastic life were developed. At the forefront were the historical Buddha, the Dharma (teachings), and Sangha (the community). These are the foundations of Hinayana Buddhism, the "Smaller Vehicle"—"smaller" because as a strictly monastic form it can only be followed by a minority of people. The goal of a Hinayana monk is to become an "Arhat" (one who is worthy), someone who, according to Buddha's teachings, stands on the fourth and highest step, that is, just before perfection. (Perfection itself can only be achieved by a single person within each world cycle, namely the Buddha.) Of the original schools of Hinayana Buddhism, only Theravada Buddhism ("Way of the Elders") survives; today it is practiced primarily in Thailand, Burma, Sri Lanka, Cambodia, Laos, and Vietnam. The center of Hinayana (Theraveda) today is Sri Lanka.

Mahayana Buddhism

Unlike Hinayana, Mahayana Buddhism—the "Greater Vehicle," which emerged in the 1st century BC—seeks to be a vehicle to salvation for as many as possible: nuns, monks, and lay people. In Mahayana, Buddha is a supernatural being in whom the faithful take refuge to be saved. They hope for redemption through mercy, not monastic asceticism.

King Ashoka and peace

Two hundred years after Buddha's death, King Ashoka (268–232 BC) assumed the throne. The brutal king, who until then had oppressed and exploited his people in India, became acquainted with the teachings of Buddha and underwent a complete transformation. Ashoka wished to achieve enlightenment for himself. He was the first ruler in world history to renounce war and oppression as political tools. From that time on, tolerance and humanity ruled in his kingdom. He championed the peaceful propagation of Buddha's teachings and supported the culture of his country. After Ashoka's death, the influence of Buddhism in India waned. Only many centuries later did Gandhi once again adopt Ashoka's commitment to non-violence.

Mahayana Buddhism demands that its followers live a life that is pure in thought, word and deed. They are taught to lovingly revere the Buddha, to invoke the Enlightened One, to emulate the Buddha in his infinite compassion for all creatures, and to meditate on Buddha's perfection. The highest goal in Mahayana is not to achieve perfection—to become a Buddha—but rather to become a Bodhisattva, a person who delays his or her own entry into Nirvana until all other sentient beings have become enlightened (bodhi). Mahayana therefore trains its followers in selfless action. Mahayana also recognizes other gods to whom its followers pray; its practice extends through China, Korea and Japan, the latter being the birthplace of Zen Buddhism.

Bodhisattvas

Mahayana Buddhism makes a distinction between incarnate and transcendent Bodhisattvas. Modern followers believe that transcendent Bodhisattvas are supernatural beings who accompany and help them in their lives. They are characterized in the temple through symbols and particular gestures, and they take human suffering upon themselves when called upon to do so. As soon as they themselves become incarnated into human beings through birth, they follow the path to enlightenment as it is taught in the Buddhist schools. A Bodhisattva must pass through ten grounds until, in a last life, he or she can achieve enlightenment.

The goal of Mahayana Buddhism is to be a "vehicle to salvation" for as many people as possible. Mahayana Buddhists do not strive to become Buddhas themselves.

Tantrism

Origins and evolution

Tantrism (Sanskrit *tan* = to propagate, to continue, to multiply) is a philosophical and religious movement whose origins date back to 4th-century India. Its influence later reached other Buddhist countries, particularly Tibet and Japan, for example, in the form of Vajrayana, the Tantric aspect of Mahayana Buddhism. In Tibet, it brought about a fruitful renewal of local Buddhist practices.

Tantrism developed primarily in the border region between India and Afghanistan and in the eastern area of Bengal. However, its roots have still not been fully explained. It contains parallels to Daoism, Gnosticism, alchemy, and the Greek mysteries. Initially, Tantrism was a doctrine of salvation for the lower Indian castes in particular; Hindu and Buddhist Tantrism have many elements in common. Central to both is the cult of the Great Mother: Kali, Shakti, or for the Buddhists, Prajnaparamita.

The Gods of Indian Tantrism

Shiva and Shakti play a major role in Tantrism. Shakti is the power that manifests itself as dynamic energy in all worlds. She is the creative or "birth-giving" principle. For this reason, women are more highly esteemed in Tantrism (in contrast to Brahmanism). Shiva, the man, exemplifies the serene intellect. The two figures are, in essence, one; however, they appear to be separate. The goal of Tantrism is to restore the fundamental unity of Shiva and Shakti, spirit and world, the union of all objects.

Tantric practices

In Tantric Buddhism, the female principle embodies transcendent wisdom. Therefore, both women and men can achieve enlightenment. Many female Tibetan Tantra masters are outstanding examples of this feminine spirituality. The techniques of the Buddhist Tantra are primarily focused on direct experience, incorporating daily life. In the West, Tantrism is often reduced to a conversion of sexual energies. However, not all forms of Tantrism (especially Buddhist, but also Hindu Tantrism) incorporate an actual ritualized sexual act. Under certain conditions, followers believe it is possible to achieve enlightenment in this way—although sexual climax is not the primary goal. Rather, the focus is on the energies that are roused during the sexual act. By "attaining" or "awakening" these energies, it is possible to meditate more intensively on emptiness (Sunyata). Here, the flow of male semen is seen as an obstacle. The precise demonstration of these Buddhist Tantric methods and work with physical en-

In Tantrism, Shakti is the female elementary power of the universe; at the same time, she represents active energy. Thanks to the Shakti cult, women are respected and honored in Tantrism, and women also become enlightened.

ergies—which are not without risks—is reserved for Buddhist masters.

There are many levels of Tantrism, and the Tantric texts range in sophistication from crude magic to advanced metaphysics. Although Tantrism reached its developmental apex around 1000 AD, it has continued to survive and have a significant influence on religious movements up until the modern era—for example, in the teachings of Bhagwan Sri Rajneesh (1931–1990).

The four classifications of Tantric doctrine

Tantric teachings are tailored to the developmental stages of the person or people practicing it.

1. Kriya Tantra focuses on the Tantra of ritual practices, sacrifices, and purification ceremonies;
2. Carya Tantra demonstrates that external actions have inner, spiritual counterparts within human beings;
3. Yoga Tantra emphasizes meditation and spiritual understanding of the world; and
4. Anuttara or Yoga Tantra is the highest form of Yoga.

Left: Bhagwan Sri Rajneesh, also known as "Osho," was influenced by various spiritual doctrines, including Tantrism and Zen Buddhism.

Below: The study of Tantric texts conveys new insights. However, the techniques of Buddhist Tantrism are focused on direct experiences in daily life.

Vajrayana Buddhism

Striving for enlightenment

Opposite page: A person on the quest for enlightenment. According to Tibetan Buddhism, human beings must free themselves from the cycle of rebirth in order to fully depart into the state of namelessness—that is, Nirvana.

A further branch of Buddhism is Vajrayana, "the Diamond Vehicle." It developed in India in the 7th century. Enlightenment in Vajrayana means following the path of emptiness and love for all living creatures, supported by the six "Paramitas" ("that which has crossed over," or virtues): patience, meditation, wisdom, effort, morality, and generosity. Believers aim to achieve enlightenment with the help of Yoga and Tantra techniques, mandalas and mantras, opening of the chakras and countless rituals, as well as of a spiritual leader (a lama or guru). In Vajrayana, every area above and below the earth contains its own demons, spirits, and deities: devilish creatures, ghosts, animals, people, demigods, and gods. A person may experience a deity as wrathful or gentle, helpful or misleading. For example, a Yidam is a protector god whose nature is nevertheless extremely complex; he displays characteristics which are similar to the Ishta-deva in Hinduism as well as to the guardian angels of the Hebrew Bible. He is a focus of meditation as well as being an embodiment of Buddha at some stages of existence.

Right: Mandalas such as this one have a religious value primarily in Vajrayana Buddhism. They are intended to help believers achieve enlightenment.

Tantrayana Buddhism

Some later Buddhist schools also recorded their texts in the Tibetan and Chinese languages. Buddhism only reached the Tibetan highlands for the first time in the 7th to 9th centuries; a belief in ghosts and demons had predominated until that time. The strains of Buddhism that emerged here—Tantrayana, "the Vehicle of the Tantra Texts"—incorporated traditional folk beliefs, gods, and demons; it mixed mythical deities and ritual practices with the concepts of overcoming passions and those of the Eightfold Path.

Far right: Belief in demons is an important element of Tantrayana Buddhism, which incorporated traditional folk beliefs into its doctrine.

Tibetan Buddhism

The origins of Tibetan Buddhism

Tibetan Buddhism is a branch of Chinese Buddhism that began to evolve from Vajrayana Buddhism in the 8th century, and has developed into a specifically Tibetan expression of the religion. Currently, Tibetan Buddhism is most widespread in areas that are inhabited by Tibetan and Mongolian nationalities (Tibet, Nepal, and the Himalayan region of India and Mongolia). Buddhism gained its first followers in aristocratic circles; however, with the passage of time, the common people were won over to its beliefs as well. In this way, Buddhism merged with the native religion of spirits and demons. The title "Dalai Lama" was first conferred by a Mongolian prince in 1578.

The cycle of reincarnation

In Tibetan Buddhism, as in other forms of Buddhism, redemption means a complete departure from the cycle of rebirth and release into Nirvana. In his "truth of the origin of suffering," Buddha answers the question of what drives the cycle of reincarnation. For Buddha, it is craving that binds us to Samsara ("wandering on"). Craving, hate, and delusion are the impulses for further reincarnations. According to the Buddha, there is a correlation between our unbridled desires and our actions in the world. This leads to rebirth and continued suffering. Elimination of cravings will bring about the end of suffering. Craving or greed must be understood as the realization of the ego in the world. Greed does not mean craving for candy or money, but rather, participation in the game of the world and society. Through Buddha, followers aim for the self-discipline to achieve a lack of cravings and obtain serenity and knowledge of true life. The world does not exist; rather, it occurs. Everything is becoming; nothing endures. Countless texts in Tibetan Buddhism express this religious philosophy.

The eleventh Panchen Lama

If he is still alive, Gedhun Choekyi Nyima, the eleventh Panchen Lama of Tibet, would be 17 years old in the year 2006. Since 1995, he has been in Chinese custody in an unknown location. The Chinese government does not recognize the boy as the eleventh Panchen Lama. Instead, a few months after Gedhun Choekyi Nyima was kidnapped, officials declared the then five-year-old Gyaltsen Norbu to be the Panchen Lama.

A large number of monks and nuns who refused to disavow the boy whom the Dalai Lama had proclaimed to be the true Panchen Lama were arrested, convicted, and expelled from religious institutions. While images of the Chinese-elected Panchen Lama are prominently displayed in the main cloisters and tourist hotels in Tibet—as Tibetan refugees and Western tourists have since reported—pictures of the Dalai Lama and of Gedhun Choekyi Nyima are strictly forbidden in most parts of Tibet.

There are numerous sects in Tibetan Buddhism which can be distinguished, among other things, by the color of their clothing. The Yellow Sect has the largest number of followers.

Sects in Tibetan Buddhism

There are various sects in Tibetan Buddhism: the Red Sect, the Flower Sect, the White Sect and the Yellow Sect, depending upon the color of their clothing, the headwear of the priests, and the decoration of their temples. The Yellow Sect was founded by Tsong-khapa (1357–1419) in the early 15th century. Under the leadership of his two disciples, the third Dalai Lama (who did not yet hold that title at the time!) and the first Panchen Lama, the Yellow Sect became the dominant group, with the largest number of followers. Religion still plays an important role in the daily lives of Tibetans—despite the facts that the Chinese Communists curtailed Buddhism in Tibet and persecuted its followers, and that the present Dalai Lama has lived in exile in India since 1959.

The Panchen Lama

The Panchen Lama—or *Panchen Rinpoche* (Tibetan, "great scholarly jewel")—is an in-

The present Dalai Lama

Born in July 1935 in northeastern Tibet, he was recognized as the reincarnation of his predecessor, the 13th Dalai Lama at the age of 2. After the Chinese People's Liberation Army began its conquest of Tibet in the summer of 1949, sovereignty over Tibet was conferred upon the 15-year-old Dalai Lama in November 1950. On March 10, 1959, the Tibetan people rose up in a popular revolt against the Chinese occupation; around 90,000 Tibetans paid with their lives for this final rebellion. The Dalai Lama escaped through the Himalayas into India. He founded a democratic government in exile in Dharamsala and since that time has attempted to alleviate the suffering of Tibetans both inside and outside of Tibet, as well as working to gain international support for the Tibetan cause. In 1989, he was awarded the Nobel Peace Prize for his tireless commitment to the Tibetan people using non-violent methods. Despite countless attempts by the Tibetan spiritual leader to initiate a dialogue with China, no direct talks with the Chinese government have taken place up to now.

fluential spiritual teacher and thus a figure of great authority in Tibetan Buddhism. He plays a role in recognizing the reincarnation of the Dalai Lama, with whom he is connected in a teacher-pupil relationship. According to tradition, a lama is a reincarnated being. The appointment of the Panchen Lama was introduced in Tibet during the Qing Dynasty (1644–1911); initially, it was an office which could be achieved through merit. The Panchen Lama is understood as the reincarnation of the Buddha Amitabha, the "Buddha of Boundless Light." On May 14, 1995, the Dalai Lama announced that Gedhun Choekyi Nyima was the reincarnation of the late tenth Panchen Lama. Three days later, the six-year-old boy disappeared and has not been seen since.

The Dalai Lama, a Bodhisattva

The childhood of the present Dalai Lama became familiar to Westerners through the film *Seven Years in Tibet*, based on the book by Austrian mountaineer Heinrich Harrer (1912–2006). During World War II, he was one of the first Europeans to live in Tibet and befriended the then very young Dalai Lama during those seven years. The protector of Tibet, the Dalai Lama is not a Buddha but the embodiment of the Bodhisattva Avalokiteshvara ("Infinite Compassion" or "the Love of all Buddhas"), also known as Chenrezig. His goal is to take all the suffering of the world upon himself. He has foregone his own entry into Nirvana and will continue to be reborn until all human beings have been saved.

The Panchen Lama is a high authority in Tibetan Buddhism. His portrait— here, the tenth Panchen Lama—can be seen at many Buddhist sites.

dhist sanctuary in Tibet. The Puning Temple is a large monastery built in the symmetrical style of the Tibetans.

Chinese Han architecture in a Tibetan monastery

The 367,000-square-foot (33,000 m²) monastery is divided into a front and a back section. The buildings in the front section—the entrance gate, the bell and drum tower, the Hall of the Heavenly King, the Mahavira Hall as well as the two auxiliary palaces on the

A replica of a Tibetan temple in China

In the Far East, there are many colossal statures of the Bodhisattva Avalokiteshvara. One of the largest is in Chengde.

Chengde, a small city approximately 150 miles (250 km) northeast of Beijing, is home to a well-known summer residence of the Qing Dynasty (1644–1911). Its construction took a total of eighty-seven years, and was initiated by the Chinese royal family of the time. Twice during this period, rebellions were staged by Mongolian tribes north of the Tianshan Mountains. The Qing government detached troops in 1755 to put down the rebellion. In celebration of the victory, in the same year, a lama monastery was built next to the summer residence near Chengde: the famous Puning Monastery. The name Puning means "universal peace." According to the emperor's orders, this temple was built as a replica of the Samye Temple, a holy Bud-

Left: Every year, thousands of tourists from all over the world visit the 367,000-square-foot monastery in Chengde, which has been declared a UNESCO World Heritage Site.

east and west sides—were built in the Han Chinese style (Han Chinese make up the country's largest ethnic group). The Mahavira Hall is the main building in the front part of the monastery. Here stand Kasyapa, the Buddha of the past; Shakyamuni, the Buddha of the present; and Maitreya, Buddha of the future. On either side are figures of the eighteen Arhats. Episodes from the lives of eighteen Arhats and eight Bodhisattvas are depicted on the eastern, northern, and western walls. According to legend, these eighteen Arhats where Buddha's best pupils, while the eight Bodhisattvas were all outstanding spiritual leaders in the history of Buddhism who postponed their own entry into Nirvana in order to help others along the way to redemption. All of these impressive figures and wall paintings have been preserved in their entirety.

The Tibetan section of the temple

The rear section of the Puning Monastery is built in the Tibetan style and rests on a stone slab platform that stands 30 feet (9 m) high. Its main building is the Mahayana Pavilion, a symbol of Mount Sumeru, the center of the Buddhist world. Buddhists believe that the sun and moon revolve around the Enlightened Ones on either side of Mount Sumeru. Thus, a rectangular Moon Hall is located on one side of the Mahayana Pavilion, and directly opposite it is the Sun Hall. Surround-ing the pavilion are four small halls and eight white, three-story terraces in widely varying shapes. These represent the four large and eight small continents which exist in Buddhist tradition. A Lama pagoda stands on each of the four corners of the pavilion-each one representing one of Buddha's four stages of development. The southeastern pagoda is painted red and decorated with lotus flowers, symbolizing Buddha's birth. The northeastern pagoda is painted black (Buddha's enlightenment), the northwestern is white (his first sermon), and the green southwestern pagoda symbolizes Nirvana.

Below: The architecture of the Puning Temple was modeled after the Samye Temple, the oldest Buddhist monastery in Tibet.

Zen Buddhism

Lao Tzu and Chuang Tzu

A Zen garden promotes inner composure and meditation. The goal is to clear the mind of all thought, because habit is deadly. The primary contributors to Zen thinking were Lao Tzu and the great philosopher Chuang Tzu.

"The purpose of a fish trap is to catch fish; once you have caught the fish, you can forget about the trap. The purpose of a sling is to catch a rabbit; once you have caught the rabbit, you can forget about the sling. The purpose of words is to convey ideas; once you grasp the idea, you can forget about the words. Where can I find the person who knows how to forget the words so that I can exchange some words with him?" (2) Chuang Tzu Zen is a centuries-old tech-nique that uses gestures, sayings, stories and unsolvable puzzles to lead the mind away from well-worn paths. The goal is to clear the mind of thoughts, because habit is deadly. The roots of Zen are undoubtedly found in China—where it is called Ch'an—and are closely related to the teachings of Lao Tzu and the great philosopher Chuang Tzu (author of one of the essential texts of Taoism; see the chapter on Taoism). Two variations of Zen spread to Japan: first, the ideas of the Tendai monk Eisai (1141–1215) that became known as Rinzai Zen; and

secondly, the teachings of the priest Dogen (1200–1253), the founder of Soto Zen. Soto Zen emphasizes meditation as an important element of Zen practice, while Rinzai Zen focuses primarily on Koans—meditation on puzzling texts and paradoxical statements.

A third school

Yet another master attempted to combine the meditation techniques of Soto Zen (seated meditation, called "zazen") with the "confounding of the mind" through corresponding techniques of Rinzai Zen. In this way, Harada Sogaku (1871–1961) developed a new form of meditation which also integrates knowledge from the Rinzai Zen School. "A monk once asked Master Dongshan, 'What is the Buddha?' Dongshan answered, 'Three pounds of hemp'." (2) In Zen, practitioners aim to consciously disrupt understanding and logical thinking in order to allow the "Great Emptiness" to gain entry.

The doctrine of the suddenness of enlightenment

Zen—or in China, Ch'an—assumes that anyone can experience sudden enlightenment. There is no need to fast for forty-nine days or castigate oneself. Enlightenment can come without warning, for example, through a text. Zen developed as a result of the interaction of Buddhism and Taoism over centuries. Thus, the wisdom of the Enlightened One

Left: Lao Tzu was the founder of Taoism, but like Chuang Tzu, he had a major influence on Zen Buddhism. The instructional book Tao Te Ching is attributed to him: it deals with the way of Tao—a universal principle—and describes how human beings can follow this path.

mingled with the "wit" of Chinese masters such as Lao Tzu or Chuang Tzu. Their cleverness lies in their ability to sell people their seemingly banal stories: "I want to tell you about these things very innocently, so listen to me very innocently," says one of Chuang Tzu's characters (2); and the spiritual "punch line" might trigger hearty laughter and thigh-slapping. However, a second glance revealed the true, deeper meaning of the master's ostensibly harmless story, as the following Zen saying demonstrates: "First there is a mountain. Then there is no mountain. Then there is." (2) It slowly seeps into a person's mind…and becomes clear.

Below: Shaolin monks are famous for their skill in martial arts. The Shaolin Monastery on Mount Song is also considered to be the birthplace of Zen Buddhism.

Shaolin and Zen

According to legend, the martial art of Kung Fu was developed by Buddhist monks in the Shaolin Monastery on the sacred Mount Song. The monastery itself was founded in 495 AD. Here, in the sixth century, numerous Indian texts (Sutras) were translated into Chinese. This is also where Bodhidharma, a man from the West (which in this case, meant India), sat facing a wall and meditating for nine years. In Chinese Zen, Bodhidharma is a well-known monk (ca. 470–543 AD, also called the "Barbarian from the West") who helped Ch'an achieve high standing in China. The Shaolin Monastery is famous for its martial arts, but there are no records as to whether the Zen masters were also skilled in this field.

cannot clap; therefore, it cannot make any sound. But what does the master want to tell us here? The answer is never revealed. This is the task of the listener. Such sayings as this last one demonstrate dualistic thinking—that is, thinking in contradictions—taken to its limits. The master's aim is to lead his pupil away from his or her dualistic view of the world. Enlightenment could suddenly be reached if he or she would raise the question "What is the sound of one hand clapping" to the level of emptiness (Sunyata) and it would seem to answer itself.

A wise person does not wish to gather knowledge

The Zen master Bodhidharma once said of himself, "This is why a wise person is like an empty cave. He does not harbor any knowledge. He lives in a world of changes and usefulness, and yet he remains in the realm of 'non-doing' (Wu-wei: see Taoism). He dwells inside the walls of the nameable, and yet he lives in the open country of that which goes beyond words. He is silent and alone, empty and open, so that his condition cannot be clothed in words. There is nothing more that can be said about him."

On beatings and cries

Buddha himself never claimed that the path to enlightenment is not a thorny one. Human beings are, by nature, lazy and comfort-seeking and tend to trust in their well-worn habits. Nor is it easy, at every moment and in every situation, to remain conscious of the fact that the world and one's own self are nothing but an illusion.

In China—and later in Japan as well—the Zen or Ch'an masters radically altered their methods of instruction in order to make Bodhi clear to their pupils: without Bodhi there is no awakening; without cries, kicks and beatings one cannot let go of the illusion of the world.

The ultimate method of enlightenment

In China, the teaching methods of Master Deshan Xuanjian have been described as follows: "Thirty blows when you have something to say. Thirty blows when you have

Some Zen masters, such as Bodhidharma, are somewhat peculiar characters who consciously use drastic methods—sayings and even beatings—to provoke their pupils. Their aim is to break through inner habits.

Zen masters and their way of thinking

Someone asked Master Yunmen Wenyan (864–949), "How old are you, Master?"—"Seven times nine equals sixty-eight."—"How can seven times nine equal sixty-eight?"—"I deducted five years for your sake." (2) All Zen masters have more or less perfected this type of absurd humor and paradoxical thinking. Their conclusions are logically paradoxical, but extremely pleasant on an existential level. Nevertheless, it can sometimes take years for a pupil to grasp what his or her master was trying to say. "What is the sound of one hand clapping?" A single hand

nothing to say." (2) Thus, the pupil had no chance of escaping the master's brutal methods. The master did not want to discuss anything with him, not because he might not have known the answer, but because in this Ch'an school it was a part of the method that enlightenment should come upon a person suddenly—without questions and without answers. The self, the monk's personality, needed to be shocked in order to break free of its previous conditioning. Everything that he had learned, experienced, heard from his parents, any education he had enjoyed and any traditions which had been passed down to him up to that point, and everything that he himself believed, hoped or wished for was to be shattered with a blow to the back. In other Zen monasteries, this was achieved through kicks, a cry or the like. The masters were not interested in inflicting torture, but rather in promoting release! Some great Zen masters were born at the moment that their

teachers slapped them in the face: the pupil would laugh because he had suddenly achieved insight. In Japan, the master's illuminating cry is "Ho!"

Atisha, a Buddhist reformer and master

The Indian Buddhist master Atisha (ca. 982–1054) was responsible for the reintroduction of pure Buddhism in Tibet. Although the religion had first been brought to that country over 200 years earlier, the practice of Buddhism had been largely extinguished through the anti-Buddhist activities of the Tibetan King Langdharma (ca. 836 AD), a follower of Tibet's ancient Bön religion. A later Tibetan king asked Atisha to map out a Dharma that everyone would be able to follow. At the same time, he was asked to demonstrate how all the paths of Sutra and Tantra could be practiced together. Hereupon, Atisha wrote his "Lamp for the Path to Enlightenment,"

Below, left: Zen Buddhists are thought of as jovial people with a great deal of humor. Their wit consists primarily in telling listeners their seemingly banal stories, all of which have a double meaning.

Below, right: According to Zen, it is possible to achieve absolute enlightenment in a split second, as if out of the blue, for example, in the moment when one realizes the hidden meaning in the question about the sound of one hand clapping.

which became the basis for all the instruction that followed. Atisha's followers call themselves Kadampas. The word *Kadampa* is made up of the syllable *ka*, meaning "word," referring to Buddha's teachings, and *dam*, meaning personal instruction and refering directly to Atisha's form of teaching, called the "Steps in the Path." The best Kadampa teachers (Kadampa Geshes) are not only great scholars but also spiritual practitioners who tutor their pupils directly in meditation techniques.

Modern Kadampa

Atisha's instructions were handed down from teacher to pupil, passed on both verbally and in writing. They spread across many countries, even in the Western World. Buddha's teachings, known as "Dharma," have been compared to a wheel which moves from one country to another, adjusting to the changing conditions and the karmic tendencies of the

The Dharma, wheel of wisdom. Buddha's teachings are known by this name, because they move from one place to another like a wheel. Dharma is also taught in Kadampa.

beings that live there. Today there are many Kadampa centers in the USA as well as England, France, Spain, and Germany.

Meditation in Kadampa

In meditation, the mind should be constantly and thoroughly focused on a particular object. The aim of Buddhist meditation is to overcome inner problems caused by anger, envy, clinging, and uncertainty. A person controls his or her mind and thus achieves inner peace. Meditation aids people in acting morally—in doing good and refraining from evil. According to the teachings of Kadampa, a person can advance to ever higher spiritual levels through meditation; finally, he or she will reach the highest level of all: the state of being a Buddha.

Correct instruction in Dharma is an important element in the preparation for meditation. A person should think about the meaning of what he or she has heard and

read. Buddhism differentiates between two types of meditation: analytical meditation and placement meditation. In analytical meditation, the practitioner purposefully examines or considers a specific theme. Its various aspects are analyzed and evaluated from different points of view. Here, the highest level of meditation is considered to be the clear visualization of the object in one's mind.

Placement meditation

In placement meditation, the mind ultimately merges more and more with the object. For example, if a person begins by meditating analytically on the suffering of all living creatures, distinct feelings of empathy will enter the mind. As soon as this happens, placement meditation can familiarize the mind with the empathy one step at a time. Finally, empathy and the human mind become one. The goal of this meditation technique is to broaden the human mind in all of its thoughts and actions, at all times, through empathy toward living beings (people, animals, plants).

Above: Around 1000 AD, Atisha wrote Lamp for the Path to Enlightenment in a Tibetan monastery. This work became the basis for all subsequent instruction in Kadampa Buddhism, which spread beyond Tibet.

Left: During meditation, a great deal can be learned about oneself and one's feelings toward one's fellow human beings. Analytical meditation on the suffering of all living creatures can be helpful. It helps stimulate understanding for the suffering of others.

Between Zen and Taoism: The Old Man from Han Shan

The unknown person who lived on Han Shan, in a spectacular mountainous region of China, consciously fled a world he found too hectic. In his chosen solitude, like the Christian hermits, he sought the eternal.

*"I live on the mountain,
no one knows me.
Between white clouds,
I am always alone." (3)*

He is called Han Shan, the "Old Man from the Cold Mountain," who is thought to have lived in the 7th century AD and about whom nothing is known. Han Shan had a profound influence on the American Beat Generation of the 1960s and 1970s, as well as later in Europe. His approximately 300 surviving poems interweave lyricism and observation of nature, the teachings of the Taoist classics and Zen Buddhist thought. The unknown author and hermit who withdrew into the mountains also confidently proclaimed his own immortality: "The man from the cold mountain will be here forever. He lives all alone, without birth or death." (3) Han Shan lived the Taoist ideal—to withdraw from the world in order to find emptiness. While Buddha sought enlightenment surrounded by his disciples, this stranger chose a different path.

Flight for the sake of enlightenment

He fled from the world never to return to it again. All he left behind him were his poems, in which he tells of his solitary life, his thoughts, and his philosophical observations of the world. His Zen observations made Han Shan an enlightened person among China's lay Zen followers (he was not a member of any monastery). He describes his reasons for doing so as follows: "Ever since I withdrew one day onto Han Shan, I have been living on wild fruits. A peaceful life, what cause have I to worry? In this world, everything runs its predetermined course." (3)

Finding inner and outer peace

"I will leave it to you to change the world. I am sitting in contented silence between the cliffs." (3)

Han Shan wishes to let go of everything, to hold on to nothing so that nothing can hold onto him. He has made himself free for the

The Beat Generation

The Beat Generation took its name from a group of young, "wild" American authors during the period from 1944 to 1960. Its most famous representatives include Jack Kerouac, Allen Ginsberg and William S. Burroughs. Their heavily autobiographical works stood in sharp contrast to the American literary establishment. "We are 'beats'!" they cried; this expression was a symbol for their "craziness." They wanted nothing to do with bourgeois society and its morality. The Beat Generation was equally interested in Mayan culture and in the slang language of Canadian lumberjacks. But above all, they discovered Zen Buddhism for themselves and read the Old Man from the Cold Mountain with great enthusiasm, because this unknown Chinese hermit had consciously turned away from a life within civilization.

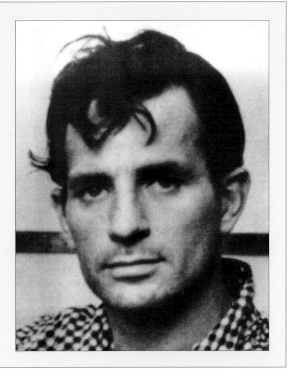

Left: American author Jack Kerouac (1922–1969) was fascinated by the poems of the Old Man from the Cold Mountain because he saw his own vision of life reflected in them.

Below: Two authors of the Beat Generation, Gary Snyder and Allen Ginsberg, who certainly would have liked to follow in the actual footsteps of the Han Shan poet. Although they both liked to travel, China remained closed to them at that time.

Tao. As simple as it may seem to be, as familiar as he had become with solitude, it would still be very difficult for him to follow the path from the ego to the self (Tao). The only things that could help him were complete self control and firm resolve to achieve his goal. Truth, wisdom and emptiness are the goals for which Han Shan lived. A further text clearly illustrates the Old Man from the Cold Mountain's objective:

Self-abandonment

The current—flowed,
The moon forgot its light—and I forgot
Myself as I sat here
By the vines.
The birds were far away,
Suffering was far away
And there were no people. (3)

The poems of Han Shan continue to carry a great fascination for everyone who studies Zen Buddhism and Taoism. This is equally true for Europeans, Chinese, and Japanese—even thought Han Shan does not offer a recipe for a better life. Some of his thoughts are shocking and mysterious. Each individual must find the way for him or herself, he advises his readers.

Buddhism in the West

Places of peace and meditation

Even in the West, it is possible to learn about Buddhism in its various forms. One can visit the temples and places of worship of Asian Buddhists, or meditate and study in one of more than 100 centers and groups, where people of many faiths and worldviews come together for shared practice and meditation.

Although the outer rooms contain impressive Buddha statues made of wood or bronze and there is a convincing atmosphere of peace and serenity, most of the people who meet here are not faithful Buddhists in the normal sense—even if they may silently assume the posture of the faithful and sit on the floor in a lotus position! One may be an avowed Buddhist, another may simply come to get away from it all, or yet "another, to combine these exercises with their Christian faith. For the teacher who is present, this is frequently only of minor importance. More important is the practitioner's readiness to devote him or herself to the exercise with perseverance. One cannot become Buddhist through baptism or by joining a church, which doesn't even exist in that sense. It is sufficient for to speak the words 'taking refuge in the Three Jewels,' either alone or to others. In this way, practitioners demonstrate their faith in the Enlightened One (Buddha), who followed the path to teaching (Dharma), the path of understanding, and the path to the community (Sangha), which accompanies and supports." (4)

Modern directions in Buddhism

The traditional distinction between the "Smaller Vehicle," the "Larger Vehicle" and the "Diamond Vehicle" is now largely obsolete. Today, the following currents co-exist as equals: Theraveda, which stems primarily from the traditions of Thailand, Sri Lanka, and Cambodia; Zen Buddhism, Amida Buddhism (Chinese Buddhism), and Tibetan Buddhism. All have centers and many followers in Western countries. The most widespread form in the West, however, is Zen Buddhism.

The Lava Viva meditation center in El Golfo on the Canary Island of El Hierro is just one of many in the West. Today, Buddhist monasteries and centers can be found throughout the world.

Zen in the Western World

The spread of Zen

At the beginning of the 20th century, Zen became known in the United States and later in Europe. Japanese scholars discovered similarities between Zen and Christian mysticism of the Middle Ages. Zen is not bound to any particular culture (even though opinions differ about its connection to Buddhism). Three important men were instrumental to the propagation of Japanese Zen—especially Soto—in the West. Shunryu Suzuki (1904–1971) is considered the pioneer. He came to San Francisco in 1959 to serve as priest for a Japanese-American congregation. Working in small groups, Suzuki began making the daily practice of Zazen a fundamental part of their lives. His book *Zen Mind, Beginner's Mind* contains a collection of his lectures; it has been translated into a dozen languages.

A messenger of Zen

Another communicator of Soto Zen was Taisen Deshimaru (1914–1982). He came to Paris as a Zen monk in 1967, eking out his life in poverty and earning a little money by offering Shiatsu massage. Above all, however, he practiced Zazen—and soon had assembled a group around himself. Shortly afterwards, he led the first gatherings in Provence. As the number of participants increased, Deshimaru decided to purchase a castle in the Loire valley; it was renovated and expanded and could soon accommodate approximately 400 people for instruction in Zazen. Deshimaru became a highly proficient writer and acquired a large following of pupils, especially in France, Germany, and the Netherlands.

Above, left: In the Western World, Zen Buddhism first became popular in the United States. Shown here is a Soto Temple in San Francisco.

Above, right: The presence of Japanese Zen in Paris. A major exhibition held there in 1994 made a great deal of information about Zen accessible to the people. Zen became widespread not only in France but also throughout Europe. The book Zen and the Art of Motorcycle Maintenance by Robert M. Pirsig contributed to its popularity.

Zen in Europe

Today, many Westerners also meditate in Soto temples all over the world. Walking meditation is just one of many techniques.

Today there are still centers in France, Spain, Germany and the Netherlands that follow the teachings of the Zen Master Deshimaru. Simi-lar to Bodhidharma, who brought Zen from India to China 1400 years ago, and just as Dogen took Zen to Japan 700 years ago, Master Deshimaru brought Zen to Europe. His legacy is carried on by the International

Dogen Zenji, the shining light of Soto Zen

Dogen Zenji (1200–1253) brought the tra-ditions of the Soto School to Japan. There, even today, he is considered one of the country's greatest religious figures and is honored as a saint or a Bodhisattva by all the schools of Buddhism. In 1223, Dogen traveled to China, where he had a deep experience of enlightenment and received the seal of a master in the Soto Zen tradition. In 1227, he returned to Japan and lived in Kyoto for ten years in two different monasteries; later he retreated to a hermitage in the mountains. Over time, his hut evolved into a large monastery— the Eihei-ji—which, next to the Soji-ji, is the most important monastery in Japanese Soto Zen. His chief work, the Shobogenzo, is considered one of the most profound texts of Zen literature. In it, he praises his form of Zazen and calls Zazen "an exercise without thoughts and without ideas."

Zen Association (AZI). The third teacher in the Western world is Fumon S. Nakagawa (b. 1947). He is a Japanese master in the Soto tradition who has been associated with a temple near Munich, Germany for over twenty years. He is considered to be a representative of the official Soto tradition—that is, the Japanese institution. What makes him particularly outstanding is his knowledge of Eastern culture combined with his many years of experience with Western cultures.

The art of Zazen

According to Dogen, the primary elements of Zazen are the sitting posture, the breath and the collection of the mind. When practicing meditation, the practitioner should choose a quiet place, eat and drink moderately and eliminate day-to-day concerns from the mind. A thick mat should be spread out for sitting on, and a round cushion placed on top of it. The individual then sits down in a full or half lotus position. In the full lotus position, the practitioner first places the right foot on the left thigh; the left foot then rests on the right thigh. In the half lotus position, the left foot simply lies on the right thigh. Clothing and belt should be loose and unrestrictive.

Instructions for practicing Zazen

Dogen wrote: "Sit upright, leaning neither to the left nor the right; do not bend forward or sink backward. Your ears and your shoulders, your nose and your navel should all be in line with one another. Your tongue should be placed against the roof of your mouth and your lips and teeth closed firmly; but your eyes should be open at all times. When you have adjusted your posture, now regulate your breathing. If a thought arises, take note of it; then, when you have done so, release the thought! With extensive practice, you will forget about the object and achieve concentration automatically. This is the basic art of Zazen. This is the Dharma gate to great peace and joy. [Author's note: *"Dharma" means all things—that is, the universe.*] Once you have grasped the sense of the exercise, your body will automatically feel light and calm, your mind alert and sharp; right thoughts become clearly defined, taste for the Dharma feeds the mind; silence and genuine joy prevail, and daily life attains its natural state." (5)

In Zazen meditation, the practitioner sits with an upright body in the lotus position. It is important that the ears and shoulders, as well as the nose and the navel, are in line with one another.

Buddhist Beliefs and Philosophy
The Five Skandhas

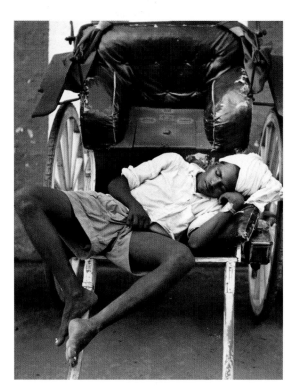

Buddha's Four Noble Truths

All of existence is unsatisfying and filled with suffering. Everything is suffering, because humans are constantly in search of something that cannot be found in the world of senses and experience. Therefore, everything is suffering: birth, illness, death, and the five groups of things that people cling to—called the aggregates—which make up the personality.

The five Skandhas—
a Buddhist model of personality

The five *Skandhas* (Tibetan, "bundle" or "collection") refer to the five aggregate conditions of "clinging" or "attachment" which define a person. As soon as people recognize these individual facets of themselves, they begin the work of realizing that every idea of themselves as a person is nothing more than an illusion. The ego is not endur-

ing. Since people in general (but especially in Western cultures) believe in a real entity that is personality, we identify this as part of a specific picture of ourselves. If we recognize that the idea of such an entity is only a habitual simplification, we can free ourselves from this habit and become—in the Buddhist sense—free.

1. The aggregate of form or matter (rupa)

Buddhists define form or matter as all the things that we can perceive with our senses. They make a distinction between "causative form"—that is, the four elements of earth, water, fire, and wind—and "perceived form"—the five senses (eyes, ears, nose, tongue, sense of touch) with their corresponding perceptions (sounds, smells, tastes, visible and tangible objects) as well as the form for mental consciousness (see also page 194, the aggregate of consciousness).

2. The aggregate of sensations (vedana)

The salient characteristic of sensation is the experience. In Buddhism, a distinction is made between three types of sensations: pleasant, unpleasant, and neutral. Sensations may apply either to the body or to the mind. Mental sensations are experienced, for example, during meditation. Fearlessness, joy, and empathy are identified as absolute sensations, since they correspond to the nature of the psyche. All other feelings are relative, since they are the result of varying conditions.

3. The aggregate of perception (sanna)

Special emphasis is placed on this Skandha because perception is exceptionally important to the development of views of the world and opinions. Buddhists speak of nameless perception on the one hand—when something cannot be identified—and of perception with a name, on the other, when something can be named and evaluated on a moral level.

4. The aggregate of mental formations (sankhara)

These consist of six groups of mental events that are classified into subgroups. Mental formations are identified as all positive, negative, and changeable conditions within the psyche. There are five "omnipresent factors" that accompany every mental experience; among these are intention and contact. There are five "determining factors" that direct the mind to particular objects, such as aspiration, estimation or mindfulness. Next, there are eleven "positive" or "virtuous factors" including, trust, respect, and humility; six "primary afflictions" such as doubt, desire, and hate; and twenty "secondary afflictions" like animosity and bearing grudges. Finally, there are four "changeable factors" which may be positive or negative, such as sleep and regret. Theraveda recognizes forty-seven mental factors; Mahayana counts fifty-one. All these factors can be subdivided further.

Left: As one of the four elements, fire is counted among the causative forms.

Below: Buddhists meditate frequently in order to collect their feelings. Most feelings are relative, since they are dependent upon differing conditions.

An illustration of Samsara,
the endless cycle of life with
its various possibilities for
reincarnation. Only a person
who has achieved release can
escape the cycle of rebirth.

5. The aggregate of consciousness (vinnana)

I. Here, physical aspects of consciousness
(man, woman, house) are distinguished from
those which are more abstract (soul, love,
hate). Nevertheless, it is always a single consciousness which perceives all objects, defines
them, and recognizes them as a thing or not
a thing. In Theraveda—and to a degree in
Mahayana—consciousness is classified into six
aspects: the five types of physical consciousness as well as mental consciousness.

II. The cause of suffering is desire. Human beings crave sensual pleasure, becoming and
passing away. This desire—identified as
thirst—enslaves a being to the cycle of existence: Samsara, the circle of life and death.

III. Without desire, there is no more suffering; the end of the world.

IV. The means of achieving this is the
Eightfold Path.

The cycle of reincarnation

Samsara, Karma, Maya, and Dharma are key
terms in Buddhism. Samsara is the endless
cycle of life: through death and rebirth, the
creatures of this world exchange their forms.

Despite all the dying, death does not exist in
Buddhism. Rather, it is a transformation of
that which exists, because with every death,
life is converted into new forms. Karma is
part of the path of life. Whatever remains
unfinished in this life forces a person to be

reborn. Good deeds will bring about a better reincarnation than bad ones. Only a person who can achieve release will escape Samsara and no longer be reborn. This person will attain weightlessness, coming to a place of ultimate clarity and motionless silence—to Nirvana. Nirvana is a condition, a happy departure. Maya is the deceptive condition of the world. Maya is illusion, a veil which separates the real from the unreal. Part of the path of the human being is to tear apart the veil and recognize the illusions of the world. Buddha refrained from speaking of God; instead, he instructed them in Dharma, the universal, absolute law. A person who brings his or her Karma into accord with Dharma will reach Nirvana.

Below: According to Buddhist belief, every human action carries consequences—not necessarily immediately, however, but in the next life. These figures are thought to foster good Karma.

Above: Buddhists do not think of desire first and foremost as erotic yearning. Desire refers to the wish to live and thus to tap all the available possibilities for sensual pleasure.

The Sacred Texts of Buddhism

The Sutras

It is believed that in the first century BC, a canon of holy scriptures from Theraveda Buddhism—the "Old School of the South"—was compiled in the Pali language. This Pali canon (called *Tripitaka*, or "Three Baskets") contains three types of texts. The first of these are Buddha's sermons, the Sutras (*sutra* means "thread," because a thread connects the Sutras to one another). One much-loved Sutra is the Lotus Sutra, which is one of the most important texts in Mahayana Buddhism. The Lotus Sutra is based on traditions that originated in India more than 2000 years ago. Its aim is to offer help to all people, regardless of their social status. This text, consisting of twenty-eight chapters, expresses inner freedom and indestructible faith in the redemptive power of Buddha. The Sutra portrays the Buddha as the personification of cosmic order, the eternal Dharma. His earthly presence serves to spread his good deeds among all those who suffer.

The Vinaya texts contain Buddha's monastic disciplines. Other texts, such as the Abhidharmas, contain various commentaries and essays on Buddhist theories and precepts.

Buddhist feasts and holidays

The Buddhist year is measured by the lunar calendar, in which each month has twenty-nine or thirty days. In February, light processions are held in memory of Buddha's sermon. More important are the feasts commemorating Buddha's birth and enlightenment and his entry into Nirvana in the month of May, at full moon. In October, Buddhist monks celebrate the end of the fasting period. In November, another great light festival is held at full moon. In addition, every country celebrates smaller holidays that honor particular holy scriptures, temple rites or relics.

The Jatakas

The second "basket" of the Tripitaka is the Vinayas, which contain Buddha's monastic disciplines; the third "basket" is called the Abhidharmas. It includes various commentaries and essays on Buddhist theories and precepts and thus represents pure doctrine. In later times, Buddhist texts written by Chinese and Japanese high priests were also added to the Buddhist canon. In addition, numerous Sanskrit texts—as well as the Shastras—have been preserved, and contain commentaries and treatises by various authors. Finally, there are the Jatakas—the "Birth Stories"—which are tales of the Buddha's earlier incarnations. Among other things, they relate many embellished stories about Buddha's life.

The Stupa

Buddha, the Enlightened One, was cremated after his death; his ashes were distributed to various princes who constructed grave mounds—stupas—to contain the relics of the founder of Buddhism. These cupola shaped monuments can be found throughout India

and other South Asian countries. They serve as memorials to the Enlightened One as well as gathering places for the faithful. Instructional Buddhist texts, holy scriptures, and depictions of events in Buddha's life decorate the interiors of these Buddhist holy places. The actual reliquary holding the remains of the Enlightened One lies in a hemispherical container. Buddhists always circle the stupa clockwise. The largest of these sites is in Borobudur in Indonesia (even though the majority of that country's population is Muslim). In Korea, China, Thailand, Sri Lanka, Burma, and Japan, believers build pagodas instead of stupas. Their separate levels are surrounded by typical umbrella-shaped roofs and always total an uneven number. The individual levels represent the varying steps toward perfection; the highest level takes the form of a sphere on the tip of the pagoda.

Stupas are cupola-shaped monuments. They can be found primarily in India and other South Asian countries. They serve as memorials to the Enlightened One as well as gathering places for the faithful—like this one in Burma (Myanmar).

Prayer wheels and flags

The Buddhist prayer wheel consists of a cylinder containing sacred texts written on a strip of paper. The cylinders are placed in monasteries, where the faithful turn them as they walk by in order to bring their prayers to life. However, there are also large prayer wheels which are housed in buildings of their own. Prayer flags are inscribed with mantras and other sayings. When the wind blows through these flags, the words are thought to be carried in all four directions of the compass.

Prayer wheels are religious objects that are placed in Buddhist monasteries, waiting to be set in motion.

Death, the Hereafter, and Reincarnation

This child in the Tibetan Buddhist monastery at Sonada, Darjeeling, is thought to be an incarnation of Kalu Rinpoche. That master chose the path of returning to the world in order to help other people achieve release.

Buddha's alternative to death in Hinduism

In India, detailed concepts of what happens at the point of death were (and still are) dominant. At the hour of death, a person should try to meditate and concentrate fully on the god Vishnu. This deep concentration will help achieve union with the god. "In this way, you will go to the lord—to him who gives light and who is the Most High." (6) In other words, people believed that something like a personal soul remained, which would merge into a union with Vishnu.

The historical Buddha was also probably familiar with this religious belief. According to his original teachings, release from the cycle of reincarnation occurs through dissolution of the self and the entry into Nirvana. The idea of what awaits a person who has achieved release, and thus receives the title of "Buddha" remains quite vague. After the monk has abandoned happiness, abandoned suffering, following their previous abandon-

ment of comfort and discomfort, the monk attains the fourth level of immersion, involving painless, joyless, absolute purity of composure, and mindfulness—and remains there. In contrast to Hinduism, the soul—that is, the personal ego—does not survive after death. That which Westerners call the self, the soul, or the personality has no permanence in original Buddhist teachings. Even during Buddha's lifetime, people were bothered by this idea. How can a soul be reborn if it does not endure after death? Buddha's answer is sobering: there is no transmigration of the soul. Rather, a person's previous existence sets the conditions for his or her subsequent existence. It provides an impersonal impulse which drives the "wheel" of Samsara forward.

The secret wisdom of the Tibetan Book of the Dead

In addition to the wheel of life, Buddhist beliefs also include the wheel of rebirth. The goal of Buddhist faith is to break through the cycle of becoming and passing away. One of the best-known collections of Tantric texts—the *Bardo Thodol*, better known as the Tibetan Book of the Dead—provides detailed descriptions of the soul's experiences during death, in the state following death, and during rebirth.

But where does this knowledge of the after-death state come from? Tibetans are convinced that certain people have been able to remember what happened to them after death; these memories served as the textual basis for the Tibetan Book of the Dead. Thus, the central theme of the *Bardo Thodol* is humans' fear of death and their inability to recognize that the projections of their subconscious minds are exactly that—projections that come into effect in the after-death state. Therefore, the Tibetan Book of the Dead accompanies the deceased person from the moment of death until their rebirth.

The period between existences

The period of time between death and re-birth is stated as forty-nine days; during this time, a lama or a good friend of the dead person repeatedly whispers the text in his or her ear: "0 nobly-born [name], the time has now come for you to seek the Path to reality. Your guru has already set you face to face with the Clear Light, and now you are about to experience it in its reality in the Bardo state, wherein all things are like the void and cloudless sky…" (7)

Tibetan Buddhism departs from Buddha's concept that the soul also dies at the moment of a person's death. The soul of the deceased Dalai Lama is already embodied in the Dalai Lama. The identity of the new Dalai Lama is discovered when a baby or small child is presented with objects that belonged to his predecessor mixed with objects that did not belong to him. The Tibetan belief in reincarnation assumes that the newborn child will remember his previous life; he will therefore recognize the objects that once belonged to him. If the child reaches for such an object when it is held in front of him, the priests in search of the reincarnated Dalai Lama will see this as a significant initial sign.

Left: The Tibetan Book of the Dead, a collection of Tantric texts, describes the dying process, death, and reincarnation.

Below: A Tibetan monk sings prayers and rings a bell. This forty-nine-day-long ritual, like many others, is described in detail in the Tibetan Book of the Dead and has been practiced in this way for centuries.

The reward for good deeds

If a person has done many good deeds during life, he will be fairly well-armed. Bad deeds, on the other hand, will hurl him into the hell of ignorance. This is the very fate from which the lama attempts to steer him on his deathbed. The dead person cannot reach his family by crying out. To his dismay, he realizes that he has a second, subtle body which only he can see, and which separates him from the world he knew. He is overcome with despair, and the lama tries to calm him: "The body which you now have is called the thought-body of propensities. Nothing which now appears to threaten you can harm you. You are incapable of dying. It is sufficient for you to recognize that all the things you see are your own thought-forms. Recognize this to be the Bardo." (7)

However, these words do not bring any comfort, and the dead person despairs still further. Peaceful and wrathful deities appear to him. Many of them begin to torment him, and he tries to run away but is unable to do so. When the Lord of Death asks him whether he was a good person or a bad one, he lies—whereupon "the furies of the Lord of Death will cut off his head, rip out his heart, pull out his intestines, lick out his brains and drink his blood." (7)

Neutral Karma and Loka

However, other people's Karma is neutral; the good and bad deeds balance each other out. They therefore experience a colorless state in the Bardo. Nevertheless, one thing is the same for all the dead: at the end of the Bardo, the soul-body takes on the color of the sphere in which it will be reborn. The soul has no power over whether it will be return to earth as a person or as an animal. This is determined solely by Karma.

> ### The mourning period
> In Buddhist practice, the intensive period of mourning lasts for forty-nine days. During this period the deceased soul makes its journey through the afterlife (Bardo) and requires spiritual support. Buddhist ceremonies are held to mark the end of each week. The funeral celebration at the temple—in which a wider circle of relatives and acquaintances take part—is also held during this period. Nowadays, mourning attire is black, but in earlier times it was white. At particular intervals—after one, three, seven, or thirteen years—Buddhist memorial celebrations are held in honor of the deceased. After this, at least in Japan, it is assumed that the soul has finally entered the afterlife.

A wall illustration shows two men who are forced to eat hot coals in the afterlife. This is their punishment for bad deeds committed during their lifetimes. Similar punishments can also be found in Islam and Christianity.

The situation of the deceased

The deceased is in a terrible situation, because he believes everything he sees is real. If he were to turn immediately toward the "clear light," he would be released. He would then tear the veil of Maya and immediately enter Nirvana, because all his visions would be revealed as shadows of his incomplete consciousness. Usually, however, he lets himself be affected by the appearance of terrifying beings, and his own torments and fears lead him away from the clear light into the deep darkness. This proves to be his undoing.

Buddhist burial rituals

Corpses are burned, since Buddhists believe that the body should be completely destroyed. The ashes are scattered into a river or ocean—or they may be preserved, like those of Siddhartha Gautama, the Buddha.

In China, Korea, and Japan, burials are one of the most important ceremonies in Buddhism. After the deceased person's body is cremated, the ashes are brought to a family grave. Sutras are recited, and the funeral ceremonies can sometimes last for days.

Buddhists prepare for death throughout their entire lives—for the process of dying and the time after death. The way a person behaves after death will affect how they are reborn. The Tibetan Book of the Dead describes the behavior of the deceased and explains the various conditions of the afterlife that can result, depending upon the Karma they have collected. If the dead person is able to recognize that the demons or angels who threaten him or welcome him joyfully are creations of his own consciousness, he may even achieve release.

Above: After a body is cremated, the ashes are scattered or—as shown here—entombed in a family grave at a cemetery.

Below: According to Buddhist practice, the body of a dead person is cremated. Buddhists believe that the soul separates completely from the body during cremation. Only so can it be prevented from remaining enslaved to the earthly world.

Life in the Buddhist Faith
Religious Practice in a Tibetan Monastery

Monastic life

Buddha himself advised his followers to be "homeless" and to travel from place to place as itinerant monks. Nevertheless, after his death, religious orders and monasteries were founded very quickly. In Tibet, the most important of these is the Gelugpa Order, to which the Dalai Lama himself belongs. The daily routine in a monastery of this order can be seen as typical for a Tibetan monastery. There are religious rituals that are repeated every day; the monks carry these out together in the assembly hall. They include the recitation of sacred texts at dawn, accompanied by ritual activities. This is followed by a meditation on a particular mandala depicting a deity. The monk visualizes the deity in question and merges with it in his mind in order to travel beyond the Maya and glimpse true reality.

The interpretation of texts

Frequently, at a later assembly, the abbot (the Tibetan "Khenpo") selects a text which he then interprets. To begin with, particular attention is paid to the newer and less well-trained monks. A communal midday meal

Women in monastic life

Buddhism is open to all people who seek redemption. Even in Vajrayana, from which Tibetan Buddhism evolved, sexuality had a different significance than in the original form of Buddhism. Very early on, women proved to be great masters in Vajrayana and Tantric Buddhism. Nevertheless, there were, and still are, very few nuns in Tibet. Today, as in the past, convents are subordinate to men's monasteries and the abbot of the men's monastery holds authority over them—a situation which fully reflects Tibet's strongly patriarchal society.

Right: The Thiksey Monastery of the Gelugpa Order is 600 years old. It contains twelve levels and a total of ten temples.

Opposite page: Even today, a Buddhist convent is subject to the authority of a male abbot. Female emancipation in this field has proven difficult for Tibetans, too.

and independent reading and study in their cells are also part of the monks' daily routine. In the evening, various guardian deities are invoked, or the deceased are honored with prayers. In the Gelugpa Order, less emphasis is placed on liturgical practice than on intensive study of sacred texts. In addition, the monks study astrology and astronomy, medicine or calligraphy. The Gelugpa Order stresses scholarship over meditation, and analyzes the holy scriptures very thoroughly.

The Dharmas

Buddhism teaches that there is neither matter nor a soul which endures after death and preserves the personality of its carrier (the individual ego) forever. Nor is there a creator god or an impersonal source of the universe that calls every living creature to life. Rather, life emerges solely from the Dharmas—the driving powers that generate everything that exists and are nearly impossible to describe in any greater detail. What is important to understand is that they generate Karma as the driving force of an individual, based on his or her good and bad deeds; after the person's death, this Karma becomes the foundation for a new life. As long as a human being does not recognize that everything is transitory, without substance, and full of suffering, the cycle of becoming and passing away will continue to exist. The remedy for this is the Eightfold Path, which leads to the elimina-

tion of the sources of suffering. Greed, hate, and delusion must be overcome. Originally, Buddha intended this path to release to be reserved for wandering monks, who had rejected society. In the period that followed, it applied exclusively to monks.

Right: In addition to studying sacred texts, monks in the Gelugpa Order are trained in other skills, such as the art of calligraphy.

Meditation, prayer, conversation and discussion of the phenomena of the world are handled in various ways in the monasteries. Some orders emphasize deep meditation, while others value clever debate.

Sunyata—emptiness

Emptiness is a central term in Buddhism. Becoming and being are dependent upon one another, since everything is merely illusion and therefore not real. They are certainly present, as humans are made aware every day, through pain or happiness. But Sunyata alone is the true essence behind all things, behind all the appearances in this world. There are various teachings about the make-up of emptiness or Sunyata. Tibetan Buddhism works from the following assumption: every non-Buddhist perceives the world and everything in it as real. This person does not grasp that Karma alone produced the world. The greatest truth, on the other hand, is Sunyata. It cannot be expressed, only experienced. A person who can achieve this will recognize—if only for an instant—that the universe and he himself do not exist.

No self, no world—but consciousness

Using various techniques, monks train themselves to recognize the dependencies that cause a phenomenon to occur. At the same time, the intellect is trained to recognize every argument and explanation as contradictory. Nothing is certain. The opposite of anything that one could actually assume to be certain is always possible. Only consciousness is considered to be real. The self, the personality, and the things that surround us are creations of this consciousness. The self is understood to be a product of the consciousness. It craves life, success, wealth, health, etc. An example of this, according to Buddhism, are the mental experiences that the self lives through but which, in fact, only give us the illusion of being real. For instance, when a person is in love, we are led to believe in something that does not really exist. As soon as we free ourselves from this, we "wake up" and realize what a fool we have been. It is the same with everything, says the Buddha.

The dangerous Chöd ritual

The Chöd ritual is familiar from Tibetan monasteries. It is described in magical literature and was practiced by the French-born explorer Alexandra David-Neel (1868–1969) in the early 20th century. This intrepid researcher of Tibetan culture studied Tibetan occultism extensively during her fourteen-year stay in that country. As the literal meaning of the word implies (*Chöd* means "to chop off"), the Chöd ritual means that a person "cuts off" their erroneous idea of a self once and for all. The ritual helps to train practitioners in fearlessness and develop empathy with all creatures—even demons. The latter are invoked when the yogi envisions his own body being cut up and offered as a sacrifice to the demons. The body is imagined as fat and ugly, a hook on which all desires hang. The practitioner visualizes a goddess of wisdom who cuts off the head and chops the rest of the body into pieces.

Deep immersion in meditation

The Chöd ritual is practiced in a state of deep meditative immersion. In further visualizations, the body pieces are thrown into a bowl, the practitioner's own skull, which is imagined as a cooking pot over a fire. The unimaginable astral light emitting from this sacrifice attracts a host of spirits and demons. The Chöd ritual demands extreme self-discipline and is often practiced in cemeteries and burial grounds. It is considered a dangerous magical practice that—if carried out improperly—can lead to psychosis.

Left: With enormous courage and completely on her own initiative, Alexandra David-Neel conducted research into the religious world of Tibet in the mid-1930s. She wrote numerous books about her experiences as the first white woman in Tibet.

Below: The study of Thangkas and sacred texts is essential for experiencing Sunyata, a major goal in Buddhism. Sunyata is the true nature behind all things, behind all the appearances of the world.

Voluntary entry into the cloister

Since 1999, women from all over the world have been given the opportunity to live as Buddhist nuns in a convent in Sri Lanka. First, however, they must be completely familiar with the teachings of this religion.

In some Buddhist countries today, it is possible to enter a cloister for a brief period of time. However, this is only comparable to a limited degree to a stay in a Christian cloister in the Western World. In Burma (Myanmar) for example, boys between ten and fourteen years old trade in their jeans and sweatshirts for red monks' robes, have their heads shaved and spend long periods of time in a monastery without their parents' supervision. They are not required to obey the rules of the order and may terminate their stay in the monastic community at any time.

For the children, this is an experience that will influence their future lives: they are introduced to the simplicity of monastic life and the search for truth above and beyond the structure of society. In the course of their lives, many adults repeatedly spend several weeks at a time in a cloister. Meditation, singing and the retreat into a world that encourages confrontation with one's own ego are among their motivations. They attempt to find a balance between their day-to-day life and spiritual experience. At the same time, they can deepen their knowledge of the philosophical aspect of Buddhism.

A Modern order of Theraveda nuns in Sri Lanka

The opportunity Buddha provided for nuns to enter religious orders was brought to an end in Sri Lanka approximately 1000 years ago by a campaign of destruction by Tamil conquerors from India. Since Buddha taught that nothing lasts for all eternity, many Asian Buddhist women (as well as monks) have been attempting for decades to reintroduce the full ordination of nuns into their respective traditions and countries. This movement seems to have succeeded in Sri Lanka—a country whose Dharma tradition is considered to be particularly tradition-bound and conservative. Since March 1999—since the full ordination (Upasampada) of twenty nuns (who were required to take ten vows) by a group of the country's high-ranking monks in the famous Raja Maha Vihara—women from all over the world once again have the opportunity to live and work as nuns in Theraveda Buddhism. The Raja Maha Vihara is near the capital city of Colombo, and is the most sacred Buddhist temple in Sri Lanka. According to legend, it was once visited by Buddha himself.

Breaking a taboo

Since the recent ordination of women, the path has been has been cleared for additional orders to be established. One of Sri Lanka's largest monastic traditions—the Amarapura fraternity—now supports the full ordination of women. The people accept this new-old movement, since nuns have long enjoyed an excellent reputation in Sri Lanka. The extremely popular radio host and university instructor Bhikkhuni Kusuma had already become Sri Lanka's first Buddhist nun three years earlier. The news of her ordination in 1996 thrilled the entire country and represented the decisive breaking of an old taboo.

Left: Modern monks may even own cell phones—especially if they have voluntarily placed themselves in the care of a monastery for a limited period of time. Here, they hope to discover far-reaching insights that will help them later in life.

Below: Similarly to Catholic nuns, Buddhist nuns also have the hair shaved from their heads. On a deeper level, this serves as an outwardly visible symbol of their complete renunciation of the world.

JUDAISM

The Origins and History of Judaism
Judaism – The Oldest Monotheistic Faith in the World

The Jewish faith

The fact that Abraham, the first patriarch of the Israelites, is prepared to sacrifice even his own son, Isaac, to God, exemplifies the Jewish belief in the covenant between people and their creator.

The oldest monotheistic religion in the world is more than 3000 years old. The God of the Tanakh, or the Hebrew Bible, acknowledges no other god but himself and entered into an eternal covenant with his chosen people, the Israelites. He gave his people two tablets bearing the Ten Commandments, which are binding tenets of the Jewish faith. All other commandments, obligations, and rituals were primarily recorded in the Torah (first five

books of the Bible) or passed down by oral tradition. The afterlife does not play a big role in Judaism; instead there is the deeply anchored hope that one day the Messiah will come to transform the people of the world into God's holy people. This will be accompanied by the extermination of all evil. Israel itself is God's chosen people, chosen to set an example of holiness and ethical behavior for the rest of the world. Until God's rule finally dawns, devout Jews try to live their daily lives according to the commandments, dedicating their lives to God.

The first patriarch

Jews trace the origins of the Israelite people and their religion back to Abraham. He is considered the founder of their faith and the first patriarch of the peoples of Israel: Abraham, along with his son, Isaac, and grandson, Jacob, are often referred to as the patriarchs. Islam also reveres Abraham, or Ibrahim in Arabic. Along with his first son, Ishmael, he is seen as the one who restored the monotheistic cult of the Kaaba. The Bible records that Abraham left his hometown of Ur in Chaldea, in southern Mesopotamia (present-day Iraq) in the early 2nd century BC. Abraham wandered through the desert of Arabia until he reached God's "Promised Land" of Canaan. He gave up the polytheistic practice of his people to believe in the one true God, the creator of the world, whom he could only find in the land called Canaan.

Abraham, Isaac, Jacob, and Joseph

According to the Tanakh, Abraham journeyed as a nomad through Canaan with his clan and his herd, in a constant search of fertile grazing land. God had called this man to be the father of many descendants and the founder of a great people, yet only very late in life did his wife, Sarah, bear him a son, whom he named Isaac. His maid Hagar also

Interpreter of dreams

The twelve sons of Isaac's son, Jacob, are the forefathers of the twelve tribes of Israel. The name "Israel" is from Jacob, who wrestled one night with an angel of God and thus received the nickname *Israel* ("he who wrestles with God"). Jacob's son Joseph was sold by slave dealers to Egypt, where he was kept in the pharaoh's prison. But Joseph possessed the gift of interpreting dreams, and the pharaoh summoned Joseph to interpret his dreams. Joseph revealed that seven years of plenty would be followed by seven years of famine in Egypt.

bore him a son, Ishmael. After Isaac's birth, Ishmael and Hagar were banished into the desert, while Isaac took on a significant role in the Jewish faith. When God demanded of Abraham that he sacrifice his beloved son Isaac, Abraham did not hesitate. The bloody deed was never performed: an angel stopped Abraham and a ram caught in nearby bushes was sacrificed, instead (see Genesis 22). Apparently, God only wanted proof of his unswerving obedience. After his wife's death,

Abraham bought the cave of Machpelah to add to the property he owned in the town known today as Hebron. There he buried Sarah, and he and later his son Isaac were also laid to rest there. The cave subsequently became a Jewish holy site, although a mosque now stands on that spot.

Above: According to the Hebrew Bible, after Abraham's wife, Sarah, had gave birth to Isaac, Abraham banished his first-born son Ishmael and his mother, Hagar, into the desert.

Left: A Jew prays at Abraham's grave in Hebron, the final resting place of both Abraham and his son Isaac. The site is a holy place for both Jews and Muslims.

The Exodus from Egypt

Back to the Promised Land

The depiction of Moses as a horned figure, here by Michelangelo, can be traced to an inaccurate translation. the Hebrew word "keren" (beam of light) was mistaken for the word "karma'im" (horn). The error was later corrected.

The sufferings of the Israelites are thought to have begun under Pharaoh Ramses II, as related in the second book of Moses (Exodus). Ramses II (1279–1213 BC) was the third pharaoh of the 19th dynasty in ancient Egypt. Under his rule, the Israelites were forced into hard labor and treated like slaves. It was Moses who led them back into the Promised Land of their fathers, Canaan. They saw him as the servant of God, their savior. The Bible describes their eventful exodus from Egypt. Miracles such as the parting of the Red Sea, which they were able to cross without getting their feet wet, while the pharaoh's soldiers were swept away by huge volumes of water that suddenly rushed over them, showed the Israelites that God is with them and will protect them.

The question as to whether natural laws were suspended by the power of the Creator, or things actually occurred quite differently, has continued to give rise to all kinds of theories and attempted explanations even into the 20th century.

Who was Moses?

Moses is known as the man who led the Israelites out of slavery in Egypt and entered into a covenant with God. It was through Moses that the Israelites received the Ten Commandments. The first five books of the Bible are called the books of Moses in his

---

Freedom fighter around 1300 BC

What is the truth about Moses? Egyptologist Rolf Krauss is convinced that the biblical hero was really Amunmasesa, an Egyptian viceroy of the 13th century BC, who instigated a rebellion against the pharaoh. The Bible preserved the memories of the rebellions—and simply rewrote them. The Egyptian became an Israelite, and the ringleader against the pharaoh a freedom fighter. "In the opinion of contemporary researchers, Egyptian memories of the Israelites form part of the biblical belief in one God. Pharaoh Akhenaton (1364–1347 BC), a religious revolutionary before the time of Moses, had already abolished all gods but one—the sun god Re." (1) Akhenaton's theory was quite radical, for he claimed this was a loving God.

Crossing the Red Sea

A mirage is caused by the behavior of light beams when they travel through layers of cooler and hotter air. On a hot road or in the desert, our eyes will perceive a seemingly clear, though wavering, reflection of the sky. In the desert, this makes endless sand dune landscapes appear to turn into seas. This leads some scientists, like American physicist Alastair B. Fraser, to wonder whether the Israelites' successful crossing of the Red Sea could be explained by such a mirage. Fraser presumes that Moses' route ran north of the Red Sea— ideal terrain for mirages. The people who fled from Egypt could hardly have been familiar with such apparitions.

honor. But did this famous figure ever exist? Archaeologists continue to hunt for traces of him to this day. The search for the historic Moses leads to Egypt. Did one of the pharaohs really enslave the Israelites there? Some modern scholars, like Israeli archaeologist Israel Finkelstein (born 1949), the biblical story is really about an ancient people from Asia Minor that settled in the Nile Delta around 1700 BC, the Hyksos ("rulers of foreign lands"). They even held power in Egypt for a time (during the 15th and 16th dynasties, around 1600 BC), until they were eventually defeated by the pharaohs.

Above: God appears to Moses in the form of a burning thorn bush and entrusts him with the task of leading his people out of slavery.

Below: The miracle of the parting of the Red Sea by Moses is a sign to the Israelites that God is with them on their flight from Egypt. Some researchers attribute this miraculous story to a mirage.

Forty years in the wilderness

Before the Jews arrived in their Promised Land, they reached Mount Sinai, where God gave them the Ten Commandments, handed to Moses on the mountain as a sign of the covenant between God and his chosen people. The second commandment makes it clear what God expects of his people: "You shall have no other gods before me." The Israelites spent forty years in the desert and Moses died before they entered the promised land. In Canaan, bloody battles with the local peoples ensued, especially the Philistines, who had formed an alliance of five cities (including Gaza). The Greeks and Romans named this land after them: Philistia (Palestine) or Palaestina Tertia. The Philistines had iron weapons and dealt the Israelite tribes a series of crushing blows. Only King David was able to eliminate the threat they posed.

On Mount Sinai, Moses receives from God two stone tablets inscribed with the Ten Commandments, intended to seal the covenant between God and the Israelites. The Ten Commandments regulate how people should behave toward God and each other.

God's Ten Commandments

The Ten Commandments Moses received on Mount Sinai are recorded as follows (Exodus 20 and Deuteronomy 5):

1. I am the LORD your God, who brought you out of the land of Egypt, out of the house of bondage.

2. You shall have no other gods before me. You shall not make for yourself a graven image, or any likeness of anything that is in heaven above, or that is in the earth beneath, or that is in water under the earth; you shall not bow down to them or serve them; for I the LORD your God am a jealous God, visiting the iniquity of the fathers upon the children to the third and fourth generation of those who hate me, but showing steadfast love to thousands of those who love me and keep my commandments.

3. You shall not take the name of the LORD your God in vain; for the Lord will not hold him guiltless who takes his name in vain.

4. Remember the Sabbath day, to keep it holy. Six days you shall labor, and do all your work; but the seventh day is a Sabbath to the LORD your God; in it you shall not do any work, you, or your son, or your daughter, your manservant, or your maidservant, or your cattle, or the sojourner who is within your gates; for in six days the LORD made heaven and earth, the sea, and all that is in them, and rested the seventh day; therefore the LORD blessed the Sabbath day and hallowed it.

5. Honor your father and your mother, that your days may be long in the land which the LORD your God gives you.

6. You shall not kill.

7. You shall not commit adultery.

8. You shall not steal.

9. You shall not bear false witness against your neighbor.

10. You shall not covet your neighbor's house; you shall not covet your neighbor's wife, or his manservant, or his maidservant, or his ox, or his ass, or anything that is your neighbor's.

David and Solomon

King David, The Beloved

King David (Hebrew, "the beloved," ca. 1004–965 BC) was the first ruler of Israel who was able to unite the land and extend its territorial boundaries. He is famous for defeating Goliath of the Philistine tribe (known as "the giant" due to his huge size), killing him with a slingshot. According to tradition, David was a shepherd, musician, and weapon-bearer for King Saul and belonged to the tribe of Judah. By marrying Saul's daughter, Michal, he became part of the ruling family. Though a rivalry soon developed between him and Saul, he remained loyal to Saul for a long time. It was not until he turned 30 that David became king of the whole of Israel.

The Star of David

The Star of David (or "shield of David" in Hebrew)—two interlocking equilateral triangles—symbolizes the joining of the tribes of the Northern and Southern Kingdoms to form a united Israel. David is credited with bringing the separate tribes of Israel together to form one people. But as far as we know, the six-pointed star was not an exclusively Jewish sign in antiquity; other peoples also used it. Some even ascribed it magical qualities, such as the power to ward off demons. The Star of David is now the national symbol of Israel, featured on the nation's flag.

His historical legacy

David understood his role as primarily that of extending the Israelite kingdom. Through successful battles with neighboring peoples like the Moabites, Ammonites, and Edomites, he extended his powerbase and also led Israel to economic prosperity. Historians describe David as a cruel ruler who did not spare his captives. After his victory over the Moabites, for example, the captives had to lie on the ground: "Two lines he measured to be put to death, and one full line to be spared." (II Samuel, 8:2).

Jerusalem became the new capital; with the Ark of the Covenant on Mount Zion, it grew to become the religious center of the realm. David founded a dynasty that would rule for many centuries to come. His musical talent led him to become the author of many biblical Psalms, through which he expressed his love of God.

It was said that the Messiah, too, would one day come from the House of David and finally usher in the rule of God on earth.

In his early years, David, who became King of Israel at the age of 30, killed the giant Philistine, Goliath, with a simple slingshot.

The Ark of the Covenant

David and the Ark of the Covenant, which was presumably destroyed with the Holy Temple of Jerusalem; yet the search for it continues to this day. The Ark of the Covenant is said to have contained the stone tablets bearing the Ten Commandments.

During the Israelites' sojourn in the desert, the Arc of the Covenant was "The House of God," or the holy shrine binding all Israelite tribes together. King David brought it to Jerusalem, and when Solomon built the Holy Temple there he placed it in its inner sanctum. Some historians assume the Ark was destroyed with the Temple in 587 BC when Jerusalem was conquered by the Babylonians, but the search for it continues to this day: in Ethiopia, under the Temple Mount in Jerusalem, and even in the south of France.

The Ark is described in great detail in the Bible. It is a rectangular chest roughly 3¾ ft (115 cm) long and 2⅓ feet (70 cm) wide and high, made of acacia wood and gilded. It was carried by means of staves inserted in four rings attached to its lower corners. Its sole contents: the two tablets bearing the Ten Commandments. Its lid, made of solid gold, was adorned with two cherubim with outstretched wings—a symbol of God's protection and presence in the Ark.

King Solomon, The Wise

The Wisdom of Solomon is proverbial, and he is famous for his legendary knowledge. The Bible credits King Solomon (ca. 965–926 BC), son of King David, with cavorting with 700 women and 300 concubines. Thanks to a clever political strategy, he safeguarded the borders of his kingdom by marrying the daughters of foreign rulers. Solomon finally took the daughter of the pharaoh to be his wife in order to avoid war with Egypt. The symbol of his power was a magical ring featuring a hexagram, a popular talisman to this day.

Left: The Queen of Sheba on her visit to Solomon's court in Jerusalem. It was in her honor that Solomon later sang the Song of Solomon.

The wisdom of Solomon and the Queen of Sheba

Solomon is said to have been a peace-loving and wise man, and the Bible cites an example of his wisdom. Two women came to the king. Each had borne a child, but only one baby had survived; both insisted they were the mother of the living child. Solomon ruled that the child should be cut in half, and each woman given half. One of the two renounced her right, thereby revealing herself as the true mother, as she put the child first—Solomon granted the child to her. The Bible records that the Queen of Sheba came to Solomon's court to test the ruler with some riddles. Solomon solved all the riddles posed by the mysterious woman, who clearly came from Ethiopia. In the book of Proverbs, Solomon lets Wisdom speak for herself: "The Lord created me at the beginning of his work, the first of his acts of old. ... before the beginning of the earth."—Wisdom's self-testimony that she existed before all creation.

Solomon and the Queen of Sheba are seen as a mystical couple, whose joint wisdom has to do with the mystery of the union of male and female. The Song of Solomon— a text celebrating erotic love—is also to be understood in this sense.

The building of the Temple and the death of Solomon

King Solomon had many buildings erected. The first Holy Temple in Jerusalem, whose origins are shrouded in mystery, was built in the mid-10th century BC. Sacrificial ceremonies were the only form of worship held in the Holy Temple, and only the High Priest could enter the inner sanctum. After the death of Solomon, his son, Rehoboam, ruled the kingdom, but he was not able to maintain the successful policies of his father for long, and the kingdom of the twelve tribes thus disintegrated.

Below: Solomon is famous for his wisdom, which was particularly manifest in his response to the quarrel of two women over which of them was a child's true mother. This has gone down in history as the "Judgment of Solomon."

Religious Groups in Judaism at the Turn of the Era

Apart from the enigmatic community in Qumran on the Dead Sea, known as the Essenes, three other Jewish groups from the turn of the era are known, and mentioned in early Christian sources.

The Sadducees

In the year 70, not only was the Holy Temple of Jerusalem destroyed by order of Emperor Titus, Roman troops also seized the menorah and took the seven-branched candelabrum back to Rome as spoils of war.

The Sadducees presumably named themselves after the High Priest under Solomon, Zadok, who was in charge of the Holy Temple. This religious group is said to have originated from an old priestly aristocracy and was part of the Jewish priest nobility in the period around 150–70 BC. The Sadducees emphasized the supremacy of the Torah. They were opponents of the Pharisees, who, unlike them, believed in the continued life of the soul after death and were convinced of the existence of angels and spirits. The Sadducees also rejected any divine intervention in human affairs through miracles, dismissed oral tradition, and placed God's divine plan above human free will. They rejected any hope of resurrection such as that described later by the apostle Luke (Luke 20:27). The Sadducees declined after the Romans destroyed the Holy Temple in Jerusalem in the year 70, leaving only the "Wailing Wall," which has survived to this day: their religious beliefs were too closely dependent on the continued existence of the Temple and the Jewish state. They also lacked widespread public support, because their teachings and interpretation of the laws were too strict for most Jews.

The Pharisees

Among the teachings of the Pharisees was belief in the immortality of the soul and in angels, and the resurrection of the dead, just retribution in the next life, and humans' free will coupled with God's divine plan. The influence of Hellenism—the Greek philosophy that was spreading through the eastern Mediterranean at the time—is apparent in these ideas. The Pharisees were apocalyptic in their approach and hoped to experience the coming of the Messiah in their lifetime, as the fulfillment of Jewish history in accordance with the Torah. The Pharisees insisted on strict observance of Biblical commandments and extended the canonic law by adding an "oral Torah," called Mishnah. They sought a balance with the ruling power (Rome) to ensure the survival of the Jewish people. For this reason they were denounced as "hypocrites" by the Zealots and other radical groups. This negative characterization of the Pharisees, which incidentally only ap-

pears in the Christian scriptures, resulted in the proverbial use of the word. Many scholars, however, see them as the forerunners of a modern, tolerant, and worldlier Judaism.

The Zealots

After Judea had been subjected to Roman rule, opposition toward the occupying forces came from the Zealots. They were radical in their methods and unafraid to risk their own lives in the battle against oppression and to secure national and religious independence for the Israelite people. The Zealots refused to pay taxes to the Romans and lived as freedom fighters. Many of them came from Galilee. In the year 70, when they saw their battle was lost, the last Zealots committed collective suicide during the siege of their mountain fortress, Masada, on the Dead Sea.

Below: The Jewish itinerant preacher now called John the Baptist also preached to the Pharisees, but they were not converted.

Above: The Romans' siege of the mountain fortress Masada on the Dead Sea sealed the fate of the Zealots. This impressive site in Israel is today a destination for many tourists who come to visit the ruins.

The Essenes – A Community in Qumran at the Time of Jesus?

with the life of a community presumed to have lived in Qumran, who hid the texts in the caves around 70 AD to keep them safe from the Romans. One of the texts includes the words "war of the sons of light against the sons of darkness." Researchers presume that "sons of darkness" was a reference to the Romans. According to research findings following excavation of the ruins, until its destruction in the year 68, Qumran itself may have been the center of a strictly disciplined faith community similar to a religious order. The authors of the scrolls in the pottery vessels are presumed to have been members of the same community, the Essenes. Some

The Dead Sea scrolls

Above: The valuable scrolls were hidden in these caves near Qumran, presumably to keep them from the Romans. It was not until 1947 that they were accidentally discovered by a Bedouin boy.

In 1947, a boy from a Bedouin tribe found rolls of text hidden in a tall pottery vessel inside a cave near the Dead Sea. The place where they were found is less than a mile from a site on the southwest shore of the Dead Sea called Khirbet Qumran. In the years that followed, additional texts were found in other caves nearby, clearly dealing

What is known about the Essenes

The Essenes rejected the idea of temple worship and priesthood in Jerusalem and hoped to bring about the reign of God by leading lives of strict penitence. The poor and the sick did not belong to the community. The Essenes led a disciplined, austere life and considered themselves the last generation before the arrival of the Messiah. Much of the way they thought and lived their lives is reminiscent of Jesus of Nazareth. They obviously believed in a "teacher of justice," who preached love, although they did advocate armed resistance against the "sons of darkness."

Far right: Some of the documents—like this excerpt from the Isaiah Scroll—date from the first century BC. The scroll containing almost the entire Book of Isaiah is the most substantial manuscript among the Qumran finds: it is more than 25 feet (7 m) long.

of the manuscripts date from the first century BC. The most substantial text is the 25-foot (7.3-m) long Isaiah Scroll, the manuscript of the biblical Book of Isaiah.

Archaeological research in Qumran

In the year 2000, the latest archaeological finds in Qumran were debated by experts. For Qumran itself, it was determined that there were three main periods of settlement, from the so-called Israelite Settlement Period in the 8th/7th century BC (Iron Age) to the third and last period from 68–73 AD. Huge water reservoirs constructed in an extremely impractical way, with almost half the storage volume taken up by elaborate flights of stairs, have been the subject of much discussion ever since they were uncovered. In their shape and design, they resemble *mikvah,* or Jewish ritual baths. For many years it was assumed that only male skeletons had been found at the community cemetery—for scientists an indication that it had been a community of monks. Objects resembling

tables, 16 feet (5 m) long, and three large inkwells were also found. Qumran thus quickly came to be seen as the location of the Essenes' faith community.

New developments

However, new findings made public in 2000 have since given rise to a new interpretation: Qumran was a winter villa, a trading place with a tax office, a military stronghold, a leather tannery, an agricultural landowner's residence, and the Essenes' equivalent of the temple. The discovery of female skeletons also led to new look at the whole theory. The population has since been estimated at around 200 to 300 people of both sexes and all ages, when the latest data and current number of known gravesites are taken into account. Khirbet Qumran was farmed along the lines of the oriental oasis culture and provided its population with an adequate living standard. That it was populated by members of the Essene sect has been neither archaeologically proven nor disproved.

No one can say with certainty who lived at Qumran. For a long time it was presumed to be the Essenes, but since new finds such as female skeletons have come to light, doubts have been raised about that theory.

Different Persuasions of Faith in Judaism

Haredi Jews wear black clothing, a hat, beard and long temple locks. The proportion of Orthodox Jews in Israel is thought to be about 20 percent.

Over the course of more than two thousand years, numerous currents have developed within Judaism, with the borders between them quite fluid at times. Generally speaking, a distinction is made between Orthodox, Conservative, and Reform Judaism.

Orthodox and ultra-Orthodox Jews

For Orthodox Jews, literal interpretation of the Torah and the Talmud is of the utmost importance. Orthodox Judaism developed in the course of the 19th century (primarily in Eastern Europe)—with the aim of living life completely in accordance with the instructions of the holy books. The *haredi* are a highly conservative subgroup of Orthodoxy, recognizable by their black clothing, hats, beards and long ear locks. Their religious belief includes mysticism or Kabbalah and, like all Orthodox Jews, they observe strict separation between men and women during worship. Physical separation of the sexes (by a barrier) is also evident at the Wailing Wall in Jerusalem. While Israel has no official state religion, religious matters are referred to the Chief Rabbinate, represented by two Orthodox head rabbis, one from the Sephardic tradition and one Ashkenazi (see p. 223)

Conservative Jews

Conservative Judaism is a relatively recent form of faith that bridges the gap between Orthodoxy and Reform. Conservative Jews believe and follow the commandments and laws of the Talmud and Torah, though interpreted less strictly, tempered by their view that God's word was recorded by men, and thus open to error and interpretation. They believe the law can be adapted to current circumstances, while maintaining Jewish values. There is no separation of the sexes in their synagogues.

Reform Judaism

The majority of Jews in the United States are Reform. They adapt their religious life to the modern world and in their religious beliefs tend to support a social ethic rather than strict observance of the Talmud and Torah. Like all Jews, they believe in the immortality

of the soul and reject the notion of physical resurrection. In Reform synagogues, men and women worship together. Their attitude to Kashrut laws governing the ritual preparation of food is more lenient and the Sabbath is not as strictly observed. While Orthodox Jews do not drive or switch on a light (since something is created thereby, i.e. light; see page 253f), Reform Jews drive and perform other everyday activities on the Sabbath.

Reform Jews, who have adapted their lives to the modern world, are particularly prevalent in the United States. This photo shows the interior of a synagogue in Savannah, Georgia.

Sephardim and Ashkenazim

Sephardic Jews are those who originated in Spain (*Sefarad* in Hebrew) and Portugal, from which they were expelled in 1492 and 1497, respectively. Ashkenazi Jews, in contrast, trace their roots first to Germany and then to other countries of Eastern Europe, in particular. Now they have spread much further and are a major presence in the United States. Theologically there are hardly any differences between them, but over time they developed a number of distinct traditions and prayers due to the varying historical and regional contexts each group experienced.

Distinctive features of the Jewish tradition of Eastern Europe are the Yiddish language and klezmer music. The Sephardim, or Jews of the Iberian Peninsula, were heavily influenced by Islam during the Moor period and greatly contributed to alchemistic and other scientific texts of the Middle Ages. After the Jewish people were expelled from Spain and Portugal, they settled in North Africa, Italy, and the Middle East.

The two Chief Rabbis of the State of Israel represent the Sephardic and Ashkenazi communities respectively.

Right: The klezmer band "The New Orleans Klezmer All Stars" have performed at such high-profile events as the jazz festival in Hollywood.

Hasidism

Jewish Revival Movement

Hasidism (Hebrew, "the pious ones") developed among the Jews of Eastern Europe as a revival movement in the face of rabbinical tradition. They recognize not only the scholarly rabbi as authoritative, but also the *zaddik*—an intermediary between the earthly and heavenly spheres. The Hasidim wanted to enliven a religion that had become rigid, bogged down in laws and commandments, with no sense of spirituality, mysticism, magic, and joy. The founder of Hasidism in south Poland and Lithuania was Rabbi Israel ben Eliezer (1700–1760), who is also known as Ba'al Shem Tov. This unusual man was a wandering preacher and worker of miracles, who felt the presence of the divine in all earthly phenomena.

Ba'al Shem Tov

The teachings of Ba'al Shem Tov (Hebrew, "Master of the Divine Name") are based on the belief that the natural world and the supernatural world interact with each other constantly. The creator is found within the world, which is merely his cloak. "No place without him": this phrase from the Kabbalah (Jewish mysticism) forms the starting point for Hasidic teaching, in which God and humans look each other in the eye. Many Hasidic stories and legends of Ba'al Shem Tov and other "Masters of the Divine Name" relate this, as the following example illustrates. After intensive study, Ba'al Shem Tov was anxious to do good works for the people of the land. Ba'al Shem healed the sick on his travels. Once he is said to have saved the life of a fatally ill boy, by attaching a small wax plaque bearing the child's name to a tree in the forest. Then he lit the wick and recited a long saying that has not been handed down. The light is said to have burned the whole night long, and in the morning the boy was well again.

Mystical flight of the soul

According to Ba'al Shem Tov, people have the capacity to penetrate into the core of all life; only then will we know why creation ever occurred. This search for the meaning of everything works best—according to Ba'al Shem Tov—through a mystical flight of the soul to reach the upper or otherworldly realm of the hereafter. According to the Kabbalah, the cosmos has a hierarchical order. In a state of ecstasy, according to Ba'al Shem Tov, when the soul leaves the body, we can reach through all of creation, from the bottom to the top (the final stage being God). Thus, we also learn that death does not exist. Ba'al Shem wrote a longer text on the

subject in which he recounts a personal experience: "On New Year's Day of the year 5507 my soul soared, as a result of incantations that you are familiar with, and I saw wondrous things face to face that I had never before encountered since I became a man. And what I saw and learned when I ascended there cannot be expressed or explained in words. But when I returned to the lower paradise I saw many souls of the living and the dead, some known and some unknown to me, countless of their number without measure ascending from world to world on that beam of light known to those who have experienced it in secret wisdom.... But among the things I learnt there were three special words, three holy names of God, which are easy to learn and explain. But I was not permitted to disclose them." And Ba'al Shem Tov explains that "every letter contains worlds, souls, and the divine, and they ascend and combine and connect with each other and later the letters combine to form words and become united in the true union of the divine." (2)

Hasidic students still receive instruction from rabbis in this mystical form of Judaism, which includes the belief that the natural and supernatural worlds are in constant interaction.

Theodor Herzl and Zionism

Theodor Herzl, author of The Jewish State, made a key contribution to the foundation of the state of Israel in 1948. His remains were transferred to Israel in 1949 and interred on Mount Herzl, in Jerusalem.

Theodor Herzl and his *Jewish State*

Theodor Herzl (1860–1904) grew up in a Jewish family in Budapest, where tradition and religion played a secondary role. He studied law in Vienna and then became a journalist. He moved to Paris in 1891 as a correspondent of a liberal Viennese paper, the *New Free Press*. In 1896, Herzl wrote *The Jewish State, an Attempt at a Modern Solution to the Jewish Problem*. In it he suggested three possible locations for the foundation of a Jewish state: Argentina, Uganda, and Palestine. In his novel published six years later, *The Old New Land*, Herzl described his vision of a Jewish state led by aristocrats.

The land of Zion

Zion was originally the name of one of the seven hills of Jerusalem as well as a fortress built atop it. Later the term came to be used to denote the Holy Land. Zionism has been a nationalistic and ideological movement of the Jewish middle class since the end of the 19th century, with the aim of creating a separate Jewish state on the soil of Palestine.

Anti-Judaism and anti-Semitism in Europe

For centuries, the general image of Jews was characterized by anti-Jewish prejudices. Theological hostility of Christianity toward them—the Church held Jews responsible for Jesus' death—helped to cement the Jews' social image. Jews had been excluded from most professions, leaving them little choice but to turn to tax collecting, money lending, and other "undesirable" work that only served to increase tensions. In medieval society, Jews were tolerated, but not accepted as full citizens; they were expelled from a number of countries. The image of the "exploitative" Jew was deeply rooted in society by the turn of the 20th century. In Eastern European countries, there were increasing incidences of violence against Jews from about 1880 onward. This triggered a wave of European Jewish emigration from Eastern Europe to the "Holy Land of Zion." The period of National Socialism (1933–1945) in Germany and the events of World War II brought anti-Semitism to a feverish pitch and marked the attempted extermination of the Jewish people in Europe. During the Holocaust (Hebrew *Shoah*) almost six million Jews were murdered.

Zionism

Jews' longing for a state of their own initially grew out of the destruction of the first

Temple in Jerusalem by the Babylonians in 587 and the subsequent period of Babylonian captivity. It was associated with their desire to practice their own religion in peace and without conflict with other peoples.

At the end of the 19th century, Theodor Herzl became the founder of political Zionism. He convened the first Zionistic World Congress in Basel, Switzerland in 1897, in an atmosphere influenced by the so-called Dreyfuss Affair. In 1894, a distinguished French captain of Jewish origin, Alfred Dreyfuss, was arrested and unfairly convicted of treason, becoming a prominent victim of the anti-Semitic policies of his country.

The Balfour Declaration

After Herzl's death, the Zionist movement continued to grow, and found its strongest advocate in British Foreign Minister Lord Arthur J. Balfour.

On November 2, 1917, Lord Balfour made a written pledge in the name of the British Crown—the Balfour Declaration—to help the Zionists establish a free Jewish national state in Palestine, an area the British had controlled since World War I. The result was the immigration of numerous Jews to Palestine. Due to the increasingly vicious persecution and then the wholesale murder of Jews in Europe, the number of people immigrating to Palestine swelled immensely in the following decades.

Division and creation of a state

At the end of World War II, Great Britain brought the "Palestinian Question" before the United Nations. On November 29, 1947, approval was given for the division of Palestine into a Jewish state and a Palestinian/Arab state. On May 14, 1948, the Jewish National Assembly proclaimed the State of Israel.

Above: From the time of their Babylonian captivity, the Israelites longed for their own state.

Below: On May 14, 1948, the first Prime Minister of the new National Assembly, David Ben Gurion, proclaimed the State of Israel.

Jewish Beliefs and Philosophy
The Holy Books and Scriptures

One of the oldest Jewish synagogues in the United States, Temple Mickve Israel, in Savannah, Georgia, preserves several holy Torahs. They are all wrapped in the mappah, a simple cloth, and covered in an embroidered cloak.

The Tanakh

The Tanakh (or Tenach) is the Hebrew Bible and consists of thirty-nine books, subdivided into three main parts: Torah (the five books of Moses, also called Pentateuch), *Nevi'im* (books of the Prophets), and *Ketuvim* (the Writings; additional scriptures). The word Tanakh is derived from the first letters of each of these three parts.

Only some parts of the *Nevi'im* and *Ketuvim* are regularly read aloud in the synagogue—especially on holy days and special occasions after the Torah reading. The scriptures were written from 950 to 550 BC. The Tanakh with its many different books also offers various Torah versions.

The Torah

Passages from the *Torah* (Hebrew, "teaching, doctrine, instruction") are read out loud during worship in the synagogue; it is the main source of Jewish law, Jewish ethics, and a guide to the thinking and way of life of practicing Jews. In addition, it defines the rules for relationships between people and

The Pentateuch

God, and for human relationships in general. Passages of the Torah are recited on every Sabbath and holy day and on Mondays and Thursdays over the course of the year; then the cycle begins anew. The reader recites the passages to the congregation from a hand-written parchment scroll that is wrapped around two rods. The congregation stands when the Torah is removed from, or put back into, the Torah shrine (the "Holy Ark").

In the Torah there are a total of 613 individual commandments (*mitzvot* or *mitzvah*). These are subdivided into 248 positive mandates (one for every bone in the human body) and 365 prohibitions (one for every day of the solar year). It is the duty of every faithful Jew to uphold them, and in so doing, to live his or her life in accordance with God's will.

The books of the Torah have many names. They are known as the five books of Moses, the Pentateuch (Greek: *penta* = "five"; *teuch* = "scrolls"), and their Hebrew names are taken from the opening word or phrase of each book:

1. The Book of *Bereshit* ("In the beginning") contains the creation story (Genesis in English).
2. The Book of *Shemot* ("The names") contains the story of the exodus from Egypt, the long journey through the desert and the Ten Commandments (Exodus in English).
3. In the Book of *Vayikra* ("He called") the stories are about the sacrificial services of the priests and basic laws (known in English as the Book of Leviticus).

Above, left: The Torah scrolls are kept under lock and key, as they are seen as sacred and not something people should have free access to. This Torah is from the Great Synagogue in Jerusalem.

Above, right: During worship, a reader recites from the Torah. No one may touch the Torah with bare hands.

Ten Commandments and a summary of the creed. The English name for it is the Book of Deuteronomy. According to the findings of experts in biblical history, the Pentateuch grew out of older sources in the period 950–550 BC, and was first recorded in written form around 450 BC.

Other books of the Tanakh

Among the other books of the Tanakh are the *Nevi'im*, or the books of both the early and later prophets. The "early" prophets contain historical books—for example on the Israelite possession of land in Canaan—and describe the lives of the prophets, Joshua and Samuel, and the judges in ancient Israel. The prophets saw themselves as delivering the message of God and were considered by the Israelites to foretell the future. The "later" prophets are divided into three large and twelve small books (which are grouped together). The authors of the total of fifteen books come from various segments of the population and draw together God's words, teachings, and prophecies, as well as reports of the life and work of the prophets Isaiah, Jeremiah, Ezekiel and twelve lesser prophets. Their messages to the rulers and people of Israel are quite similar: they denounce social inequality and the forsaking of God for foreign cults; the country's rulers, however, seldom approved of their words.

The Ketuvim: the scriptures

The *Ketuvim* form the third part of the Tanakh and are used in various ways in Jewish worship. These scriptures date from the time of Babylonian captivity (587–537 BC). During this dark time, the Israelites were banished to Babylon and lived there in slavery for fifty years. The *Ketuvim* include, among other things, the Psalms, the Book of Job, and the Lament of Jeremiah. They were presumably adopted into the Tanakh around the year 100, and by about 190 many documents of the Ketuvim were already considered holy scriptures.

Construction and layout of a Torah scroll

Trained and experienced writers inscribe the text of the Torah on parchment using goose

Torah scrolls intended for holy worship are generally handwritten by a specially trained and experienced scribe called a "sofer" and, as shown in the photo above, they are edited in the same way.

4. The Book of *Ba-midbar* ("In the desert"), or the Book of Numbers, is about the Israelites' journey through the desert, which is why many scholars take it to be the oldest book of the Pentateuch—or at least older than the second book of Moses (Exodus).

5. In the Book of *Devarim* ("The words"), the farewell speech of Moses to the people of Israel is found along with a repeat of the

quills and ink without any metal additives. This parchment is handmade from the skin of a ritually slaughtered animal. Every Hebrew letter is written in a special way, and even the tiniest mistake makes the scroll unsuitable for ritual use. Old scrolls are not simply thrown away, but first corrected by painstaking handiwork. Only when a scroll can no longer be corrected is it buried in a Jewish cemetery.

The Torah is wound around two rods that symbolically form the "Tree of Life" (see page 253, box). When reading from the Torah, a pointer (*yad*) is used—a silver pointer with the outstretched finger of a hand attached to it. The scroll is rolled to reveal each paragraph as it is read out loud during worship. The *mappah*, a long narrow cloth, holds the two rolls of the Torah together like a belt.

The Torah is kept in a "Holy Ark" on the eastern wall of the synagogue behind a curtain. The shrine itself usually faces in the direction of Jerusalem.

Left: Just one error in transcription makes the Torah unsuitable for ritual use. But such Torahs are not simply discarded; they are buried—as here in Hebron.

Below: The books of the prophets, the Nevi'im, are also part of the Tanakh. Here God is shown appearing before the prophet Ezekiel, an event that plays a major role in the Jewish Kabbalah.

Talmud and Mishnah

These Jewish men are reading religious books, but not the Talmud, one of the most important works of Judaism. There are two editions: the Babylonian Talmud and the Jerusalem Talmud.

Talmud is the written form of what was originally oral law. Religious debate and interpretations of Jewish legal scholars were passed on orally from the days of the Babylonian captivity until they were set down in

writing in the third century. Sixty-three tracts include rules governing ritual cleanliness, doctrine, the Sabbath, marriage, holy days, and criminal law. These are the *Mishnah* (Hebrew, "repetition").

Discussion and interpretation of all the traditions and laws recorded in the Mishnah continued, and was recorded between the 3rd and 5th centuries in the *Gemara* (Aramaic for "completion"). This contains explanation and commentary on the Mishnah by various scripture scholars.

There are two versions of the Talmud: the Jerusalem and the Babylonian Talmud. The Jerusalem Talmud, written in the 4th century, is shorter, containing only Gemara, or interpretation of Mishnah, written by scholars who lived in Israel. The Babylonian Talmud, compiled in the 5th century, includes both Mishnah and the Babylonian Gemara. It differs from the earlier Talmud on some points, and is the more influential of the two. The Babylonian Talmud comprises twelve thick volumes addressing every aspect of humanity between heaven and earth.

The rabbinate

Originally, a rabbi was an unpaid teacher of the Torah, but since the 14th century rabbis have been salaried scholars in the service of a Jewish congregation.

A rabbi's role has less to do with ritual functions than a priest or minister, instead focusing on interpretation and teaching of scriptures and law, disseminating religious teachings, offering spiritual guidance to members of the congregation, and making decisions on religious issues. Since early Judaism, rabbis have always been encouraged to marry. The first female rabbi, Regina Jonas, was ordained in 1937. She was murdered at Auschwitz.

The Sabbath

Day of rest and prayer

"On the seventh day of the week you shall rest," is the essence of what the Hebrew Bible says. The sacred nature of the Sabbath (also called Shabbat), when all work should cease, is one of the most important commandments of the Jewish faith. The day of the Sabbath is reserved for honoring God. Traditionally, work of any kind is prohibited, meaning any productive, creative work; for even God rested on the seventh day of his creation. The Sabbath is to be devoted to prayer, rest, inner reflection, and contemplation of the Creator.

The Sabbath begins at sundown on Friday evening and does not end until Saturday evening. Sunday is the start of the week in the Jewish calendar, and Saturday marks the end of it. It was Christianity that moved the end of the week to Sunday.

Observing the Sabbath

The Sabbath is welcomed with the lighting of two candles and celebrated accordingly, "like a beloved bride." In families, a plaited wheat bread, the *challah,* is blessed (in Hebrew *bracha*) and broken. The meal recalls the manna the Jews received from God to fortify them on their long journey through the desert, the so-called "manna from heaven." Traditional dishes of the Ashkenazim on the Sabbath are soup, vegetables, potatoes, meat, and fish (often pike). At the end of the Sabbath meal, the *Havdalah* (Hebrew, "distinction") is recited as a blessing, accompanied by wine and fragrant spices to distinguish between the sacred and the ordinary. In religious households, the meal for the following day is prepared on Friday and kept warm, since no work can be done on the Sabbath itself.

Above: Three generations take part in this Sabbath ceremony of lighting the Sabbath candles while the parents bless their children.

Left: A traditional meal on the Sabbath includes the plaited bread called challah. It is broken while being blessed by the head of the household before it is eaten.

The Synagogue

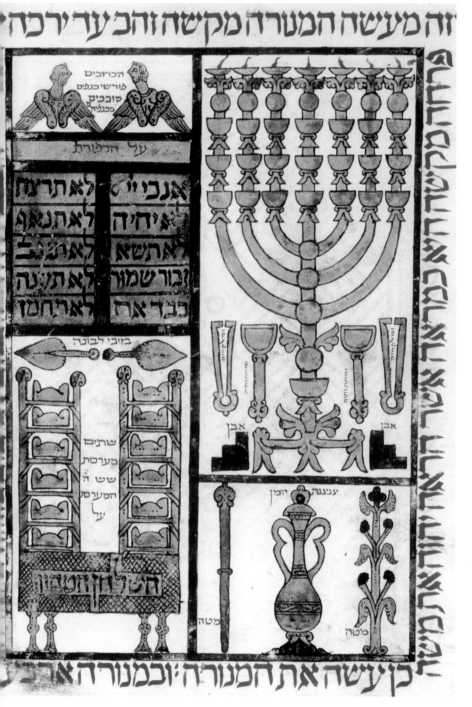

זה מעשה המנרה מקשה זהב עד ירכה

Various holy objects, of which the menorah is the most readily recognizable. The seven-branched candelabrum, with the Ark of the Covenant or the table for the bread in the Holy Temple, is one of the earliest ritual objects in Judaism.

Place of congregation and instruction

The Jewish place of worship serves as a place of congregation and learning for the faithful. The term "synagogue" comes from Greek and means "the community that congregates." The first synagogues emerged after the Holy Temple in Jerusalem was destroyed by the Romans, and synagogues usually face Jerusalem in honor of it. The architectural development of the synagogue was influenced by various building styles of the times, with the result that there is no typical building style. Inside, however, one finds the same objects associated with ritual practices: the Ark in which the Torah scrolls are stored, a podium, an Eternal Lamp and possibly a menorah. The oldest remaining synagogue in the United States, dedicated in 1763, is in Newport, Rhode Island.

The service of worship in the synagogue

Worship services may be held in the morning, midday, and evening and, in the Orthodox tradition, at least ten religiously mature men must be present in the synagogue. This constitutes a *minyan* (quorum; women may or may not be counted toward it). During the service, there need not be a rabbi present, since no facilitator between God and people is required, according to Jewish religious understanding. The head is covered to show respect for God; this covering of the head is called the *kippah* or *yarmulke*. The service runs according to the *siddur*, or prayer book, which contains a collection of excerpts from the Torah, as well as Psalms and proverbs. The reader or cantor and the congregation take turns reading aloud from the siddur. Selected parts are spoken while the congregation stands, and the worship service usually ends with a prayer for the future.

Left: The Great Synagogue (Heichal Shlomo) in Jerusalem. The headquarters of the Chief Rabbinate are located right next door to the synagogue.

The Prayer Shawl and Tefillin

The *tallit* (prayer shawl) and *tefillin* (phylacteries) play an important role in the religious life of many Jews. The prayer shawl is worn to remind them to follows God's commandments. The tallit is decorated with thirty-two embroidered threads and tassels, symbolizing the commandments and prohibitions of the Torah. It is worn by men during all morning worship services, but also on the Sabbath and holy days. The tallit should be large enough to cover most of the upper body. Many strictly observant Jews cover their head with the tallit before they pray, to help them concentrate.

Women are exempt from wearing the tallit according to the Talmud, as they often look after their family during the day and do not need to attend worship to pray during the day.

Tefillin are also highly significant. They are two small leather pouches or boxes containing parchment with selected handwritten passages from the Torah. Four Torah passages for the tefillin worn on the hand are written on a single piece of parchment, but each text for the tefillin worn on the head is on its own piece of parchment. Each text must be handwritten.

All the boxes hang on leather straps; like the parchment, the straps must be made from kosher animals. "The strap for the box for the arm has to be wrapped around the left arm seven times by the right-handed, and vice versa by the left-handed, as the Psalm verse (145:16) consists of seven words in Hebrew. The end of the straps is then wrapped around the hand three times and three times around the ring finger and middle finger to form the Hebrew word *Shaddai*, which means God." (3)

Women are also exempt from wearing the tefillin, though in some traditions they do. Tefillin are worn to morning prayers, but not on the Sabbath or High Holy Days.

Tallit (prayer shawl) and tefillin (phylacteries) are worn to remind Jews to follow God's commandments.

Commandments and Prohibitions

first and foremost toward behavior. The two basic principles on which Judaism is based are also reflected throughout this body of laws: the omnipotence of God and the sacredness of the individual.

A path that one takes

Halakhah is the entire body of Jewish law. It is based not only on the commandments of the written Torah, but also oral Toral (see Talmud, page 232), rabbinic laws and their instructions and commentaries that have been recorded over the centuries; a final layer is customs that have taken on the binding quality of law. This means the *Halakhah* ("the path one takes") is all about practice, not theory; religious obligations rather than religous insights. It is concerned with the correct application of commandments (*mitzvot*) in every situation.

This is why the Halakhah, as the Jewish legal system, includes every aspect and every relationship in life—be it among people or between people and God.

Commandments for every aspect of life

The Halakhah is not only concerned with areas that are considered part and parcel of ritual and religion, but also with areas that non-Jewish scholars would tend to define as matters of moral or civil and criminal law. The Halakhah is therefore all encompassing, like the Jewish religion itself. No human concern is outside the scope of this religion. It issues clear instructions about everything, and every aspect of life is regulated by a direction in the Halakhah—whether it be eating habits, sex life, business ethic, social life, entertainment, even artistic expression.

These precise instructions are followed to the letter only by Orthodox Jews today; nonetheless, the spirit of the Halakhah is to perform even the smallest actions spiritually, ever mindful of God.

Halakhah: the heart of Judaism

Every area of Jewish life is governed by the guidelines of the Halakhah, including wedding ceremonies. This bridal couple is marrying under the tallit, the traditional Jewish prayer shawl.

The Jewish religion defies systematic classification, despite many attempts to set up such a system. These attempts were bound to fail, because a systematic, logical structure of its teachings has never been as important in Judaism as living according to God's laws. Therefore, the priority has always been to develop a collection of customs, practices, rules, and traditions that establish what it means to live a religious life.

The Torah (the first five book of Hebrew scripture) imposes a total of 613 such religious obligations. Rabbinic scholars throughout the ages have set themselves the task of providing specific interpretations of these laws—but not with the aim of formulating a fundamental Jewish dogma. Jewish theology, such as it is, is contained in the Halakhah, the body of Jewish laws, which is geared

Adonai

In religious texts (the Torah and Talmud) God's mysterious name is expressed in the Tetragrammaton YHWH, four Hebrew letters now pronounced "Yahwe." The Tetragrammaton represents God's true name, but it is no longer clear exactly how to pronounce it. In worship, Adonai (Hebrew, "Lord") is one name used in place of the sacred Tetragrammaton, which is neither spoken nor written by devout Jews; *Ha-shem* ("the Name") is another. "Ado-shem" is used when Torah or Talmud texts are sung outside of services (e.g. at practices), so as not to reduce God the Creator to human terms by mention of his name.

Reasons for the multitude of commandments

A prodigious amount of literature testifies to Jews' interest in explaining the reasons for all the laws and rules and customs that have developed in the course of Jewish history. The scriptures themselves do not offer reasons for most of the commandments. The reason devout Jews should observe such strict rules in daily life is simply that by doing so they demonstrate their obedience to God. That has never stopped Jews from trying to understand the reasons behind the laws and commandments, and in the course of Jewish history, many rabbis have racked their brains over them. Their very search for the answers, regardless of their success, is always an expression of their efforts to come closer to divine intention.

Above: Pious Jews do not enunciate God's true name when praying.

Below: Practicing Jews and rabbis alike constantly discuss the reasons behind the commandments imposed by the Halakhah.

Death, Burial, and the Hereafter

Concentration on this world

Jewish religion is more firmly focused on life in this world than any other religion. If a dying person is capable of inner reflection, he or she should prepare for their imminent death by praying, repenting any sins, and blessing their offspring. Immediately prior to death, family members should join the person to profess their faith in the oneness of God. The dying words of a Jew, ideally, should be *Shema Yisrael,* the single most important declaration of God's sole sovereignity. The Shema Yisrael, or "Hear O Israel" is the most important prayer in daily life and is recited every morning and evening and in other times of crisis or transition.

Once a Jew has died, the body should not be touched immediately; later it is placed on the ground and candles are lit. The body is washed and covered with a simple linen cloth. Until the burial, the body is never left alone, out of respect for the deceased. Usually a *shomer* ("custodian") sits next to the body and recites Psalms.

Sheol, the Day of Judgment, and Life after Death

What happens after we die and are buried (see box, below) is not a major focus of Judaism, and Jews hold a wide range of beliefs. Still, some general comments can be made. A concept of the hereafter has always been part of Judaism; however, only the Pharisees believed in life after death. In the Bible, the bleak, dark place under the earth where all people go after death is called Sheol. This is a place of desolation, darkness, and anarchy, where everyone—rich and poor, master and slave, kings and princes, great and small—go when they die. It is part of the journey to the hereafter. Devout Jews believe that on Judgment Day, the dead will

Whenever possible, the deceased should be buried on the day of their death, or no later than the day after death.

Burial

Wherever possible, the deceased should be buried on the day of their death and no later than the following day. Observant Jews reject the practice of cremating the body. Because of the Biblical commandment, "You shall return to dust," the body is often only wrapped in shrouds, or holes are drilled through a coffin to allow contact with the earth.

Though the body is treated with the utmost respect and care, it is at the same time ritually impure, and anyone in its presence must wash themselves. At the funeral service a rabbi says a eulogy, then a relative of the deceased says the *Kaddish* (prayer of mourning). Before the burial, relatives may tear their clothing as a sign of their grief—

usually done symbolically these days by ripping off a ribbon attached to the outer clothing.

The mourning period lasts a total of one year. During the first seven days (Hebrew *shivah*) the family stays home—no one goes to work—and sits on low stools to receive visitors. In the first thirty days after the death, the family members do not cut their hair, and no weddings take place.

Jewish graves may not be destroyed, moved, or dissolved, as is done in many Western countries, where cemeteries may change hands. In Jewish cemeteries, the dead must remain without any further interference from the living to disturb their peace, until the Day of Judgment arrives and God's reign begins.

Left: The prophet Elijah ascended to heaven in a chariot—and the righteous shall do the same.

appear before God, who will allow only the righteous to rise again, as is written in the Psalms, while the godless face eternal death.

The traditional concept of the resurrection of the body remains a fundamental tenet of Orthodox Judaism. Progressive Judaism, on the other hand, has largely abandoned the idea in favor of belief in immortality of the soul.

Waiting for the Messiah

Jews live in expectation of the coming of the Messiah (Hebrew *mashi'ah*, "the Anointed"). This expectation is associated with the redemption of Israel from all evil and the reconstruction of the Holy Temple in Israel. Images of what the new world of God will look like are not permitted in Judaism. The Jewish prayer book includes the following: "He will send our Anointed One at the end of time, to save all who await the final goal of redemption" (4).

End of the world

The end of the world (apocalypse) will be determined solely by God. To devout Jews, it is coupled with the hope of God's rule coming on earth—both for the people of Israel and for all other peoples of the world who fulfill God's will, provided they recognize God's supremacy. The Israelites will be redeemed from their suffering and torment; all persecution, degradation, and contempt will cease. By "redemption," it is not sin and guilt that is meant, but a form of national freedom and peace for all peoples. When the earth is renewed, the dead will also be resurrected. This is why they have to remain in the earth and not be cremated. Misery, hunger, and poverty will end for all time. Yet what form this redemption will take, may not be imagined by anyone, as God alone shall determine this.

Below: Sheol is a land of desolation, darkness, and gloom, where everyone goes when they die.

Life in the Jewish Faith
The Jewish Calendar

The new moon as the measure of time

The origins of the Jewish calendar (Hebrew: *lu'ah*) date back to biblical times. The Israelites' year already had twelve or thirteen months at that time. From the time of the Babylonian exile (from 587 BC), the names of the months were borrowed from the Babylonian language via Aramaic.

To determine the beginning of each month by observing the moon, a calendar council came together on the 29th day of each month to hear the statements of reliable witnesses about the visibility of the moon's crescent. The day after the sighting of the first crescent of moon was declared the *Rosh Hodesh*, or the first day of the month. The news of the start of a new month was then publicized by beacons.

The Jewish calendar

As the Jewish calendar developed, time was measured from the year of the creation. Based on the Bible, this was determined to be 3761 BC. The year 2007 is thus the year 5767 according to the Jewish calendar. The current Jewish calendar is a combined luni-solar calendar. Months are calculated according to the moon—thus the length of a month varies from twenty-eight to twenty-nine days—and the year according to the sun—a year can therefore have 353, 354 or 355 days. This is regulated seven times over a cycle of nineteen years by adding an extra month (leap years). The Jewish calendar presumes a twelve-month year and a thirteen-month leap year. This means all feasts occur in the same season every year.

The current Jewish calendar is a combined luni-solar calendar. In the calendar shown here from the 19th century, the menorah and the Tree of Life are both clearly visible.

Converting to Judaism

Religion with no missionary zeal

While some other religions actively recruit and welcome every new believer—even those converting from another faith—Judaism does not proselytize. In fact, people who apply for conversion are initially discouraged. Becoming Jewish means taking on a lot of responsibilities. Anyone serious about becoming a Jew has to learn a great deal about the Jewish religion and pass an examination by a three-person rabbinical court (*Beit Din*); once that test has been passed, both men and women must be submerged in a ritual bath called a *mikvah* to become ritually pure.

Circumcision

Anyone whose mother is Jewish is, by Jewish law, a Jew from the moment of birth. The covenant of God with the Jewish people—once sealed by Abraham's willingness to sacrifice his son—is symbolically renewed through the circumcision of every newborn son in accordance with Genesis 17:9–14 on the eighth day after birth. This involves the ritual act of removing the boy's foreskin with a knife. In this rite, God guarantees the fertility and prosperity of his chosen people. Circumcision is the visible sign of the covenant between God and the Israelites. Circumcision of boys is also an integral part of religious life in Islam.

Marilyn Monroe became a Jew

In 1956, American actress Marilyn Monroe (1926–1962) converted to Judaism before marrying the Jewish writer Arthur Miller (1905–2005). To do so, she had to learn Hebrew so she could understand the Torah. In addition, she also had to concern herself with the strict food regulations, observation of the Sabbath, and Jewish holy days.

Rabbis work from the principle that people wishing to convert have to grow into the Jewish way of life through a gradual process. They need to experience the cycle of holy days and readings, and may need several years to become familiar with all aspects of religious Judaism.

The state of Israel guarantees all Jewish people the right to immigrate to Israel. However, Orthodox Jews regard all non-Orthodox conversions with a high degree of suspicion.

Actress Marilyn Monroe converted to Judaism before marrying her husband, Jewish author Arthur Miller.

Jewish High Holidays

Ketubah and chuppah: elements of a Jewish wedding

The *ketubah* is the marriage contract, in which the wife's right and the husband's responsibilities are enumerated. It is traditionally written in Aramaic, often in beautiful calligraphy. The wedding celebrations begin with the *ketubah* and reach an important climax when the rings are exchanged under the wedding canopy, or *chuppah*, symbolizing their new home together. The groom breaks a glass with his foot, recalling the destruction of the Temple. The rabbi or the couple says seven marriage blessings and the bridal couple drink a sip of wine.

Bar Mitzvah and Bat Mitzvah

Above: At the age of 13, the Bar Mitzvah marks the day that a boy is accepted into the adult world, while a girl reaches this point at the earlier age of 12 years and a day. Both have to show convincing proof that they are conversant with the Jewish faith.

At the age of 13, boys celebrate their entry into the adult world with the *bar mitzvah* (Hebrew, "son of the commandment"). As of that time, they are granted the rights and duties of a Jewish man. Girls celebrate the *bat mitzvah* ("daughter of the command-ment") and enter the adult world at the age of 12. In all but Orthodox congregations, they become full members of the synagogue community: they may read from the Torah, recite the blessing, and wear the tefillin on their arm. Before the bar or bat mitzvah, young people receive special instruction and an introduction to the traditions of Judaism.

Right: Only after the Bar Mitzvah may the tefillin be worn. Beforehand, the art of putting on the long prayer strap and the phylacteries worn on the arm and head must be practiced with the parents at home.

It is written in the Mishnah that 13-year olds should be welcomed as full members of the community, but the term *bar mitzvah* can only be traced back as far as the 15th century. The bar or bat mitzvah celebration with family and the congregation is a significant highlight in the life of Jewish young people. The bat mitzvah wasn't introduced until the 19th century, and the first bat mitzvah to be celebrated in the United States was in 1922.

Rosh Hashanah and Yom Kippur

Each fall, Jews celebrate their New Year. It is a feast that lasts one or two days and is devoted to reflection and self-examination (sometimes white clothing is worn on both days). Rosh Hashanah, according to Jewish belief, is the day the world was created and also the day of divine judgment over all the earth's people. Ten days of penitence and soul-searching follow the day of celebration, reaching their climax on Yom Kippur, the Day of Atonement, with twenty-five hours of fasting, confession of sins, and atonement.

On Rosh Hashanah and after Yom Kippur, the shofar is blown, an instrument made from a ram's horn. Ashkenazi Jews blow it without a mouthpiece, while Sephardic Jews use a simple mouthpiece. There is also a Tashlikh ceremony on the afternoon of the first day of Rosh Hashanah. After a prayer for forgiveness of sins, these sins are symbolically cast off by the act of throwing stones or breadcrumbs into flowing water. The meals on Rosh Hashanah contain fruit (especially pomegranates) and honey, to symbolize a sweet New Year.

The shofar is traditionally blown on Rosh Hashanah. This wind instrument from biblical times is carved from the horn of a ram and can be blown with or without a mouthpiece.

The Menorah

The menorah, a seven-branched candelabrum that stood in the Holy Temple, is one of the most important symbols of Jewish identity. It was one of the earliest ritual objects in Judaism (see Exodus 25:31 ff). When Romans destroyed the Temple in the year 70, it was taken and disappeared without trace. The menorah today has symbolic value. A huge version of it stands in front of the Knesset, the Israeli Parliament, and it appears on Israel's seal. The menorah used in services have six or eight arms, or nine at Hannukah, but not seven.

Sukkot, the Feast of Booths

Sukkot is a cheerful feast that calls for great creativity: many harvest symbols, such as fresh fruit, are used to decorate the sukkah, or booths.

Sukkot commemorates the deprivation the Israelites suffered in the wilderness. It can be traced to a harvest thanksgiving festival and takes place six days after Yom Kippur, or the Day of Atonement. In preparation for Sukkot, the faithful build booths or tabernacles (Hebrew *sukkah*) where they eat, pray, and, if the weather allows, sleep. These booths recall the temporary shelter the Israelites erected during their period of exile in the wilderness, as well as symbolizing the impermanence of all material possessions and the everlasting nature of faith. Sukkot is a light-hearted feast, where creativity is welcome.

These days a *sukkah* might consist of wood, tent walls, and mats. The roof is made of palm branches, but the sky should still be visible (i.e. it is not weatherproof). During the Sukkot week, people spend as much time as possible in the booths. On the last day of the Feast of Booths, (*Hoshana Rab-*

bah), prayers are offered for a good harvest in the year to come during services that include ceremonial processions.

Simhat Torah

Simhat Torah (Hebrew, "rejoicing in the Torah") is the name of the last of the holy days begun by Sukkot. This day marks the end of the annual cycle of Torah readings in the synagogue and the start of the new. The Torah is carried around the synagogue; readings are accompanied by festivities and children join in the celebration.

Hanukkah

Hanukkah, an eight-day festival of lights in December, celebrates the miracle of the oil (a tiny supply of undefiled oil lasted eight days) when the Temple was rededicated under Judah Maccabee in 165 BC. On each of the eight days of the festival, one of the

Left: During Sukkot, a procession takes place near the Wailing Wall in Jerusalem. The faithful carry palm, willow, myrrh and lemon tree branches.

Below: Hanukkah is the eight-day Festival of Lights that begins in mid-December. Each day, one more light on the nine-branched Hanukkah candelabra is lit to commemorate the reconsecration of the Temple of Solomon in the year 165 BC.

candles of the special (nine-branched) Hanukkah menorah is lit.

Hanukkah does not have its origins in the Torah. According to the legend of its origin, in 168 BC King Antiochus IV prohibited circumcision and tried to forcibly convert the Jews in his kingdom to Greek polytheism, or the belief in many gods. As a result, the priest Mattathias and his son Judah Maccabee led the battle against the tyrannical king for three long years (Seleucid revolt).

Antiochus IV had installed a statue of Zeus in the Temple of Solomon and in doing so defiled the sacred place. Jews were driven out of their homes and reduced to fighting as outcasts for their homeland, their religion, and their desecrated and defiled temple. In 165 BC, they finally defeated Antiochus IV and succeeded in restoring and reconsecrating the Temple that had since been plundered. According to legend, they only had oil for one day. Amazingly, though, the light continued to burn for eight whole days.

Purim: The story of Esther

Purim, which Jews celebrate at the end of February or the beginning of March, is one of the most festive Jewish holidays. Masquerades are generally frowned on in Judaism, since they often led to men and women swapping clothes, which is prohibited by the Torah. Despite this, everything seems to be different at Purim. This is the day when people dress up, especially children, and celebrate a joyous feast that actually has its origins in a rather somber event. Purim is derived from *pur* (plural, *purim*) and means "lot" or "drawing a lot." Haman, the vizier of the Persian king, persuaded the king that the Jews posed a great threat, whereupon Haman cast a lot in the 5th century BC to determine the day of the Jews' extermination. This was prevented, however, by the king's brave wife, Esther, who was Jewish, and her uncle Mordecai. In the end, Haman was executed instead. And so, what might have been a day of indescribable despair for the Jewish people came to be celebrated as the festival of deliverance, when Jews eat, drink, and are merry, give each other gifts, and donate to the poor.

The Passover seder

Pesach, more commonly known as Passover, lasts seven to eight days and commemorates each year the Exodus of the Israelites from Egypt. It is celebrated on the first full moon of spring, which is usually in April. The symbolism of this festival relates to people who are on the move, referring to the Israelites' journey from Egypt to the Promised Land. *Pesach* means "to pass by or spare" and points to God's sparing of the Israelites when he caused ten plagues to fall upon Egypt. During the tenth plague that befell the land on the Nile, the Angel of Death went from door to door killing all the firstborn children. The only ones spared were the firstborn of the Jews, as the Israelites had marked their doorposts with the blood of a lamb.

On the first night of Pesach, Jewish families observe the *seder*, a very special meal in which every component has symbolic meaning. Because the Israelites had no time to let their bread rise, unsalted, unleavened bread called *matzah* is eaten. Other symbolic foods on the seder table include bitter herbs and horseradish to

Dressing up for Purim

The first costumes at Purim are said to have been worn in the late 15th century by Italian Jews who were influenced by the Catholic pre-Lenten Carnival. This custom spread, and today costume parties are common all over the world. A festive meal and alcoholic drinks for the adults are all part of the Purim festivities, celebrated in memory of the victory won by Esther, which also began with a banquet of food and wine. Children love dressing up and reenacting the ancient story on the stage.

Children, in particular, love to dress up and parade through the streets during the Purim Festival

signify the bitterness of the time spent in slavery, and saltwater as a reminder of the Israelites' tears in Egypt.

Shavuot: The Festival of Weeks

On the fiftieth day after Pesach, in January or February, the two-day Shavuot is celebrated, also called the Festival of Weeks. Israel's release from Egyptian captivity, which began at Pesach, reaches its fruition forty-nine days later at Shavuot—and the Torah, the divine instruction, is revealed to the people when God reveals himself on Mount Sinai and gives Moses the Ten Commandments. Thus Shavuot is the festival of the "giving of the Torah" as well as a harvest or "first fruits" festival, since it takes place at the time of the wheat harvest. Certain Torah passages are read during Shavuot; no work is done on either day and everyone should have fun. As a sweet reminder of this occasion, they receive honey cake, on which verses of the Torah are written.

All the food on this richly laden table for the seder, or Passover feast, has symbolic significance. The meal commemorates the Israelites' release from captivity and the Exodus from Egypt, and is a joyous occasion celebrated—as seen here—in the company of as many family members as possible.

Ritual Purity Laws

Above: Ritual impurity is known in many religions, including Judaism. In order to become ritually pure, a particular form of cleansing must take place, such as ritual cleansing with running water in a well before praying at the Wailing Wall.

Right: Since plant foods are usually considered kosher (pure) and may be combined with both milk and meat products, a wide variety of sweet and savory specialties can be found in Jewish bakeries.

Taharah and Tumah

There are two basic concepts around ritual purity in Judaism: *taharah*, ritual purity, and *tumah*, ritual impurity. The origins of both go back to the Torah; they relate to the Temple cult and are seldom practiced today outside of Orthodox Judaism, except for a few aspects (such as menstruation and death). *Taharah*, ritual purity, has to do with physical cleanliness—but primarily in relation to dead bodies one may have come into contact with. In addition, *taharah* is also meant in a sexual context—particularly personal impurity caused by male semen or female menstrual blood. For this reason, both men and women can be ritually unclean.

Kosher means "fit" or "proper"

According to Jewish purity laws (Hebrew *kashrut* = "appropriateness"), only certain animals are suitable for eating, such as

The mikvah

In earlier times, almost every Jewish community had a Jewish ritual bath, or *mikvah*. Historic mikvah can still be found in a few places—like Speyer, Worms, or Cologne. The construction and use of a mikvah is governed by strict rules. The water must be pure running water, meaning only spring water, ground water, or collected rainwater is permitted; almost all medieval mikvah used ground water. The bath must contain a certain amount of water. Anyone who gets into a mikvah must be fully naked—no lipstick or nail polish or bandages are permissible—and the body must be completely immersed, including the head and hair. Traditional rules dictate the practice for men and women. Men should immerse themselves in the bath before the Sabbath or before Yom Kippur, the day of atonement. Women should take the mikvah before their wedding, and after menstruation or the birth of a child. Even today Torah scribes must immerse themselves in a mikvah before they begin their work. These days mikvah are similar to modern bathing pools, and non-Orthodox Jews are finding new meaning in the experience.

calves, sheep, and goats; but not pigs. Similarly, creatures with no bones are not kosher—like snakes, insects, snails, mussels, and other seafood—and only fish that have scales as well as fins (i. e. no eels) may be eaten. Animals are ritually slaughtered with an especially sharp knife (*halaf*) and the jugular vein must be allowed to drain. One of the most important rules forbids the mixing of milk and meat. Deuteronomy 14:21 says: "You shall not boil a kid in its mother's milk," and this is why meat and milk products may never be combined with each other or eaten at the same meal. For this reason, Jews who observe *kashrut* use separate cooking utensils for each type of food. Special kosher rules also apply to cheese.

Impurity of objects

Both objects and rooms may be unclean. In traditional Jewish households, new cookware is made kosher by immersing it in the *mikvah*, or ritual bath, before it is used. To restore their ritual purity, impure individuals must first wash thoroughly before immersing themselves fully in "living" or running water. This has been performed in the *mikvah* since time immemorial. Pure, flowing water plays an important role in many passages of the Torah. "The Midrash also refers to the living water of Miriam's well, which accompanied the people of Israel on their journey through the desert." (3)

The Kabbalah: Recognizing the Presence of God

A hidden wisdom

Kabbalists consider it their calling to unlock all the mysteries of the universe with the help of the Kabbalah. This takes years of practice in the company of like-minded scholars.

The term *Kabbalah* encompasses the esoteric teachings of Judaism—particularly the forms that have emerged since the Middle Ages. The subject of the Torah is the will of God, to be followed by every devout Jew. The subject of the Kabbalah is fathoming the inner essence of God, from which all life emanates. According to the Kabbalah, God can best be perceived through contemplation and illumination, for he constantly conceals and reveals himself. The Kabbalah considers itself to be the hidden wisdom of all spiritual life—a store of knowledge that can unlock all the mysteries of the universe. However, since this mystic knowledge can so easily be misinterpreted, dissemination of it must be restricted to those who have achieved a certain level of scholarship.

The nature of the Kabbalah

The basic teachings of the Kabbalah attempt to shed light on the mystical essence of God and the cosmological structure of the world. Kabbalists perceive God as the power of all reality, although the Spanish Kabbalists associated with the creator of the *Zohar* considered the Devil to be his mighty opponent. It is up to people to decide which side to take. To the initiated, the Kabbalah provides an opportunity to recognize the "connecting links" between humans and the universe or between creature and Creator. These "connecting links" are viewed as "forces" (spirits) through which creation can also be formed by human hand; only, however, if we are able to make them work for us. Certain forces (angels, spirits, demons) have to be invoked. All forces of the universe, according to the *Zohar*, can be awakened and reawakened by names and symbols. To the Kabbalist, names are not simply random labels, but reveal the innermost essence of that which is named. Those who know the true name of something have power over it. In the Kabbalah there are twenty-two forces of creation (corresponding to the letters of the Hebrew alphabet), which are effective in the written and also the spoken form, to summon the energies of the universe and put them to work.

Left: The Chamsa, or open hand, in the Israeli city of Safed, once a center of Jewish mysticism. It is a Kabbalistic symbol and represents the hand of God that shields and protects humankind.

Below: The Kabbalah has become very popular again. Numerous works on Jewish mysticism can be found in bookshops these days.

The Zohar

The main work of the Kabbalah is the *Zohar*, a mystical doctrine that first appeared as a written manuscript in 13th-century Spain. It was presumably produced by the Kabbalist Moses Ben Shem Tov de Leon (1250–1305), who compiled a summary of all Kabbalist teachings from the first century to that time. The *Zohar* was first printed in 1558 in Cremona. Written in Aramaic, it contains 2400 densely written pages. Among other things, these deal with the hierarchy of evil, or the so-called unholy Sefirot. These form a counterpart to the ten divine Sefirot, which bring happiness and blessing—a divine world of light—to humankind and human life. These ten stages of the manifestation of God are the focus of interest for the Kabbalah.

Gematria, or the practical Kabbalah

Gematria teaches the knowledge and use of esoteric meanings through numbers, and in particular numbers signifying letters of the alphabet. Each Hebrew letter has a designated numerical value. This makes it possible to add the numerical value of individual letters to determine the numerical value of words and replace them with other words with the same value—thereby revealing the hidden meaning of a text passage or a name. This system can be applied to other alphabets or languages, of course, but, according to the Jewish faith, God speaks Hebrew.

Kabbalistic interpretation of the word "amen"

To the Kabbalists, God is the "One," because he is the source and origin of all. The word for "one" in Hebrew is *ehad*. The word has three letters (since Hebrew does not have separate vowels like Latin alphabets) with the following numerical values: Alef (1) + Het (8) + Dalet (4). Adding the numerical value of all three letters together, the result is the number 13. The word *ahavah* means love and is spelled Alef (1) + He (5) + Bet (2) + He (5). The numerical value of all the letters is also 13. A Kabbalist would take this to mean that love and oneness (God) are one and the same. Not only that, if you add both together, 13 + 13, you get the numerical value of YHWH, or the Tetragrammaton of God ("Yahwe"). The word "Amen" can also be successfully subjected to Kabbalist interpretation. The origin and sense of this word, which Christians, Muslims, and Jews all use in equal measure, remains a mystery. It is usually translated as "so be it."

For Kabbalists, however, "Amen" has always been an imploring request, a plea to God. The Hebrew letters of this word are Alef (1), Mem (40), and Nun (50); they are also the initial letters of three Hebrew words used in connection with God, *Adonai, melek,* and *ne'eman,* the translation of which is "Lord, the true King!" The numerical value of the word "Amen" is 91 and the sum of the letters is 10. The number 10 is the epitome of the ten Sefirot, or in this case, clearly God himself.

The letter Alef is, like the Greek alpha, the first letter in the Hebrew alphabet. Letters, sounds, and words are the elements of creation, because God created it with the decree, "Let there be."

The ten "stages" of God

Sefirot, one of the central concepts of the Kabbalah, refers to the ten attributes of the absolute, the unlimited (*Ein-Sof*) or hidden God. The ten Sefirot are imagined as a tree (the mystical Tree of Life or World Tree) depicting stages of the divine being, in which the concealed world of the absolute one, God, is revealed. The manifestations (Sefira), from top to bottom, have the following names:

The ten Sefirot of the Kabbalistic tree

Keter—"crown" of the Godhead
Chokhmah—"wisdom" or original idea of God
Binah—"understanding" of God
Chesed—"love" or "mercy" of God
Gevurah—"power" or "strength" of God
Tiferet or Rahamim—"compassion"
Nezach—"constancy" of God
Hod—"majesty" of God
Yesod—"foundation" of all working and creating powers of God
Malkut—"ground" of God or "kingdom"

The powers of the Sefirot also live in individual human beings. Their limbs are the expression of an inner, spiritual being symbolically represented by Adam Kadmon, the primordial human being.

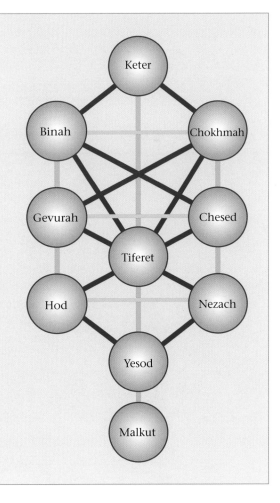

OTHER RELIGIONS

6

Confucianism
Master Kung and his Wisdom

Zi Gong asked what makes a person noble. Master Kung Fu Tzu answered, "He only preaches that which he has already put into practice himself." (1)

His name and works

Right: Master Kung is the founder of Confucianism. His teachings are just as much philosophy as they are religion and have lost none of their relevance to the present day.

In the year 551 BC, in the small principality of Lu—part of the present-day province of Shandong—a boy was born to the aristocratic Kung family. He would later be known as Master Kung, Kung Tzu, or Kung Fu Tzu. He became a great teacher of his people due to his attempts to restore order to a political world that had fallen into disorder. The Latinized version of his name, "Confucius", can be traced back to Jesuit missionaries in 17th-century China. At first glance, we seem to know a great deal about the life of Kung Fu Tzu, but in fact, we know very little, since his legend-filled biography was not written until 400 years after his death.

Kung Fu Tzu's own accounts

Below: Confucius surrounded by his pupils, whom he taught to write poetry as well as history, ethics, and decorum. He is reputed to have been an outstanding teacher.

The Master supposedly said of his own life: "When I was fifteen years old, my entire will was directed toward learning. At thirty, I took

my stand. At forty, I no longer had doubts. At fifty, I knew the will of the heavens. At sixty, everything sounded pleasant to my ears. At seventy, I follow all the desires of my heart without breaking any rules." (1) Kung Fu Tzu's teachings evoke an order in the world, an order that in his time had been destroyed. His teachings are religion and philosophy at one and the same time and draw upon China's ancient Wu religion, primarily primitive beliefs in spirits and magical rituals.

Kung Fu Tzu's biography

Kung Fu Tzu's father died early, and the young boy struggled through a difficult childhood. Kung married at the age of 19, and

Major events in the life of Confucius (more or less confirmed)

Ca. 552 BC: Birth of Confucius

549 BC: Death of his father

539–533 BC: Private instruction with his grandfather, Yan Xian.

532 BC: Marriage

532–502 BC: Various low-ranking positions, including that of granary supervisor.

530 BC: Confucius begins teaching. According to legend, he had 3000 pupils (based on today's knowledge, a number close to 70 seems likely).

529 BC: Death of his mother

523 BC: Study of music

518 BC: Confucius travels to the old Zhou capital of Luoyang, where he meets Lao Tzu, the founder of Taoism.

516 BC: Confucius flees internal power struggles and goes into exile in the neighboring state of Qi; returns to Lu one year later.

Ca. 500 BC: The beginning of Confucius' political ascent. Under Duke Ding, he first becomes Minister of Buildings (sikong), later Minister of Justice (sikou).

498 BC: Deputy Chancellor; orders the execution of the agitator Shao-zheng Mao.

497 BC: The prince of Lu receives eighty singing dancing-girls as a gift from the neighboring state of Qi, whereupon Confucius goes into exile for thirteen years.

497–484 BC: Confucius wanders through various states. The Chinese philosopher Wang Chong (27–97 AD) reports that no one could relate to Confucius during this time; he compares him to a large tree on top of a mountain.

484 BC: At the age of 68, Confucius is summoned back to Lu. Chancellor Ji Kangzi occasionally asks him for advice.

482 BC: Death of his son, Bo Yu; later, death of his favorite student, Yen Hui, and another pupil, Zi-lu.

April 11, 479 BC: Death of Confucius.

served in low-ranking administrative positions. At the same time, he devoted himself to intense study of the customs and conventions of the past. As he himself remarked, he let himself be guided by his love of antiquity and traditions. Kung's talent for teaching became apparent early on, and he instructed countless pupils in decorum, poetry writing, and history. For thirteen years, he wandered homeless from place to place, accompanied by his pupils, always in search of a position at a princely court. Finally, he returned to Lu and devoted himself to writing down his teachings and composing a book of history. He summed up the essence of his wisdom in the book *Analects*, in which he conveyed his teachings in a pedagogical style. Kung Fu Tzu died in 479 BC and was buried in his hometown with great honor by his disciples.

Honored only after his death

After his death, Kung's disciples spread his teachings throughout the country. Centuries later, ensuing generations venerated Kung Fu Tzu, and a temple was built in his honor in his hometown, where sacrifices were offered to the wise man four times a year. Over the course of centuries, Master Kung achieved an almost divine status. "Heaven cannot speak in words; therefore, it ordered Confucius to deliver its message instead." (2)

The Confucius Temple is located in Kung Fu Tzu's home city of Qufu. It was built on the site of the house where Master Kung was born.

The Teachings of Confucius

"The Master taught four things: how to understand the old texts, how to act rightly, to be loyal and steadfast, to be honest and credible." (1)

In Confucianism, everything is strictly regulated. For every situation, there are precise instructions in the Book of Rites. Thus, even a memorial ceremony for the dead (shown here), which fosters the cohesiveness of a clan, follows strict rules.

The honest sage

Legend has it that at the age of 50, Confucius was given the opportunity to put his principles of just government into practice as a civil servant in his home state of Lu. He was said to have been extraordinarily successful: merely appearing in public as Justice Minister brought criminals out of hiding and promoted righteous behavior among the people. When the prince of the neighboring state saw how Lu blossomed he was overcome with envy. He sent the ruler of Lu a gift of girls skilled in singing and dancing, as well as beautiful horses, hoping that he would give himself over to debauchery and abandon Confucius' precepts—and it worked! When Confucius saw what had happened, he resigned in disappointment. Sources report that the Master wandered homeless from place to place for thirteen years afterwards.

Following strict rules

The legend about the prince of Lu is, above all, an account of Confucius' hopes of winning people over to his strict view of life. When the prince failed in Confucius' eyes because he took pleasure in luxury, the Master left him in disappointment. "Even the ruler must abide by the common rules of virtue. Furthermore, he must be dignified and treat all people equally."(1) For Confucius, this virtue is decisive because it is the way of heaven. A prince, above all, has the responsibility to be an ethical and religious leader. He is the nobleman.

Doing the right thing: the hierarchy of Confucius

Confucius defined a hierarchy among human beings, saying, "To already have knowledge at birth—that is the highest level. To achieve knowledge through learning is the next level. To have difficulties and yet still learn—that is the level that follows. To have difficulties and not to learn—that is the lowest level of the common people." (1) People on the first level, those who at birth already know how to follow the law of the Tao, Confucius called saints. The nobility, those who lead the people, are on the next level because they know how to do what is right. This may seem idealistic, but Confucius said, "To rule means to do what is right. A person who is righteous himself does not need to give orders, and he will succeed. If a person is not righteous, he may give orders, but they will not be obeyed." (1) If a nobleman internalizes this set of ethics, his government will be effective and good.

The distinction between noble and common

Confucius distinguished between noble and common people. Commoners do not recog-

nize the orders of heaven and have no reverence for them. They scorn values and all that is good, and harm the community with their deeds. Confucius gave the aristocracy a special position in society. By nature, they are superior to non-aristocrats; however, they can fail. Confucius' ideas still sound plausible today, for example, his opinion of people who scorn religion: "A person who sins against Heaven has no one to whom he can pray." (1) At most, they could argue that they don't even want to pray in the first place.

Rituals and beliefs

Everyone should strive for modesty. Each should be friendly, restrained, loyal, moderate, reliable, and sincere. Similarly, each should seek his friends among those who are equally respectable. Following the ancient rituals and rules of decorum is important to maintain order in the world. Sacrifices to ancestors and spirits, and funeral ceremonies, must be performed with emotional commitment." (1) Confucius' moral system presents clear instructions for life in the community. The sage did not ponder metaphysical questions like life after death or the existence of a creator. Where life after death was concerned, only the nobility were lucky enough to continue living after their earthly shells had decayed—provided, that is, that

their descendents continued to perform the rituals of ancestor worship. Confucius perceived himself as one who practiced on earth the inherently harmonious and orderly laws of heaven (Tao) according to the credo that all should follow the ruler's laws—which, however, should be in accordance with the laws of Heaven. For Confucius (in contrast to Lao Tzu), the Tao is a divine law of the world and moral behavior serves to establish cosmic harmony. Harmony is established when hierarchies are maintained: "A subject honors his ruler. A younger person respects an older person. A wife obeys her husband. Children respect and obey their parents."

Festivals, ceremonies and rules

In Confucianism, nothing is left to chance. There are clear instructions for everything. The "Book of Rites" (*Liji*) lays down the rules to follow for the important celebrations in life. These include events such as birth, marriage, visits, large parties in the home, and funerals. As soon as a parent died, the children began a period of mourning lasting several years. During this time, they were expected to suspend their education or professional activities. They were not allowed to hold any office. Even widows were required to be faithful. For a long time, remarriage was forbidden.

The Central Ideas of Confucianism

Confucius said: "Learning without thinking is useless. Thinking without learning is stupid." (1)

The central concepts of Confucianism, augmented and expanded by other masters over time, can be found in nine different works, consisting of the "Five Classics" and the "Four Books" also included in the canon of important texts. Among the classics is the world-famous *I-Ching*, which dates back to pre-Confucian times. This "Book of Changes" is a significant work even today and is also consulted frequently in the Western world.

The I-Ching

The I-Ching (also called I-Ging), perhaps the oldest Chinese text dealing with philosophy, cosmology, and prophecy, was composed as long as 4500 years ago. *The Inner Structure of the I-Ching,* a book by Lama Anagarika Govinda, tells us "The most astonishing characteristic of the Book of Changes is that it

The I-Ching, an oracle considered to be one of the oldest in the world, may be practiced using fifty dried stalks of yarrow or with three coins.

The practice of the I-Ching

The Book of Changes is a collection of oracle texts that only reveal their meaning when they are read in the context of specific questions. The book should be consulted in connection with a concrete, previously unanswered question. As a preparation, a hexagram—a symbol made up of six solid or broken lines—is created, to which passages of text in the book are allocated. This is done with the help of fifty dried stalks of yarrow (or alternatively, with three coins) and the notation of several successive tossings of these items according to specific rules.

does not seek that which is eternal and unchanging; rather, it explains that change itself is the fundamental principle of the universe." (3) Thus, the Chinese discovered eternal timelessness in constant change. In ancient Greece, the philosopher Heraclitus (ca. 540–480 BC) had the same idea, as his most famous quotation—*panta rhei* ("everything flows")—implies. On this subject, Govinda adds, "For we are all mortal as long as we fear death; but we become immortal as soon as we give ourselves over to the eternal rhythm of the universe in which we live." (3)

The secret of the I-Ching

The basis of I-Ching is the polarity between the two principles, Yin (female) and Yang (male). All things and events are the result of the interaction between these two fundamental principles of the cosmos, and they explain the nature of human beings.

Other important books in Confucianism

The other classic texts of Confucianism are the *Shu Jing* (the Book of Documents, containing government texts and certificates), the *Shi Jing* (the Book of Songs), the *Liji* (the

Book of Rites) and the *Chunqiu* (the Annals of Spring and Autumn). All of these works pre-date Confucianism; however, they exemplify the character of his teachings. In addition, the canon includes the "Four Books": the sayings and texts of Confucius himself (the Analects), all set down in writing by his disciples; the book of Meng Zi (Latinized: Mencius); the writings of Chung Yung (the Doctrine of the Mean), which deals with philosophical themes; and, above all, the *Da Xue* (the Great Learning).

Some lesser works have also been mixed in with the major canon at times, such as that of Master Xun Zi (ca. 300–235 BC). Xun Zi believed human beings are fundamentally evil and that only strict morals and education can re-educate them. He thought order and structure are the appropriate means for correctly evaluating life.

Above: There are many philosophical texts central to Confucianism. Nine books form the foundation, but over time these have been augmented by the teachings of later Confucian masters.

Left: The elements of Yin and Yang represent universal forces. The principle of Yin and Yang encompasses everything that is contradictory—the one cannot exist without the other. This also includes the union of the male principle with that of the female.

Confucianism in the Modern State

The influence of other religions and thinkers

Confucianism was influenced by Buddhism and Taoism at an early stage. The philosopher Chou Tun-yi (1017–1073) adopted the principle of Yin and Yang as well as that of the five elements—water, fire, wood, metal and earth (see Taoism)—and combined them with the teachings of Confucianism. Chou Tun-yi's objective was also to realize the harmony and order of heaven on earth; however, he would incorporate the powers of Yin and Yang. Another Chinese scholar, Zhu Xi (1130–1200), enhanced Confucianism with his doctrine of two elements. For him, every aspect of life is the product of Li—the eternal, rational principle—and Qi, which is changeable, vital energy.

Even people can be equated more or less with the eternal, indestructible Li; however, a person's character is determined by the strength of their Qi. Qi, the energy of life,

Confucius and Chinese culture

South Korean followers of Confucian teachings pray in front of an altar. South Korea is among the countries where Confucian traditions and ways of life still play a major role.

The down-to-earth, humane thinking of Confucianism, directed toward liberal-minded practice and ethical behavior as well as focusing on the value of tradition, has shaped Chinese intellectual and cultural life in many ways, right up to the present day. Prior to the Chinese Revolution, Confucius was publicly honored in the country's temples and schools—although, interestingly, it was not priests but state officials who carried out the rituals. During the great Cultural Revolution in China (1966–1976), Confucianists were persecuted just as followers of all other religions. Only seeing that Confucian ideas enhanced the work ethic and family unity in other countries, such as Japan, Taiwan or Korea, made Confucianism acceptable to the Communists. who then saw it as a means of increasing productivity in China.

can be increased through constant learning (in accordance with the rightful law of heaven). One can only be considered wise when fully unified with Li—after clarifying everything that is dark or unjust in oneself.

Modern Confucianism

"One seldom finds people who love children and their fellow human beings and yet still like to resist authority." (1)

Confucius' interest in preserving and passing on old traditions—without actively seeking innovation—made his teachings a boon for many rulers. Obedience to those in power is an important pillar of Confucian teaching. The goal is to achieve harmony with everything, so a person who follows these teachings should, through effort and force of will, be able to bring perfect order into the chaos of life. In Taiwan, in particular, the old religious structures of Confucianism, along with those of Taoism, are still intact. For Confucius' followers, respect for others is the most important thing in life. As in Taoism, the individual plays a less important role in modern Confucianism than in Western traditions and religions. Both of these Asian traditions perceive individuals as merely a tiny part of a larger whole; the more the

Left: Even today, the teachings of Confucius serve as a guideline for young people in China. Discipline and the fulfillment of one's duties to the state and to one's parents are not questioned.

individual is in harmony with the laws of heaven, the better the world functions.

No reward in the afterlife

Dissolution into the great whole is the reward for a modern Confucian. There is no afterlife, no paradise, no final judgment and no hell. As Confucius said, "If you can't even really understand life, how can you understand death?" (1) In this respect, Confucianism promises no reward for a virtuous life in this world. The afterlife itself is cloaked in a mist. Nevertheless, spirits and ancestors need to be appeased, since they keep a protective and sanctifying watch over the family. Modern Confucianism does not include any theological concept of God and the world. In everyday Chinese life, the old teachings are made apparent through disciplined behavior toward the state and children's respect for their parents. Rebellion is not worth the trouble and hardly ever occurs; fulfillment of one's duty is the Confucian imperative. In today's China, Confucianism serves as a pragmatic guideline for young people, particularly in areas such as marriage and partnership, career planning, and child raising.

Far left: The Communist government in China exploits Confucianism for its own purposes, since it increases coherence and the work ethic. Not least for this reason, schoolchildren are instructed in Confucian teachings.

Master Meng, Disciple of Confucius

Confucianism and humanity

Far right: Meng Zi followed closely in the tradition of Master Kung. However, he placed particular emphasis on the idea that people are fundamentally good. It is only through life's experiences that they become corrupted.

After Confucius, Meng Zi (ca. 372–ca. 289 BC) is considered to be the second important founder of Confucianism. He was born in the state of Zou, a neighbor of Confucius' home state of Lu. His life's work consisted of making Kung Fu Tzu's teachings known in the royal courts. In addition, he placed particular emphasis in his own teachings on the idea that people are born good, and that humanity is a quality we possess from the very beginning. It is only through life and its experiences that people—if they are weak—become corrupt. "I like life and I also like righteous behavior. If I cannot have both at the same time, I will forgo life and choose righteous behavior." (2) No matter what hap-

pens to people in their lives, they must not stray from the right path! In contrast to Confucius, Meng Zi established a different hierarchy of values. For him, people come first, followed by "the gods of soil and grain; of least importance is the ruler." (2) A prince may rule as long as he acts wisely, considerately, and righteously. If not, he should abdicate; or if he proves to be a tyrant, the people have the right to assassinate him.

Right: This old man sees himself as a descendent of Master Kung. One in four of the residents of Qufu—the city of Confucius' birth—is thought to be descended from the great philosopher.

Me-Ti: antagonism due to lack of human kindness

Another famous disciple of Confucius was Me-Ti, who lived in the 5th century BC. He was a passionate opponent of war, and attributed all antagonism in the world to a lack of human kindness. He is known as a preacher of undifferentiated love. In his opinion, war, envy, malevolence, illness, and death all exist only because people do not make love the defining force in their lives. Me-Ti believed in a personal god, whom he called "Tien" (Heaven), whose will one was obliged to follow.

Famous sayings of Confucius

155. Lun Yu 1.4
"Each day I examine myself on three counts: have I been loyal to those on behalf of whom I act? Was I trustworthy in my dealings with my friends? Have I myself practiced what I have preached?"

5. Lun Yu 8.14
The Master said, "Do not discuss matters relating to a position that is not your own."

12. Lun Yu 1.16
The Master said, "Do not be concerned about others not appreciating you. Be concerned about your not appreciating others."

13. Lun Yu 17.3
The Master said, "Only the wisest and the dumbest never change."

17. Lun Yu 17.2
Confucius said, "Brought so close to each other by nature, yet kept so far apart by practice."

18. Lun Yu 15.30
Confucius said, "To make a mistake and not to correct it, is indeed a mistake."

3. Lun Yu 17.17
The Master said, "Clever talk and a neat appearance are seldom signs of benevolence."

161. Lun Yu 15.24
Confucius said, "What I do not wish upon myself, I do not do to others."

Above: Confucius' wisdom is still quoted in today's modern industrial states. The question of whether one practices what one preaches sounds like a quote from a contemporary political handbook.

Left: The Confucian Temple in Nanjing—located in the middle of a shopping district—is just one of many Confucian temples one can visit in China.

Taoism
Lao Tzu

No one knows who the wise man known to the world as Lao Tzu or Lao Tse really was. He is said to have been modest at all times and somewhat unassuming in his day.

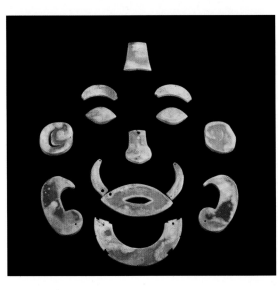

This face mask dates from the time of the Zhou Dynasty, during which cosmological ideas about heaven and earth, Yin and Yang, and the I Ching evolved.

"He who wishes to shine himself will not be enlightened." (1)

Origin and transformations

Alongside Confucianism and Buddhism, Taoism is the most important philosophical tradition in the history of China. It can be traced back to Lao Tzu, the "Wise Old Man," who is credited with writing the book *Tao Te Ching*, the classic work on "the way of Tao." In the course of the last 2000 years, Taoism has undergone several transformations caused by various influences, primarily those of Buddhism and Confucianism. Despite their quite divergent lines of thought, however, all three

Lao Tzu and the Tao Te Ching

Today, there is doubt whether the great thinker and philosopher Lao Tzu really existed at all. Even his name, "Wise Old Man," is more of a title than a real moniker. The definitive Lao Tzu biography is widely attributed to Sima Chin (145–90 BC), but his life's tale is intertwined with countless legends and is much disputed by scholars. According to Sima Chin's biography, Lao Tzu lived in China in the 6th century BC—a time of unrest and wars that nevertheless also saw the flowering of Chinese philosophy. One of the central questions posed by the scholars and wise men of the time, namely how to achieve peace and justice on earth, has lost nothing of its topicality in the meantime.

Numerous philosophers have shaped the religious world of China. The same is true of Taoism, with its communities of faith all over the present-day world.

religions (Buddhism, Confucianism, and Taoism) have melded together into a single tradition in Chinese spiritual life. They are thus commonly united under the concept of "Chinese Universalism." The three teachings have also had an enormous impact on the religion and spirituality of other cultures outside of China. In fact, due to the diverse forms of Taoism and the lack of firm lines of demarcation from other religions, it is difficult to determine the size of the community of the faith. The number of Taoists in the People's Republic of China alone remains obscure. It can be stated with confidence, however, that the center of Taoist belief today lies primarily in Taiwan.

Fruits of the Zhou Dynasty

When exactly Taoist teaching arose is lost in the annals of history, but one early flowering can be traced to the days of the Zhou Dynasty (1040–256 BC). During this period, people developed cosmic ideas about heaven and earth, the "Five Transformation Phases," the doctrine of Chi (energy), Yin and Yang, and the I Ching. Tao itself is the "path" or the "cosmic principle" according to which people should live. But Tao is also the destination toward which the individual is heading.

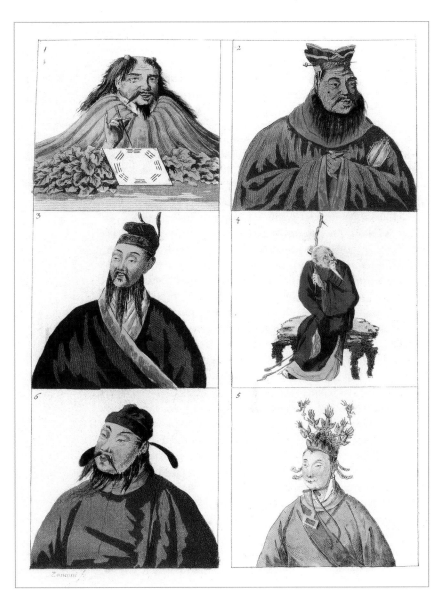

Tao and Wu-wei

The concept of Tao

The term "Tao" was in use in Chinese philosophy long before the Tao Te Ching was recorded (by Confucius, for example), but it attained its pivotal importance only with the teachings of Lao Tzu. *Tao* originally meant "path"; in classic Chinese, however, the word also connotes a "method," "principle," or "the right way." In the writings of Lao Tzu, "Tao" takes on the meaning of a principle underlying the workings of the whole world.

Tao is the highest reality and the supreme mystery, the original unity, the cosmic law and the Absolute. From Tao come the "ten

Taoism: philosophy and religion

Taoism is both a philosophical and a religious system, even though the most diverse doctrines and systems have emerged in its more than 2000-year history. To distinguish between religious and philosophical Taoism would thus be tantamount to a falsifying oversimplification—as if one were to set the mentality of the wise against the enlightenment of the religious. Taoists would only shake their heads in disbelief at such a pointless endeavor.

thousand things," the entire cosmos. Tao likewise governs the order of things, like a natural law. Nevertheless, Tao is not an all-powerful being, but rather the unity of all opposites (Yin and Yang) and by its very nature indescribable. The inexpressible unfolding of Tao gives birth to all of creation by generating the duality of Yin and Yang, positive and negative, whose transformations, movements, and interplay ultimately bring forth the entire world. Without sweetness there can be no sourness, without suffering, no happiness—and vice versa!

Above: The principle of Yin and Yang has shaped almost all religions in the Far East, including Taoism. Its traces can be found everywhere in daily life—such as on this simple wooden door.

Yin and Yang symbol

In a circle, a light and a dark side are intertwined along a curved middle line. In the center of the dark part is a bright point, and in the light part directly opposite is a dark point. Positive and negative energy hold the universe in equilibrium. But at the heart of every being, every thing, every manifestation, there is already the germ of its opposite. This belief in the transformation of all things toward harmony is ubiquitous in the Chinese cultural tradition—both on the Chinese mainland and on the island of Taiwan; it is an article of faith for both Taoists and Confucianists.

Active "non-doing": Wu-wei

One principle described in the Tao Te Ching at first sounds paradoxical, and yet elucidates the goal of Taoists: the principle of Wu-wei, or active "non-doing." Lao Tzu says that every being and every thing spontaneously recognizes its own "path" (Tao) if allowed to follow its own course, without intervention or doing anything. Wu-wei, i.e. active "non-intervention" and "non-doing," is thus a characteristic Taoist virtue. Things and their course will take care of themselves, unfolding in their own innate order. It thus seems senseless to the wise person to waste energy on actions or decisions. Living in harmony with Tao means to interfere as little as possible in its workings. Rather than exerting tremendous energy, goals can better be realized by utilizing the processes that take place on their own as governed by Tao.

What Tao demands from humanity

By allowing Tao to carry out its natural processes of transformation, the wise achieve inner emptiness. In this way, they realize the acceptance and unification of opposites, because Tao, which brings forth Yin and Yang, is the cause behind these two forces and at the same time their unifying principle. For Westerners, who are used to interfering with things, this path is not easy to comprehend at first. For Wu-wei does not mean being lazy, folding the hands, or resigning. Instead, Wu-wei means to have faith in what will come and what will develop through the power of Tao. Wu-wei also means, however, to accept what one is given. In this sense, Taoism as a doctrine demands that people cast off what is considered a virtue in the Occident: the will to consciously shape one's life and the things of the world.

Left: In the original doctrine of Tao, there are no gods. But in its popular religious variation as practiced in Taiwan by its respective priests, there are thousands of gods and spirits—here we see the Tao god of war.

Opposite page: In the works of Lao Tzu the emphasis is on describing regained unity with the Absolute. In order to achieve this, one must follow a path of undetermined length.

Ethics and Practice

Political influence of the Tao Te Ching

A great ruler, according to Lao Tzu, is one who does not actively intervene in events, but instead lets Tao unfold its effect.

The Tao Te Ching explicitly formulates its demands on rulers—and in this way exercises influence on the behavior of those in power. Whoever uses the power of Tao correctly, by non-action as called for by Wu-wei, "has an influence on what is to be," according to Lao Tzu. By maintaining harmony with Tao, Taoists thus influences both things and people, for they are connected

with the source of everything. Lao Tzu recommends that heads of state uphold this ideal of Wu-wei—in his day, these were the Chinese emperor and his officials. "He who knows how to comprehend the world wanders the earth fleeing from neither tiger nor rhinoceros; he can walk through an enemy army without armor or weapons," the great sage wrote. (1) He advises leaders not to rule their country by means of great industriousness or political intrigues, but by letting Tao run its course. A great ruler, in Lao Tzu's view, is one who does nothing. "I am without activity, and the people become rich by themselves; I do nothing and the people change by themselves." (1) Some busy statesmen will find this suggestion absurd in view of the wealth of problems in the world. But the "Wise Old Man" by no means encourages laziness; instead, he advises getting to the root of a problem by uniting with Tao and making an impact through it.

The ethics of Taoism

Taoism strives to foster inner serenity and equanimity, encouraging the individual to live and act according to the laws of Tao. In order to do so, a person must be able to push his own will into the background. This can be expressed through a question posed by Lao Tzu: "Why are heaven and earth everlasting? – Because they themselves are not alive." (1) Conversely, this means: Why does man feel mortal? – Because he lives and acts egocentrically. The ethical teachings of Taoism challenge individuals to orient themselves according to Tao. How can this done? By observing the course of the world and becoming familiar with the natural laws and manifestations of the world principle of Tao.

Surrendering oneself to Tao

Whoever devotes himself to Tao achieves harmony with it not through intellect, will-power, or conscious action, but intuitively, by adapting to the way of all things. For nothing in the cosmos is fixed; everything is subject to change, and the wise realize Tao by accomodating this constant change, the growing and becoming that govern all of the visible world. Someone who acts morally in accordance with Tao is someone who, with a pure and non-egocentric spirit, lets things happen without being blinded by their own wishes and desires. Lao Tzu says, "He who has reached the supreme peak of emptiness maintains the imperturbability of peace. He who recognizes the eternal has everything inside himself. He who acknowledges Tao, who is one with Tao, exists eternally and is safe from harm until the end of his days." The wise view "emptiness" as the ability to absolutely let go of the world. One clings to no desires, no gods, no way of thinking. "Being one with Tao" means to surrender entirely to it.

Many Chinese artists have worked in the spirit of Taoism. This has mostly resulted in the creation of moving landscapes, painted in ink. They show people in natural surroundings that embrace them protectively.

Taoist practices

Over two and a half thousand years, a number of Taoist schools promoting various teachings and practices have grown up in China. The Taoist canon of holy manuscripts was last compiled in 1442 and contains thousands of works dealing with questions of philosophy, magic, medicine, the imagina-tion, morality, rituals, and much more. The earliest texts from the 4th century BC describe an intensive form of meditation involving inner journeys to spiritual worlds. The goal of the many complex techniques (which include breathing exercises as well as various physical experiences) is to achieve harmony of body and mind—Yin and Yang—in order to return to the original unity.

Those who act in the spirit of Tao will be able to find inner peace and lead a content life. The first step is to cease allowing oneself to be led by one's wishes and desires.

Alchemy and Tao

Alchemy has at times played as great a role in Taoism, as it has in the Occident. Despite a few notable achievements, such as the discovery of gunpowder, people later devoted themselves more to an "inner alchemy" to rid themselves of bodily chaos.

Striving for immortality

Taoists from various epochs have striven for immortality, developing in the process alchemist techniques and products, for example, elixirs and pills designed to prolong life. Cinnabar, mercury and gold played a special role in their experiments. Not a few of those who hoped these pills would grant them a long life actually died of mercury poisoning; for this reason, alchemists in China tended to have a bad reputation. Nevertheless, the early alchemists could definitely boast a few successes: in the course of their research, gunpowder and numerous medicines were discovered. As they gave up the search for life-prolonging pills, they turned instead toward an interest in "inner alchemy." Instead of mixing substances in the laboratory, they came to view their own bodies and minds as an inner laboratory, and developed meditation techniques to give structure to the chaos within; and by cultivating vitality, energy, and an invigorating spirit, they hoped to realize their goal of inner emptiness and unity. This was based on the concept of the microcosm-macrocosm principle.

The five elements

The concept of the elements in Taoism is not the same as that in natural science, but takes on a metaphysical dimension instead. The five classic elements of Taoism are wood, water, earth, fire, and metal. Yin and Yang, the two central forces of the universe, gave birth to the five elements. Fire and wood are associated with Yang, while metal and water

---

Three Treasures: Jing, Shen, and Chi

From a cosmological standpoint, three forces govern the human body: the life essence, "Jing"; the mind, "Shen"; and the vital energy called "Chi." In Taiwan, these are known as the "Three Purities." Here too, Taoism calls on people to live in harmony with all three forces. Shen is situated in the head and is the faculty by which people can recognize Tao. Shen shows the path a person should follow in his or her life; through Shen we can unite with the cosmos and the laws of Tao. Allowing Tao to flow is the right path to take: not to cling to anything, but instead to let go. In the so-called Dantian (beneath the navel) is the center of Chi, the life energy—which, by means of special exercises (Qigong), can be exchanged repeatedly and held in flux. Jing is located in the pelvic area; it is the source of sexual energy and a secure foundation in life.

The microcosm-macrocosm principle

The assumption that there are analogies between cosmos, earth, and humans is a central idea of Taoism. Everything great and small, above and below, is structured in the same way according to this principle. Between these two worlds—the microcosm (the small world) and the macrocosm (the big world, or universe)—a reciprocal relationship exists. Both consist of the same elements, which correspond in every detail, although their material shape is only the visible expression of a hidden force flowing through them. Humans are therefore designed in the same way as the universe; the universe and the earth are likewise similarly structured.

It follows that the stars influence people: this is the basis for astrology, which says the arrangement of the stars has a direct influence on a person's life path. Finally, the elements are also structured in an analogous way, and thus affect individuals accordingly. This is the core belief of alchemy: the human mind can influence processes within material by the exertion of will ("mind over matter").

A person who can manipulate the powers that flow through the macro- and microcosms to their own ends is a magician. One who recognizes the interconnections in nature on the basis of similarities between outer characteristics (signatures) is a healer. These ideas are not foreign to the Occident, either. The great physician Paracelsus (1493–1541), for example, arrived at a complex, systematic view of man as a microscopic reflection of the macrocosm through his studies of the Kabbalah and alchemy; this concept was the foundation of his medical insight and his success as a physician.

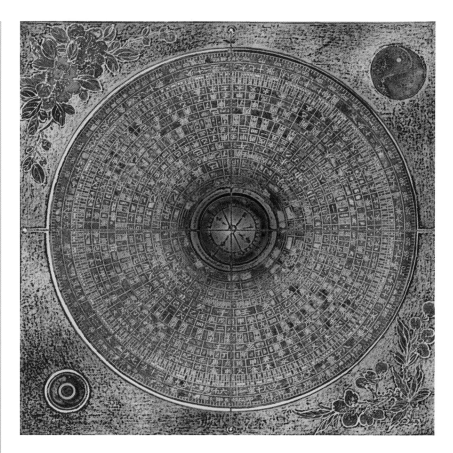

belong to Yin, and earth remains neutral. The five elements act in the cosmos in various constellations. Wood-fire-earth-metal-water brings something forth, while the cycle fire-water-earth-wood-metal destroys. "Constancy in change" is the central principle of the powers of Yin and Yang.

This idea also forms the basis of Chinese medicine, which works from the assumption that one element either blocks or promotes another. A balance between the energies in the body is therefore its primary goal.

Feng Shui: overcoming human separation from nature

The Chinese art of Feng Shui (Chinese for "wind-water") was developed by taking into consideration the five elements and the two forces of Yin and Yang. Today, many people in the West also design their surroundings and living space with its help, paying heed to the interactions between people, earth, and cosmos when deciding on the layout of buildings or rooms. Taoists in China use Feng Shui especially when choosing the best sites for buildings, graves, and temples.

Above left (box): Paracelsus occupied himself intensively with the Kabbalah and alchemy. He considered humans a microcosm whose body is influenced by its relationship to the macrocosm, the universe. This analogy shows that the great physician thought along similar lines to the Taoists.

Above right: The "luopan" is the round, magnetic Feng Shui compass. It takes into account data on astrology, the directions of underground elements, landscape forms and times of day, and identifies places in which the Chi energies of heaven and earth are in perfect harmony.

Taoism Yesterday and Today

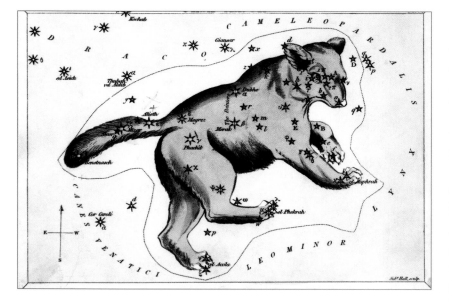

Deity worship in modern Taoism

There are no gods in the original teachings of Tao. In its popular religious variations, however, as practiced for example in Taiwan, where today Taoism is part of everyday culture, there are thousands of gods.

The gods and their veneration in this popular form of Taoism date back to a pre-Taoist era (similar to the spirits in Confucianism). These nature gods stand by people in their time of need, provided they can be persuaded to be benevolent. For example, there are gods that help one to find the right partner in life: in the Long Shun temple in Taiwan's capital, Taipei, a bearded god of wisdom is venerated for this purpose, while another god helps students taking their exams. The three Taoist forces of Shen, Jing, and Chi (spirit,

Taoism in Korea

In Korean Taoism, demons, stars, spirits, and dragons play a central role. People once believed, for example, that the constellation of Ursa Major, or the Great Bear, could prolong human life.

Taoism didn't reach Korea until 624 BC, when the Chinese emperor Kao Tsu of the T'ang Dynasty dispatched a Chinese priest to the neighboring country with Taoist manuscripts. In contrast to Buddhism, however, Taoism was unable to gain a firm foothold in Korea. Nevertheless, many Taoist elements can still be found in popular beliefs today, which is why the brand of Taoism practiced in Korea is often referred to as Popular Taoism. Demons, stars, spirits, and dragons became central elements of the teachings. For example, people believed the constellation of Ursa Major, or the Great Bear, could prolong human life. Taoist priests in Korea appear to have functioned more like civil servants than spiritual guides. The original Taoism in China recognizes religious specialists who must undertake many years of training under a master before they can work as healers. Supposed Taoist masters in Korea, on the other hand, sometimes perform all kinds of hocus-pocus to drive off evil spirits they believe are causing illness.

Taoism and modern management

From a contemporary point of view, Taoism resembles the business technique known as "Change Management." In the fields of politics and business, as well as on a more personal level, numerous examples can be found of people causing their own problems by stubbornly or even unconsciously clinging to inappropriate habits, rituals, and traditions. Taoism acts as a dynamic catalyst in such instances, helping people to part with old, entrenched structures so as not to hinder the natural course of things—in other words, the solution process.

vital life essence, and energy) are called the "Three Purities" in Taiwanese Taoism and are also illustrated as such. In nearly every house on the Chinese island, these Three Purities can be found in the form of statues. And for the Taiwanese, they by no means represent only Shen, Jing, and Qi, but also, for example, *fu*, *lu*, and *shou*—wealth, social status, and long life.

Left: There is a Taoist temple in Taiwan where the faithful enter through the mouths of a dragon and a tiger. The dragon is a symbol of happiness and represents Yang, while the tiger stands for Yin.

Above: Taoist priests like this one drive out evil spirits through rituals and prayers. They help in cases of illness, while in Korea they are also called upon when a super-market, office building, or house is to be used for the first time.

The advice of Wu-wei

Let your body rest completely—relax;
simply stop talking and persist in
deep silence;
empty your mind and cling to nothing.
Like a hollow bamboo, rest your body,
giving nothing, taking nothing;
rest your mind.
The mind that clings to nothing is Tao.
Practicing thus, you will gradually become enlightened. (2)

Taoism
and the People's Republic of China

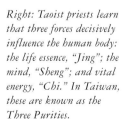

Above: In the Taoist Man Mo temple in Hong Kong hang incense spirals made of sandalwood. Their smoke is supposed to carry messages, wishes, and prayers—which are written on pieces of red paper and hung in the middle of the spirals—to the gods.

The Communist regime in China suppressed all of the country's religions and relentlessly persecuted their followers. During the Cultural Revolution (1966–1976), a great number of monasteries and temples were destroyed, holy manuscripts burned, the Dalai Lama driven out of Tibet, and monks and nuns re-educated. Today, the People's Republic of China is once again looking to its religious and philosophical heritage: monasteries and temples are being rebuilt, training courses for monks and nuns reestablished, and even research posts for studying Taoism set up at the universities. At the dawn of the new millennium, some 3,000 Taoist shrines can allegedly already be counted in China. An official version of Taoism is also propagated by the state, above all emphasizing goodwill, patriotism, and public service. Taoist training in today's China encompasses rituals, music, calligraphy, philosophy, martial arts, and the English language. There are, however, many Taoist priests who do not belong to the government organizations, so that it is hard to know exactly how widespread Taoism is in China today. The restored temples are in general well frequented, and many thousands of pilgrims gather on special occasions such as the Lantern Festival.

Old traditions

Many Taoists fled to Taiwan during the Cultural Revolution, where the political leadership has claimed ever since to be preserving Chinese culture from decline with the help of religious Taoism. In the People's Republic of China today, there are two main streams of religious Taoist tradition: the "School of Complete Perfection" (Quanzhen Taoism, also called "inner alchemy") and the "School of Orthodox Unity" (Zhengyi Taoism). Both of these emerged in the 12th century and can be traced directly back to the tradition of the old heavenly Masters.

Right: Taoist priests learn that three forces decisively influence the human body: the life essence, "Jing"; the mind, "Sheng"; and vital energy, "Chi." In Taiwan, these are known as the Three Purities.

Other Masters of Taoism
Chuang Tzu

Origin and character

Chuang Tzu (ca. 370–286 BC), also known as Zhuangzi, the most important proponent of Taoism and a brilliant writer, lived in the 4th century BC. We know little about him—only that he was supposedly poor. His works, above all the *Nan Hua Jing* (the "Book of Southern [Cultural] Florescence), demonstrate that he was a man of great learning and humility. He venerated Lao Tzu and considered himself one of his pupils. His basic attitude toward life could be seen most clearly as he was facing death. His followers wanted to bury their master in style, but Chuang Tzu told them, "Heaven and earth are my coffin, sun and moon light the way as burial lanterns, the stars are my pearls and precious stones, and all of creation will be there to mourn me. What could you possibly add?" (3)

The question of reality and truth

The central question that preoccupied Chuang Tzu concerned what constituted reality and truth. His most famous text on this question has been published countless times and yet still remains pertinent: "I, Chuang Tzu, once dreamed I was a butterfly, flying back and forth to all destinations. I knew only that I was following my whims as a butterfly would and was unaware of my human nature. Suddenly, I awoke, myself again. Now I don't know: was I a man dreaming he was a butterfly, or am I a butterfly dreaming I am a man?" (4)

In a dream one doesn't realize that one is dreaming. So what is the true reality? Only when we awaken does the one prove not to be real. But it is actually just as real as the other state.

Is a person really a butterfly dreaming it is human, or is a person merely dreaming of being a butterfly? Chuang Tzu investigated this problem, irresolvable by reason alone, and wrote many enigmatic texts on the subject.

Chuang Tzu's contribution to Taoism

In his book "The True Book of Southern (Cultural) Florescence" (*Nan Hua Jing*), also known simply by the author's name, Chuang Tzu explains the essence of Taoism using parables and anecdotes that are often paradoxical and interwoven with philosophical comments. Chuang Tzu picks up several concepts of the Tao Te Ching, but without avowing the same political objectives as Lao Tzu. The latter's original intention was to show the country's rulers a path to peace. Chuang Tzu's path, by contrast, turns away from the world. Although it is certain that such a person lived, we now know that large portions of the *Nan Hua Jing* were compiled by Chuang Tzu's pupils only after his death. It was through this work that Chuang Tzu, and the very idea of Tao, became known far beyond China's borders.

His philosophy of Tao

Almost all of Chuang Tzu's parables contain the core concept of his philosophy: timeless being. Without being bound by time, people should live in unconditional abandonment of the self. For example, when Chuang Tzu's wife died, the master reacted strangely: he sang and played the drum. In his view, life is change. People should surrender to every change and even greet death. In principle, this is the same as Lao Tzu's doctrine of "non-doing." Chuang Tzu would only add, "Be without intention!" "When the Great Emperor lost his magic pearl during a trip, he first sent out Knowledge to look for it. But Knowledge could not find it. Then he sent out Clear-Sightedness, also in vain. Then he sent out Eloquence. But Eloquence could not find it. Finally, he sent out Unintentional to look for the pearl. And it was found." (3)

Other Masters of Taoism
Lieh Tzu and the "Classic of Perfect Emptiness"

The unreality of the world

For many people, the appeal of Taoism lies in its often paradoxical images and stories, which at first tend to irritate anyone who approaches them with a Western mindset. Taoism provokes curiosity, but can also lure people into jumping to superficial, false conclusions, such as assuming that one can become successful through "non-doing." At the same time, Taoism calls reality into question and tears the veil from its face. Just like Chuang Tzu, another Taoist about whom we know very little also explored the reality of the world as we know it. Lieh Tzu probably lived about a century after Lao Tzu and left behind a book entitled "The Classic of Perfect Emptiness." Some scholars, however, believe that this manuscript originated in the 3rd century; even today, no one knows for sure.

According to The Classic of Perfect Emptiness, which is full of mystical stories, the world is neither real nor important because the truth must lie outside it. For the book's author, this means that a person thinks truth and reality are one and the same thing until their Taoist-trained mind finally sees through the masquerade of "reality." This is illustrated by the following parable.

The magician and the king

A magician invited a king to take a journey with him. The king held onto the magician's cloak and they flew up in the air, right into the center of the sky. Here they found the magician's castle. The king stayed for several decades in this place full of pleasure. Then he asked the magician to return him to earth. "When he regained consciousness, he found himself in the same place as before. His servants were waiting for him; the food was not yet cold. The magician then explained to the perplexed king, "I wandered in spirit with you, my king. Where we were, was no

less real than your castle here. You are much too accustomed to permanent states, but even they dissolve into nothing." (3) All worldly manifestations are nothing more than an illusion-and the truth lies beyond all appearances.

Left: In a Taoist story, a magician shows a king how fragile the real world is. All worldly manifestations are nothing more than an illusion - and the truth lies beyond all appearances.

Below: Whoever wanders on the spiritual paths of Taoism comprehends the world as one possibility among infinite manifestations. He will not take anything for granted, not even his own self.

The Heavenly Masters

The Five Bushels of Rice movement

In the 2nd century BC, Chang Tao Ling and his grandson founded the "Heavenly Masters" movement. This school of religious Taoism, also known as the "Five Bushels of Rice Movement" (those who wanted to join had to make a donation of five bushels of rice), was dominated by messianic and revolutionary thought: the imperial Han Dynasty should be toppled to enable Heavenly Master Chang Tao Ling to become the ruler.

Instead, after reaching an agreement with the emperor, a Heavenly-Master state, characterized by an immense administrative apparatus, existed for almost thirty years. The Heavenly Masters interpreted the Tao Te Ching along esoteric as well as practical lines—but above all on the basis of guilt and elimination of guilt. This resulted in an almost bureaucratic administration of heaven.

Petitions and prayers were written as forms and then burned in order to submit them to the appropriate deities.

Tao and Lao Tzu as gods

The Heavenly Masters Movement became a religion in many parts of China. Compulsory contributions were levied that allowed what were at first small communities to gradually grow into economically powerful organizations. In the 5th century, many nobles joined the Taoist Heavenly Masters Movement, which also attracted artists.

In Taoism, the gods are generally understood as personifications of natural forces such as wind, rain, or storm. Starting from this period, however, people began to worship Lao Tzu as a god—not as a personal deity as in the West, but more as a kind of supreme version of absolute Tao.

Right: Taoism recognizes gods as the embodiments of natural forces such as wind, rain, or storm. The Heavenly Masters Movement administered the heavenly deities in an almost bureaucratic fashion.

Far right: The Heavenly Masters wrote down their prayers and petitions and then burned them, as a way of sending them to the gods.

Eternally Valid Thoughts

Brilliant pearls of wisdom

The book of the "Wise Old Man," Lao Tzu, can best reveal its truths to those inexperienced and unschooled in Taoist thought and Wu-wei through slow, thoughtful reading. The seemingly paradoxical formulations then reveal themselves to be brilliant pearls of wisdom. The following texts are taken from the Tao Te Ching (1):

Thirty spokes converge upon a single hub,
it is on the hole in the center
that the use of the cart hinges;
A vessel is formed from a lump of clay,
it is the empty space within the vessel
that makes it useful;
Doors and windows are made for a house,
it is these empty openings
that make the house liveable.
Thus, while the tangible can be possessed,
it is the intangible that makes things useful.
The five colors blind the eyes;
the five musical tones deafen the ears;
the five flavors dull the taste;
racing and hunting confuse the mind;
difficult-to-obtain goods confuse the heart.
Therefore, the wise man listens
to his internal self
and not to his external senses.
He shuns the one
and attends to the other.
Give up on holiness
and forego wisdom;
this is a hundred times better
for all concerned.
Give up on goodness
and forego justice;
and all men will rediscover love.
Give up on resourcefulness
and forego the desire for profit;
and thieves and robbers will vanish.
These three, which are false ornament,
are not enough.

Men must have something,
that gives them stability:
Unfold what is simple and
adopt the essence
of the unhewn block of wood,
reduce your selfishness
and give up your desires.
... The work is the goal ...

The Tao Te Ching describes central questions that arise in our search for meaning and our reflections on God that are still pertinent in our modern world. People in the West who choose the path of Tao will not have an easy journey, for the way of Tao demands that elementary Western values—such as determination and striving for material success, maximizing profits at others' expense, and the search for one's own happiness to the detriment of others—be cast aside.

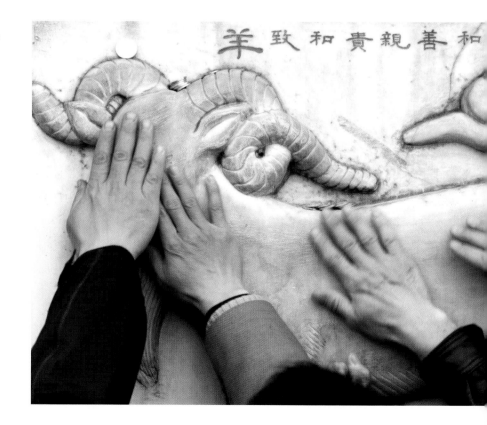

Modern Taoism also has its superstitions. Here, worshippers in a temple in Beijing touch a stone relief of a ram that supposedly brings good luck.

Shintoism
Japanese Tolerance

Religious life in Japan

In the modern metropolis of Tokyo, Shintoism is simply one religion among many. In rural Japan, however, the Shinto faith is still widely practiced.

The Japanese approach to religion is different from that of Western, predominantly Christian, countries. Religion pervades everyday life less dogmatically and demonstratively in the Land of the Rising Sun. It is natural for most Japanese to follow religious customs and even to observe detailed religious rituals without being religious in the common sense of the word. Many even describe themselves as nonbelievers, although they follow religious rites in their everyday life. Furthermore, those who visit a Shinto shrine one day may nevertheless pray in a

Buddhist temple the following day, and visa versa. For many Japanese, religious behavior is not necessarily an expression of deeply held religious conviction; it is simply a part of their day-to-day life and cultural identity. Such an attitude is only possible if the religious requirements of the individual are few and make do with forms of praxis that are small in number and quite simple.

Ritual and form

On the other hand, one finds a high degree of religious sincerity in Japan, demonstrated by the great attentiveness and care taken when performing the traditional religious and ritual ceremonies. Inner sincerity, shown when executing clearly defined traditional rituals, is most important. Religious faith is a central virtue in Japan; at the same time, it cannot exist outside of prescribed religious praxis (however, religious praxis without faith exists very well). Those who diverge from the traditional forms are quickly viewed as egoistic, which in Japan is an utterly reprehensible characteristic.

Parallels with the West

Still, there are some similarities between religious circumstances in Japan and those of the Western industrialized countries. Involvement in traditional religious institutions is generally on the decline, especially in the cities. As in the USA, new religious sects pop up regularly in Japan's great conurbations, while traditional religions continue to be deeply rooted in rural areas. As in the West, the separation of religion and state is constitutionally prescribed in modern Japan. Furthermore, there is no religious instruction in public schools and, at least in principle, any support of religious communities by the state is forbidden.

Talismans for daily good fortune

Japan has no church tax or governmental support for religious communities. Religious institutions are therefore dependent on voluntary donations, which are generated in two main ways. The first is through large ceremonies performed on the occasion of important phases of life (such as weddings, starting a business, the completion of a house, or funerals), and the second is the sale of religious symbols and talismans (mostly at public shrines). Talismans in every form are very popular—a spiritual help in everyday life. And although it may seem strange to those from Western countries (even those who are familiar with the sale of holy pictures and other objects from Christian culture), it is taken very seriously in Japan. What is more, local traditions and legends play an important role for the reliability of the good luck effects, with new legends and traditions continually being created. For the Japanese, talismans are a way of practicing religion in everyday life.

Above: A Shinto shrine in Hokkaido dedicated to fishermen. Shintoism stands out in terms of its tolerance of other religions: those who visit a Shinto shrine one day can nevertheless pray in a Buddhist temple the following day.

Left: For the Japanese, talismans are a part of everyday religious practice. Talismans in all shapes and sizes are even sold in the temples.

Origins of Shintoism

According to legend, after the sun goddess Amaterasu had retreated to a cave, she was lured out again by the other gods. In doing so she brought light back to the world. Her worship is connected with that of the Tenno, the Japanese name for emperor. He is regarded as her son.

The oldest religion in Japan

The religious needs of the individual were in the past and continue to be met mainly by Confucianism, Taoism, and Buddhism, all of which came to Japan from abroad. The original Japanese religion, however, and indeed the oldest of the island kingdom, is Shintoism. It is called *kami no michi* in Japanese, which in Sino-Japanese means "way of the gods, spirits."

The Shinto religion developed after Buddhism, or *butsudo* ("the Buddha"), came to the country in the middle of the 6th century. During the time prior to Buddhism, Shintoism was confined to a primitive worship of spirits and ancestors; only after exposure to the new religion from China did folk Shintoism develop, primarily finding its many supporters in the countryside. After numerous changes over the course of the centuries, Shintoism was elevated in 1868 to the status of the state religion as a result of a growing nationalism; as such it was forbidden in 1945 by order of the Western Allies due to its chauvinistic, totalitarian body of thought. Today Shintoism exists in Japan alongside Buddhism, Confucianism, and Taoism. These are primarily practiced independently of each other, although the Shinto faith is often used for religious dedications of national facilities and events.

The sun goddess and the Tenno

The nationalistic character of Shinto shows in that the worship of the sun goddess Amaterasu is associated with honoring the ruling emperor, the Tenno. The Tenno is regarded as the son of the sun goddess. This relationship made Shinto the national religion: a faith system immediately and exclusively related to the Japanese nation and the Tenno, its emperor.

Kami

The core of the Shinto faith, the "Way of the Kami," can be summarized by the concept of "kami": something that brings forth deep respect in people, something that is mysterious and supernatural—holy or numinous—that is elusive in the human realm. It could be the gods, spirits, or the sun, as well as the mountain Fuji (Fujiyama), in addition to stones, or the wind, or even one's ancestors or important personalities. The number of potential kami seems infinite, as new ones can be added at any time. To show how curious the list of possible kami can be, the famous bacteriologist and Nobel Prize winner Robert Koch (1843–1910) has also been included in the circle of kami because he did so much good for humankind by discovering the tuberculosis bacillus. In addition to admirable people, beautiful landscapes between cliffs or under trees are also suitable for reverence. Shintoism today—as a mixture of naturalistic spiritual beliefs and nationalism—is mainly practiced by the lower levels of society. An obeisance to the kami however, does not at all exclude the simultaneous reverence of Buddha.

Above: People who have done much for the good of mankind are included in the circle of kami, such as the famous bacteriologist and Nobel Prize winner Robert Koch, who discovered the tuberculosis bacillus.

Left: A Shinto priest at a ceremony in Ise for the sun goddess, who is regarded as one of the imperial family's ancestors. As a nationalistic religion, Shintoism requires its followers to venerate the imperial family.

The Teachings of Shintoism

A faith turned toward humankind

Shintoism has no specific founder. It takes a positive view of people and the world. According to Shinto beliefs, humanity is in principle good, and everything evil is caused by spirits that wish ill. It follows that the purpose of many rituals is to calm and dissipate these evil spirits—through cleansing, sacrificial offerings, and prayer. The rituals are performed by priests, who are allowed to marry and are only slightly organized as a group. Shintoism does not have the equivalent of a common holy book, even if the texts *Nihonshoki* (from the 7th century) and *Kojiki* (from the 8th century) have an important place in everyday faith, as they contain a large portion of the legends and stories of the religious life of old Japan.

Shinto and the imperial family

According to legend, through the play of the kami, the gods' children, the world eventually became fruitful, enabling the gods to enjoy its beauty. This shows the positive fundamental attitude of Shintoism, which sees only good in the creation of the earth. Because the gods first produced the sun, Amaterasu, people placed special significance in the imperial family. In the course of Japanese history, the legend of their ruler's deification led time and again (up until 1945) to a direct connection of the Shinto faith with the state and the imperial family.

Forms of Shinto

Through out its development, Shintoism has not produced different forms of doctrine or ethical orientation, but rather different forms of participation in traditional rites and celebrations. The different forms are distinguished primarily as Shrine Shinto, Sect Shinto and Folk Shinto.

Shrine Shinto (Jinja Shinto) is the oldest and most widely practiced form of the faith. It is strictly organized and accounts for around 80,000 large shrines throughout the country. Supernatural beings are at home in

According to legend, Japan was created by the deities Izanagi and Izanami from the floating bridge of heaven.

The rise of Japan

One of the great legends from the Kojiki, known by every child, describes the creation of Japan by a god and goddess:

"In the beginning there was the sky and the sea, each still and without any movement. The high ruler of the sky created the male and female gods Izanagi and Izanami who were to use a diamond-studded spear to create land, where there could be life and death, joy and sorrow. The two deities stood on the floating bridge of Heaven and moved the motionless sea with their spear. As the sea swirled, they pulled out the spear, from which seven drops of water fell and became the seven floating islands of Japan. To complete the world, the gods begat their children Sun and Moon, Mountains, Storm, and Fire."(1)

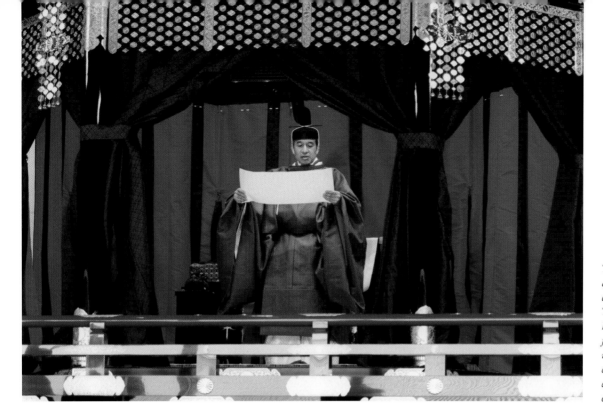

The emperor of Japan is quite conscious of his significance for state Shintoism. The photo above shows Emperor Akihito reading from a document; he is wearing the same traditional clothes as he did for his coronation as the 125th emperor of Japan.

these shrines in which the gods are honored. They are venerated through prayers, dance ceremonies, and offerings. Coming from the nationalistic forms of Shrine Shinto, the State Shinto (Kokka Shinto) developed in close connection with the Shinto of the imperial family. Modern Sect Shinto (Kyoha Shinto) includes thirteen recognized groups and countless subgroups that have arisen since the 19th century. Each of these groups fol-lows its own faith and doctrine. They were frequently founded in times of crisis by a charismatic leader, and often emphasize the adoration of a specific central deity. Folk Shinto (Minkan Shinto) is found primarily in rural areas. Characteristic for this form are rituals that provide defense against demons and fertility magic; natural phenomena and the changing of the seasons also play a major role.

A Shinto priest prepares sacrificial offerings for a ritual. The priests of rural folk Shinto have the tasks of holding rituals for the change of seasons, for fertility, and to defend against demons.

Shinto Practice

Buddhism and Shinto in comparison

Although Shintoism originally strove to dis-associate itself from Buddhism, today there is a harmonious coexistence of the two religions. While Buddhists consider the kami to be a variety of manifestations of Buddha, Shinto followers believe that Buddha is another kami.

One frequently finds Buddhist temples next to, or even inside, Shinto shrines, and Buddhist monks often take part in great Shinto celebrations. Many followers of Shinto also believe in Buddhism. Wedding ceremonies are usually performed according to Shinto practices; however, funeral ceremonies follow Buddhist ritual, since according to Shinto, death is regarded as something impure and to be avoided.

Why this is so cannot be obviously justified on the basis of Shinto beliefs, since they have not produced their own existential code. Shinto instead took on the codex of the Confucians over time and attached pri-mary importance to inner purity and integrity (*makoto*), and harmony with nature.

Shinto practice

Regular religious services are not part of Shinto practice. A large part of religious life remains a private matter. However, events are frequently celebrated and processions held that bring together the faith community. Besides the great change of season festivals, there are numerous smaller celebrations to honor specific kamis or to commemorate certain anniversaries, such as the founding of the local shrine.

The innumerable kami are not only venerated at the shrines, but in homes as well. Accordingly, one lights incense sticks or offers the respective kami rice balls and other foods, placed in front of the small household shrine. Honoring ancestors also plays an important role because, as invisible yet active members of the family, they enjoy the highest authority.

The most important and holy shrine is in Ise. It is dedicated to the powerful sun goddess Amaterasu, and consists of about 200 buildings in all. According to religious custom, the buildings are dismantled and rebuilt every twenty years.

Left: Lively celebrations such as the "Tori No Ichi" shown here, celebrating the Ootori shrine, are quite common in Shinto praxis.

Areas of influence

Shinto is closely connected with the social and cultural life of the Japanese where it is practiced. Although the influence of the West has had an increasingly adverse effect on the continuation of Shinto in large cities, in rural areas the Shinto faith has enjoyed almost uninterrupted active participation. Traditional Shinto ceremonies frequently accompany construction projects, factory openings, or ship christenings. Shinto followers have not always used shrines. Originally the rituals took place in beautiful areas, which were considered to be sacred. Small buildings were built over time to protect the participants and the altar from the weather; in this way shrines arose with prayer and offering halls. Behind the halls is the inner sanctuary, which is not open to the public. This is where the symbols for the kami—mirror, sword, dagger, or similar objects—are kept.

Below: A particularly lively event is the "mud celebration" which is carried out by young men. They run through a muddy field outside the Warabi shrine in Yotsukaido in order to bring luck.

The holy shrine of Ise

The most important place of worship is the Shinto shrine in Ise, east of Kobe and Osaka. Founded in the 4th century, it is dedicated to the powerful sun goddess Amaterasu, and consists of about 200 buildings in all. Following a religious custom, these are dismantled and reconstructed every twenty years. The present shrine buildings were rebuilt in 1993. All 200 buildings are in the classic Japanese style. The buildings are off-limits to tourists, and most of them are surrounded by high wooden fences. Every year millions of Japanese make a pilgrimage to the Ise shrine. Such a pilgrimage is also considered beneficial for the entire nation, which explains the visits of numerous politicians even in the present day.

The Torii

In contrast to pre-Buddhist Japan, the sacred entrances to the shrines—the torii—are almost always coated with bright red varnish, which also serves to weatherproof the wood. Torii can be found in old representations of the hereafter, where they delineate the different areas of the Buddhist realm of the dead. This indicates that the torii, today important Shinto symbols, are actually of Buddhist origin.

Kami and the meaning of ritual purity

Distinctive ideas of ritual purity are a general characteristic of Shinto found in the documented phases of its history. Believers are thought to incurr the bad will of the kami when the rules governing purity are disobeyed. In Shintoism, the contrast between "purity" and "impurity" is far more meaningful than the concepts of good and evil. Serious crimes, for example, are considered acts of defilement. Ritual celebrations help guard against impurity.

Death is considered a main source of impurity. The honored kami must therefore never come into contact with any sign of death, nor blood nor illnesses. Many Buddhist scholars are of the opinion that the Shinto stance toward death and its accompanying rites, such as burials, is the reason for the historical distancing of Shinto from Buddhism. This characterizes the funerary culture and the predominant concepts of the hereafter in Japan to this day. The fact that Buddhism primarily deals with death and the hereafter, while the kami are responsible for life and the present, arose from an early-established Shinto conception of itself and can be regarded as a custom derived from varying historical profiles.

Below, left: The torii of the Fushimi-Inari shrine of Kyoto are painted red like most torii. This color indicates that the torii are actually of Buddhist origin.

Below, right: A young bride signs her vows in the Shinto shrine of Meiji in Tokyo. Her clothes are white and pure. In Shintoism the contrast between "purity" and "impurity" is far more meaningful than that between good and evil.

Tenrikyo

Tenrikyo, a young religion

The history of the monotheistic religion Tenrikyo ("the teaching of the heavenly truth") goes back to its founder Miki Nakayama (1798–1887) and her revelatory experience in 1838. According to her revelation, a god unknown up until then, Oyagami (Japanese, "parental God") created the world in order to enjoy the harmonious life of the people. Oyagami merely lent the people their physical bodies; the soul, however, was to be used according to humans' free will. Egoism and selfish behavior distance people from God, and only through a cleansing of the heart can they find God once again. This return to God is achieved through selfless deeds and the giving of alms, among other things. The reward is the "joyous life" that the parental god Oyagami has planned for all people.

Development to this day

At first, the adherents of the new religion—which has been led under the governing body of the Shinto sects since 1908—were persecuted by the police and Miki was arrested repeatedly. On January 26, 1887, the founder of the religion died while performing a service in Jiba, in contravention of police orders. Her supporters believe she has only hidden her visible body, and lives on in her shrine in order to convey God's mercy to humankind. Even after her death, Oyagami continues to feel, think, and act through the deceased woman. In 1970, the community of the Tenrikyo broke loose from the Shinto sect organization and has emphasized its independence ever since. Miki's hometown, the village of Shoyashiki, has developed in the meantime into the city of Tenri. The community of the Tenrikyo runs various social and cultural services and broad missionary activities that have expanded since the faith has spread outside of Japan. Missions can be found today in Taiwan, Korea, China, Europe, South America, and the USA, among other places. The number of believers is estimated to be around four million supporters worldwide.

The origins of all things is called Jiba

The place where, according to Japanese belief, God created all humankind and where they shall return is called Jiba. It lies approximately in the middle of Japan, and was discovered in 1875 by Miki Nakayama. The main church of the Tenrikyo, located next to the founder's shrine, is open to believers day and night and services are held there daily. Ten select persons, five men and five women, using ten various hand gestures symbolically represent the ten aspects of complete protection by the god Oyagami. In a dance ceremony, "kagura zutome," the whole of God's creation is portrayed.

Kagura zutome is a dance ritual that symbolically represents the act of creation. It is performed only in Jiba and in the Tenrikyo belief is considered a step toward redemption.

Redemption and earthly paradise

The "kanrodai," a sacred wooden stand with a bowl to contain heavenly dew, is open for viewing by anyone in Jiba. This heavenly dew bestows eternal life. but will only fall from the sky when the "joyous life" is achieved throughout the world.

Also part of the Tenrikyo faith is the belief in the eternal rebirth of the soul—not, however, in the Buddhist meaning of release into Nirvana, nor in the Christian belief of a heavenly paradise, but rather an earthly paradise in which all of humanity obtains the "joyous life."

Mandeanism
The Last Gnostic Religion

The core of the Mandean faith

Mandean belief (*manda* means "knowledge") contains elements of Judaism, Gnosticism, and Christianity, such as celebration of the Last Supper and Sunday worship. They consider John the Baptist the reformer of their religion. Not only did John baptize Jesus in the Jordan River, he also baptized the Mandean redeemer, Manda d-Hajje ("Gnosis of Life") as well. The latter became the highest God (*mana rabba*), sent to earth (*tibil*) to bring the revelation of their divine origins to Adam and his wife, Hawa (not Eve). Only with this true knowledge can human beings be saved. At the end of the world, Manda d-Hajje will release all devout souls from the underworld.

A demiurge created the earth

Mandeans practice the last remaining Gnostic religion on earth, which is centered on the "knowledge of God and the Last Things" and the "gnosis of the True and Only"; its origins remain shrouded in mystery. At the same time, Gnostics assume that it was not God, but a lesser deity—a demiurge—who created the world, and this demiurge attempts to conceal true knowledge of God from humans. Here, the Gnosis brings clarity. The Mandeans are thought to trace their origins back to John the Baptist, the forerunner of Jesus, as he is identified in the New Testament. More recent studies indicate that the first Mandeans had their religious roots in the 1st century AD, influenced by Judaism, Gnosticism, and by John the Baptist. Today, the Mandeans live in southern Iraq and in Iran. They reject Christianity and consider Jesus to be a false prophet. The number of believers is estimated at around 50,000 in Iraq and about 10,000 in Iran. In both countries, Mandeans are subject to persecution from Islam.

Baptism and other rituals

In Mandeanism, baptism is the central ritual, and it may take place during Sunday worship services or on special occasions such as weddings, births, and funerals. It is performed in flowing water. The Lord's Supper consists of pita bread and *mambuha*, water that has been blessed by a priest. Mandeans do not perform circumcision. They follow the Ten Commandments and place a high value on

Above: At no time have Mandeans been allowed to participate in Iraqi society. Their refuge is the branching river delta of southern Iraq, where they live under the most primitive conditions even today.

marriage and family. A requiem Mass may only be attended by the faithful; its aim is to aid in the ascension of the dead person's soul.

In the present day, the Mandean community is a closed one: one must be born into a Mandean family; there are no conversions. Ancient sources from pre-Islamic times suggest this was not always true. The ban may be a result of the Islamic context in which they live, which led to conversions to Islam. Anyone who converted from Islam, on the other hand, was put to death. Mandeans who marry outside the religion are no longer members of the Mandean community.

The Genza

The holy book of the Mandeans is the *Sidra Rabba*, known in the West as the *Genza* ("treasure"). It consists of two parts: the mythological-cosmological texts, as well as songs and hymns. On the subject of Jesus, the Sidra Rabba states: "When John lives in Jerusalem during this period, takes the water of the Jordan and performs baptisms, Jesus Christ will humbly accompany him, receive John's baptism, and through John's wisdom become wise. Then, however, he will twist John's words, change the rite of baptism in the Jordan and preach sacrilege and deceit in the world. Christ will divide the people; his twelve seducers will travel throughout the world. In this time—beware, true followers." (1)

Left: For the Mandeans, flowing water is the true element in which people are to be baptized. Their holy text is the Genza, in which Jesus Christ is portrayed as a prophet who falsified the teachings of John the Baptist.

Baha'ism
The Last of the Revealed Religions

Babism

Siyyid 'Ali Mohammed (1819–1850) was the founder of a revivalist movement that prophesized the coming of the Imam-Mahdi, as promised in the Shia expectation of salvation. Shia Muslims associate with him the idea of a pure human being, free from sin, who is able to win political respect and greater standing for the religion.

Siyyid 'Ali Mohammed declared himself to be the awaited Imam-Mahdi and, under the name of Hazrat-i Bab, or simply the Bab, gathered a group of zealous followers around him. This was met with opposition in Shia Islam. In 1848, the community around Imam Mahdi divorced itself completely from Islam, and established a religion of its own.

After armed conflict with the government and unsuccessful attempts to divide Persia and create a theocratic state, Babism was crushed after only a few years of existence—at the cost of approximately 20,000 Babist lives. In 1850, the Bab was publicly executed.

Shortly before his death, the Bab had appointed 19-year-old Mirza Yahya Subh-i Azal (1830–1912) as his successor. When Mirza Yahya failed to unify the internally divided community, his half brother, Mirza Husayn 'Ali Nuri (1817–1892), thirteen years his senior, assumed its leadership.

Above: A Baha'i temple in New Delhi called the Lotus Temple.

Opposite page: Baha' Ullah died in Palestine. The Middle East (here a view of the Sinai Peninsula) has been a cradle of religion like no other region of the world: this is where Judaism, Christianity, Islam, Baha'ism, and Mandaeism all originated.

Mirza Husayn, recipient of a new divine revelation

Baha'ism (*baha* = "light," "brilliance," "splendor") originated in Persia (present-day Iran) during the late 19th century, but is today widely spread throughout the world. It has roots in both Shia Islam and Babism, the Shia revivalist movement.

The founder of the Baha'i faith is Mirza Husayn 'Ali Nuri. He was a passionate follower of The Bab, a Babist prophet who had prophesied in 1844 that a herald sent from God would appear nineteen years later as the "manifestation of God": Mirza believed himself to be that herald. The Baha'i believe Mirza Husayin is the last in a series of divine incarnations—Buddha, Jesus Christ, Krishna, and Mohammed are all considered his predecessors—and that the world received a new revelation through him. Mirza Husayn 'Ali began calling himself Baha' Ullah ("Glory of God"), saw himself as God's messenger, and considered Babism to be only a preliminary step toward the new religion. Baha' Ullah believed himself to be the fulfillment of the teachings of Moses, Christ, Mohammed, and all earlier religious teachings. In the course of the 20th century, this idea was developed further by adding Hinduism and Buddhism.

Above: The Baha'i Gardens shrine of Baha' Ullah in Acre. Baha' Ullah was kept under house arrest here and temporarily imprisoned by the Turks.

Persecution, death, and succession

Baha' Ullah was persecuted by the Turks, kept under house arrest in Acre (present-day Israel), and temporarily imprisoned. On May 29, 1892, shortly after his release, Baha' Ullah died in Palestine. Following his death, his quest of establishing a universal religion was carried on by his son, Abdul Baha (1844–1921), who continued to spread his father's teachings.

One of the core demands of these teachings is moral and social compensation for those worse off in society. Abdul Baha also spent many years in prison; he was only released in 1908, when many peoples of the Ottoman Empire revolted against the sultans and secured independence.

Abdul Baha himself appointed his oldest grandson, Shoghi Effendi Rabbani (1897–1957) as his spiritual successor. Since Shoghi Effendi did not leave a testament, the office of "Guardian of the Cause of God" came to an end when he died. Since 1965, an institution located in Haifa, Israel and consisting of nine members who are elected every five years has been in charge of the legal administration of the religion.

The Baha'i faith

The Baha'i faith is based on three main pillars: the unity of God, the unity of religions, and the unity of humankind. Moreover, the Baha'i faith sees itself as the ultimate and final revealed religion. According to Baha'i belief, all other religions—in particular the five major world religions—while recognized as being of divine origin, have by now lost their claim to validity.

The wide-reaching spiritual, social, and political goals of the Baha'i faith are derived from its three fundamental pillars: "A progressive divine revelation, the elimination of prejudice, the pursuit of harmonious relations between the races and religions, the equality of men and women, and the restoration of harmony between science and religion. Furthermore, the development of an international auxiliary language as well as the establishment of an international court of arbitration, a world parliament and government, are demanded." (1)

Social aspects of the Baha'i faith

The Baha'i religion demands the gradual elimination of both luxury and extreme wealth and poverty. The Baha'i see themselves as citizens of the world and reject every form of nationalism. According to Baha' Ullah, every individual should walk on the "Path of Perfection." The aim in life of each person is to act in such a way that their conduct becomes a source of abiding progress. To the Baha'i, death is the beginning of a new, better life. "The individual should perceive himself as always living, always developing." (2)

There are no rituals or priests in the Baha'i religion. The only authority is holy scripture, a compilation of texts written by the Bab, Baha' Ullah, and Abdul Baha. Every Baha'i believer is, according to ability, a spiritual teacher to the others. The most important elements of a pious life are studying the words of God, praying, and fasting.

The Baha'i calendar consists of nineteen months of nineteen days each. At the beginning of each month, the community gathers to celebrate the 19-Day Feast.

Baha'ism in the world

Under Shoghi Effendi, the Baha'i established a global organization. Today, they can count some 5 to 6 million believers, including growing communities in India and Southern Africa. In Europe, the number of Baha'i runs into several tens of thousands, and in North America there are about 100,000 believers. The religious community is banned in Islamic countries. In Iran, where about 2.5 million Baha'i live today, several early Baha'i buildings were destroyed in 2004 in an attempt to erase the traces of this religion. In 1992, the first English translation of the central text of the Baha'i, the *Kitab-i-Aqdas*, was published. Since then, the faith has increasingly spread in the West, as well. The first European

Relation to Islam

Baha'i teachings resemble those of Islam in many respects, but there are decisive differences: to a Baha'i, the holiest book is not the Quran, but Kitab-i-Aqdas, the Baha'i religious "Book of Laws." This book contains daily obligatory prayers as well as rules for the annual obligatory 19-day fast, pilgrimages to holy sites, etc. Marriage is also a duty, and polygamy was allowed for a time. Offenses are punished by monetary fines, banishment, and imprisonment.

Baha'i "House of Prayer," for example, was opened in 1964 in Hofheim-Langenhain, Germany. The most important memorial sites of the Baha'i, the sepulchers of their founder and his successor, are located in Haifa and Acre, Israel.

Below, left: A close-up of the Baha'i Shrine in Haifa. A Baha'i must perform daily prayers, observe an annual 19-day period of fasting, and make a pilgrimage to the holy sites of the religion.

Below, right: The American Baha'i center is located in Wilmette, Illinois. On the political level, the Baha'i demand establishment of an international court of arbitration and a world parliament and government.

Nature Religions
Religions of Primitive Peoples

more the shapers of nature rather than a part of it, tribal people, who are deeply connected to their natural surroundings, do not distinguish the supernatural, divine, and transcendental from the immanent, i. e., from that which we recognize as real and which constitutes their world.

In the experience of primitive people, nature is stronger than the individual. Sickness and death, weather and drought, the death of livestock, unsuccessful hunts, famines and other kinds of hardship are beyond their control. Everything that happens is the work and expression of a ubiquitous higher power that exists both in this life and in the hereafter, both in organic and inorganic nature.

A further distinctive feature of nature religions is that they are restricted to one ethnic group, while world religions cross both ethnic and national boundaries. Today, tribal societies practicing nature religions are found in Africa, but also in some regions of South America, and tribal religions are found predominantly in Asia, in countries such as India and the Philippines.

Helping healers

Ill fortune mainly is the work of spirits that are ill-disposed to an individual; either because he or she has inadvertently offended them, or just because they are evil by nature. Spirits can cause sickness in people or their livestock; this is why they have to be appeased. Frequently, this is achieved by spiritual help—and with the support of healers or shamans. An African marabout, for instance, is capable of invoking and appeasing spirits.

Marabouts and shamans can help because they have detailed knowledge of the human soul; they believe that the soul is able to detach itself from the living body, during sleep and in states of trance. In such states, human consciousness becomes receptive to

Religions without founders

Nature religions are characterized by their harmony with nature. They have no founders or organizational structures and no religious hierarchy.

The most distinguishing feature of what are known as nature religions (also called tribal religions) as opposed to other religions is that they have no founder. No one created them by introducing new ideas about God and the world. Nature religions are practiced by tribal peoples, in which people are one link in the chain of nature; while the so-called high religions, including Christianity, Islam, or Buddhism, are religious expressions of "civilized" people, who use and live off of nature. While civilized people feel they are

extrasensory perception. At its deepest level, the soul detaches itself from the body and becomes capable of soul traveling.

Power over spirits

Shamans appease, humor, or fend off spirits. Their power to do so comes from within and enables shamans to act as a vehicle for extra-human, supernatural powers while, at the same time, opposing them—a tricky balancing act. Shamans influence the spirits and control them with their own power. They send their souls traveling, and their souls leave their bodies. That leaves their bodies available as a medium for spirit powers—again a feat that is not without danger: some shamans have gone mad performing it.

The shaman

Shamans are mediators between this life and the hereafter. The hereafter and the supernatural realm are referred to as the otherworld.

Shamans are also healers; they believe that our world and our everyday reality are ruled by powers that are beyond human comprehension, but not beyond the reach of the human soul.

A person recognizes that they have the gifts necessary to become a shaman through special experiences such as signs, dreams, visions, or health crises. After an appropriate initiation, he or she then begins an apprenticeship with one or several shamans that can extend over many years.

Shamans fulfilled an important spiritual function in the archaic cultures of the hunter-gatherer peoples, long before the creation of high religions with their prophets, priests and reformers. The shaman determines what has made a patient so weak that evil spirits could invade and possess them—for example black magic performed by malevolent neighbors, warlocks, or sorcerers.

Severe sicknesses involving impaired consciousness are usually interpreted as the loss of a part of the person's soul: the soul has been abducted, and it becomes the shaman's task to locate it in the otherworld and retrieve it. To do so, the shaman enters a trance state (through dance, drumming, or drugs) and travels to the otherworld—a dangerous place where spirits and demons rule.

Asian Nature Religions

other from the underworld. In southwest China, a common theme is the belief that the origins of humankind date back to a brother and sister who were the only survivors of an all-destroying flood. At the gods' request, these two become the first parents of all humanity. In East Indonesia, on the other hand, humans was born from a marriage between the heavens and the earth. The Khmer, an Austro-Asiatic people living in Southeast Asia, Cambodia, and parts of Thailand, Laos, and Vietnam, believe that humans are descended from a frog couple and have gradually become people. The Tungusi in Siberia believe in a creator-god, who, however, does not interfere with the worldly course of events.

Supernatural beings or deities are responsible for whatever happens. They take care of the fertility of fields and people. There are sacred mountains and lakes that are home to a wide range of spirits. At times, these spirits have to be appeased, which is achieved through the help of shamans, who can establish contact with them.

Veneration of ancestors and the dead

Revering one's ancestors is important to all primitive peoples. They are keenly aware that they would not exist if not for their ancestors. Ancestors and deities together protect people and preside over the all-embracing order of things. If this is disturbed, there are consequences for the community—and it has to restore the order. This requires complex rites that can include headhunts or human sacrifice, as in Papua New Guinea until recent years. Consumption of human flesh is taboo in modern civilization, and suppresses such rites. But the tribes that practiced them did not see themselves as murderers; rather they were honoring the person they ate. When the natural habitat of primitive peoples is subjected to the forces of civilization, nature religions are fundamentally changed.

Creation myths

Until a few years ago, there were still headhunters in Papua New Guinea. Primitive peoples' notions of morality and ethics differ considerably from Western ideas; this is frequently a source of conflict.

The Bhils of India believe that their god, Bhagwan, created the entire world, but the details of the construction were the work of his assistant, the giant Nung. The heroic deeds of Nung corrected Bhagwan's creation: for instance, he shot down a second, superfluous sun, thereby creating normal living conditions on earth. Some Polynesian peoples believe the earth descended into the primordial sea from the skies, or was lifted from the ocean floor. Others believe that all things have been raised from the depths in the course of a holy battle between two beings, one from the upper world and the

Concepts of the Underworld in African Nature Religions

The Ewe's notion of the two halves of the soul

The Ewe people, consisting of many individual tribes, live in the rainforest of West Africa. They believe that the soul has a pre-existence (i. e., a prenatal life) and resides in the realm of souls, which is identical with the earthly world. Each time a child is born, a deceased ancestor is reincarnated. The soul the newborn child receives thus has two halves: the larger part, the so-called life soul, comes from the realm of souls, the world of the gods. The other, smaller part—the dead soul—is associated with the underworld.

The journey to the underworld

The life soul keeps returning to the divine home of souls. The dead soul starts out on a journey to the underworld, also known as the "House behind the River," where it meets its ancestors. The journey there is long and arduous, frought with challenges, and the soul has to be equipped with everything it may need to overcome them by means of burial objects.

Contrary to the myths and beliefs of many other peoples and religious communities, lack of food may become a problem in the underworld of the Ewe. In such cases, the souls may claim food from the living, who place it on the ground as a sacrifice.

Sometimes, entry to the underworld involves being judged: the ancestors not only ask the newly deceased about the state of affairs in the earthly world, they also question them to find out if they have committed any crimes. The results of this inquiry determine their place in the underworld. Each sphere is separated from the other, so that the evil never get through to the good.

Ritual tribal dances involve invoking the spirits of the deceased or the gods. Masks and clothing give the dancers an unusual appearance— after all, they intend to enter an unusual world.

Nature Religions in the Americas and Oceania

Native American conceptions

Right: This Polynesian spirit might appear to shamans in their dreams. Usually, its appearance involves a message.

All Native American cultures share the idea that the world consists of two spheres, a natural and a supernatural one. The natural, inhabited sphere is the disk of the earth; the supernatural heaven is located above this disk, resting on four pillars and a "Middle Tree," also called the "World Tree," connecting the human with the heavenly (the sphere of the gods, the spirits, and the ancestors). All the dead go to the same realm. It is a happy place that Native Americans refer to as the "Happy Hunting Ground," which mirrors life in this world under ideal conditions (such as ample food).

Below: The animal with which an individual most closely identifies becomes their totem animal—here a snow leopard. Totem animals represent the untamed side of human nature.

Belief in totems

The totem is the northern Native American term for a person's guardian spirit. Totem animals play an important part in nature religions such as that of Native Americans.

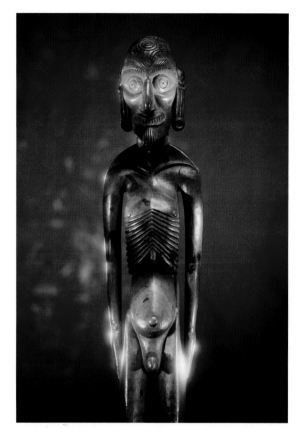

Individuals most often recognize their totem animals in a vision after a long period of fasting. They represent the characteristics and needs of a person.

Nature religions recognize two kinds of totem. The first is the central totem, which defines who or what an individual is—this is the animal that a person feels most closely connected to, whether it is a wolf, a bear, or a puma. These animals represent the wild, untamed side of human nature. The "external" totem, on the other hand, represents spirits surrounding a person that can be invoked for guidance.

In North American tribes, people frequently encounter their totem animals in dreams. During sleep, the dreamer is transformed into the totem animal and learns how to act in an imminent situation. These kinds of intense dreams are understood to be messages from a person's soul.

Animism in the nature religions of Oceania

In the nature religions of Oceania (Polynesia, Micronesia, Melanesia, and the Philippines), the reciprocal relationship between nature and humankind is symbolically expressed by the word "spirit." Spirits are real to the primitive peoples living in this region, if not in a Western sense. Spirits are symbols for real reciprocal dependencies and relationships among humans, and between humans and nature. However, the term animism, introduced by Western scholars, insufficiently describes the phenomenon of "spirits" in the nature religions of the South Seas. Today, we know that nature religions, frequently perceived and characterized as primitive and childlike, are fully developed and well-balanced belief systems. Most of them, however, are restricted to very small geographic areas or defined tribal groups.

Animism

The British scholar E. B. Tylor (1832–1917) was the first to use the term "animism" to describe the religion of primitive people, considering it to be Stone Age in nature. Animism denotes the belief in spirits that reside in every part of nature: in mountains, rivers, plants, and animals. Every phenomenon—lightning, thunder, or the sound of the wind in a forest—is associated with its own spirit. The term animism as Tylor and his successors applied it to the world's nature religions became an expression of Western arrogance. From today's perspective, Tylor's theories and understanding of the belief systems of primitive peoples are outdated.

Native North Americans experience their respective totem animals mostly in their dreams, but sometimes also in spontaneous visions.

Glossary

IMPORTANT TERMS IN CHRISTIANITY

Apostle – Title for Jesus' disciples, chosen by Christ to spread the Gospel; later also used for other missionaries.

Atheism – The rejection of belief in God and a spiritual origin of the world.

Ban (also Excommunication) – An ecclesiastical punishment that excludes a person from all church rites, sacraments, and privileges; total exclusion from the community of the faithful.

Celibacy – Life in an unmarried state, a binding obligation for priests of the Roman Catholic Church.

Church service – The rites of prayer and worship conducted within a community of Christians. Protestant services center around the announcement of the Word of God, while the Catholic Mass tends to focus on the Eucharist.

Communion – see Eucharist

Confession of Faith – Statement of a Christian community's beliefs.

Crucifix – Any representation of the crucified Jesus.

Crusades – A series of military campaigns undertaken by European Christians between the 11th and 13th centuries to regain the Holy Land from the Muslims.

Diaspora – Originally, the Jews who scattered throughout the world after the destruction of the Temple in Jerusalem; later also used (not capitalized) for other emigrant peoples.

Dogma – Formulaic statement of basic belief that is generally binding for the followers of a certain teaching.

Dualism – Belief in two powers that mutually complete or contradict each other (e.g. good and evil).

Ecumenism – (Greek: "the inhabited world") A movement calling the Christian denominations throughout the world to work together.

Eucharist – (Greek: "thanksgiving") A sacrament and the central component of many Christian services of worship: the sharing of bread and wine to commemorate the sacrificial act of Christ.

Free Churches – Protestant churches that are completely independent of the state, and whose members consist only of those persons who explicitly choose to belong; also known in Great Britain as Nonconformists.

Gnosticism – (Greek: *gnosis*, "to know") Theological and mystical knowledge, extant since late antiquity; Gnostics believe that Jesus taught a secret knowledge necessary for salvation. An aspect of this secret knowledge was the separation of spirit and matter.

Gospel – (Germanic: "good word"; Greek *evangelium*: "good news") The first four books of the New Testament, named for the four Evangelists Matthew, Mark, Luke, and John; also more generally the teaching of Jesus.

Hierarchy – Order of command within, for example, the Catholic Church, whose head is the pope. He alone can decide upon matters affecting the Catholic Church; beneath him are the bishops, and below them, the priests.

Lord's Prayer – The most important prayer for all Christian confessions; since the 5th century, it has been a fixed element in Christian worship services.

Martyr – A believer who is sacrificed for his or her faith, and is prepared to face torture and death.

Monotheism – Belief in a single god (in contrast to polytheism).

Monstrance – (Latin *monstrare*: "to show") A richly decorated, chalice-like vessel with a glassed compartment in which a Host (the Eucharistic wafer of bread as Christ's body) is displayed.

Mysticism – Systems of thought and practice supposed to lead to a direct experience of God.

Pantheism – A widely spread concept that sees God and the world as one.

Polytheism – Belief in many gods (in contrast to monotheism).

Relics – Mortal remains of saints, usually bones or other body parts, that are said to have special power.

Religious order – A group of monasteries or convents within a religious community abiding by defined laws of behavior.

Rosary – An established series of prayers within the Catholic Church; the beads on a rosary correspond to the prayers in the cycle.

Sacraments – Religious rites that mediate God's Grace. Denominations recognize different sacraments: most Protestant churches recognize two (baptism and Communion); while the Catholic Church recognizes seven (baptism, confirmation, marriage, Communion, penance, anointing of the sick, and ordination of priests).

Saint – A person who is especially close to God, and therefore the subject of prayers of intercession.

Schism – Division of a religion into two or more denominations; for example the schism between the Western and Orthodox Christian Churches.

Scholasticism – A movement in the medieval Church to unite reason and faith.

Sects – Groups within a religion, characterized by their own organization and religious content, which often come into being as a protest.

Septuagint – A translation of the Hebrew Bible into Greek, made several centuries BC.

Sermon on the Mount – A sermon in the Book of Matthew in which Jesus overturned all worldly values.

Trinity – (Three-in-one) A doctrine describing the unity of God the Father, God the Son, and God the Holy Spirit.

Vulgate – A fourth-century Latin translation of the Bible.

IMPORTANT TERMS IN ISLAM

Allah – God, the Only One, Creator.

Alms – Donations given as charity to the poor, obligatory for every Muslim.

Dervish – Islamic mystic and ascetic, follower of Sufism.

Five Pillars of Islam – The five most fundamental obligations of every faithful Muslim: *Shahadah*, *Salat*, *Sawm*, the *Hajj*, and *Zakat*.

Jinn – Spirit beings that are mentioned in the Koran.

Hadith – (Arabic: "story") The collection of pronouncements by Mohammed; the most important source of religious instructions besides the Koran.

Hajj – Pilgrimage to Mecca, one of every Muslim's five basic obligations.

Imam – (Arabic: "prayer leader") The prayer leader in a mosque, spiritual leader.

Caliph – (Arabic: "successor") official title for the successors of Mohammed since 632 AD.

Kaaba – (Arabic: "cube") The holiest shrine, in Mecca.

Koran – (Arabic: "recitation") The holy book of Islam, the revelations of God to his Prophet, Mohammed.

Mecca – Holiest city in Islam, destination of the *hajj*.

Medina – Second most important city in Islam after Mecca, location of the tombs of the Prophet Mohammed and his daughter, Fatima; also place where the Islamic calendar originated.

Muezzin – Someone who calls the faithful to prayer.

Mosque – Islamic place of communal worship.

Ramadan – Ninth month in the Islamic lunar year, a month of ritual fasting.

Salat – Ritual prayer in Islam, performed at five prescribed times a day facing toward Mecca; one of the five basic obligations of every Muslim.

Sawm – Fasting from sunup to sundown during the month of Ramadan, one of the five pillars of Islam.

Shahadah – Islamic profession of faith, one of the five pillars of faith required of every Muslim.

Sharia – Religiously founded laws and provisions in Islam, based on Mohammed's revelations.

Sura – Chapters of the Koran.

Shia Muslims (also Shiite) – "Ali's party," followers of the smaller of the two main movements in Islam (ca. 9 percent).

Sufi – Mystic, ascetic, follower of Sufism, the mystic tradition in Islam.

Sunnah – (Arabic: "custom," "tradition") Together with the Koran, the Sunnah provides the basis of Islamic law.

Sunni Muslims – Followers of the largest Islamic group; orthodox Muslims (90 percent).

Ummah – The community formed by all Muslims.

Wahhabites – Followers of a very conservative tradition within Sunni Islam.

Zakat – Obligatory alms, state tax, one of the five pillars of Islam.

IMPORTANT TERMS IN HINDUISM

Atman – Soul (not, however, in the Christian sense); a part of Brahman.

Avatar – An incarnation of a Hindu deity, usually Vishnu.

Baba – "Father"; a form of address for a holy man.

Bhagavad Gita – A central text of Hinduism. Written around 200 BC, it includes Krishna's self-revelation and his teachings.

Bhakti – Total, utter, fervent devotion to a god.

Brahma – A primary deity, member of the trimurti and Creator of the universe.

Brahman – The incomprehensible absolute; the unity of contradictions.

Brahmins – Priests, religious leaders, members of the highest Hindu caste.

Dharma – The law; religious duty.

Ishta-deva – A personal deity, an aspect of Brahman.

Karma – The summation of all one's actions in life.

Krishna – The shepherd god, an incarnation of Vishnu.

Mahabharata – A heroic folk epic, an important philosophical-religious work in eighteen chapters. Bhagavad Gita is part of the sixth chapter of this book. The *Mahabharata* was composed between 400 BC and 400 AD.

Mantra – An incantation or murmured meditation.

Maya – Veil, illusion.

Moksha – Release.

Om – (also Aum) a sacred syllable or mantra.

Ramayana – An epic Indian poem composed between 200 BC and 200 AD. It contains stories of the hero Rama, who became a god, an avatar of Vishnu. The poem also contains texts dealing with bhakti, devotion to a god.

Rigveda – A collection of hymns concerning the creation of the world, death, and rituals.

Samsara – The eternal cycle of life, death, and rebirth.

Shiva – A primary deity and member of the trimurti; a dancer, god and destroyer of creation.

Shruti – Sacred Hindu texts that are binding for all Hindus, including the Vedas.

Smriti – Sacred texts, including epics such as the Bhagavad Gita.

Swami – Form of address for a holy man.

Sadhus – Wandering ascetic monks or holy men who devote themselves fully to their spiritual path.

Trimurti – The trinity of Hindu deities: Brahma, Vishnu, and Shiva.

Tirthayatra – A pilgrimage to one or more holy places (called *tirthas*).

Vedas – Sacred texts including the Upanishads.

Vishnu – A primary deity, member of the Trimurti; the god who preserves the Dharma and the world; appears in ten incarnations.

Yoga – A path to release through certain postures and movements.

Yuga – A cycle of the world, of which there are four.

IMPORTANT TERMS IN BUDDHISM

Arhat – The goal of a Hinayana monk. According to Buddha's teachings, an Arhat stands on the fourth and highest step, just short of perfection.

Bardo – One of a total of four conditions, of which life is one; but especially the three stages of death, the afterlife, and rebirth.

Bodhi – Enlightenment, awakening.

Bodhisattva – An enlightened being who reincarnates voluntarily to assist others in achieving enlightenment.

Buddha – The Enlightened One.

Bön – A pre-Buddhist religion in Tibet.

Dharma – The law of the world; various factors of existence from which everything originates.

Hinayana – The "Small Vehicle"; an old school of monastic Buddhism.

Karma – Sum of good and bad deeds, as well as their positive or negative consequences for a person's new life.

Koan – A paradoxical, puzzling or mind-confounding saying in Zen.

Lamaism – An alternate term for Tibetan Buddhism; the manifestation of Vajrayana Buddhism in Tibet.

Mahayana – The "Greater Vehicle," a form of Buddhism also accessible to lay people.

Mandala – A harmonious, circular picture (a deity).

Mantra – A holy phrase or sound, pronounced out loud.

Nirvana – Passing into emptiness.

Prana – The greatest wisdom in Mahayana.

Samsara – The "wheel" of reincarnation.

Sunyata – Emptiness, without world, personality or being.

Sutras – The sermons of the Buddha.

Tantras – Secret teachings composed in a language of symbols.

Tantrism – The union of male and female principles by means of prescribed rituals, secret teachings, breathing techniques, as well as techniques of sexual union.

Theraveda – The oldest form of Buddhism, still practiced today.

Tibetan Buddhism – A form of Buddhism specific to Tibet that developed out of Chinese and Vajrayana Buddhism.

Vajrayana – The "Diamond Vehicle" - the third significant current of Buddhism, which developed in India.

Zen – A Japanese expression of Buddhism that emerged in China under the influence of Taoism.

IMPORTANT TERMS IN JUDAISM

Ark of the Covenant – Chest in which the tablets bearing the Ten Commandments were stored, presumably destroyed with the first temple in the year 586; model for the current Torah shrine in each synagogue, known as the Holy Ark.

Ashkenazim – Jews of German and Eastern European descent.

Bar Mitzvah, Bat Mitzvah – Ceremony marking the admittance of boys and girls into the religious community of Jewish adults.

Hanukkah – An eight-day light festival celebrated in mid-December.

Kabbalah – Mystic and esoteric doctrine of the Torah.

Kaddish – Prayer of mourning.

Kashrut (noun), Kosher (adj.) – Rules and regulations governing food, including its handling, kitchenware, and places where food is prepared.

Kiddush – Blessing, consecration, ceremony at the start of the Sabbath or a holy day.

Kippah – Skullcap, the traditional head cover for men. Also *yarmulke*.

Knesset – Assembly; Israel's State Parliament.

Menorah – A candelabrum originally with seven branches (a ritual object in the Second Temple, now lost); symbol of Jewish identity.

Mishnah – Oral tradition (law) handed down from generation to generation.

Mitzvah – Command or precept(s) or acts fulfilling them (plural: *Mitzvoh*).

Passover; Pesach – Jewish festival in April commemorating the Exodus from Egypt.

Rabbi – Jewish teacher and spiritual leader; "Rabbi" is the form of address.

Sabbath – Ritually observed last day of the week, a day of rest on which no work should be done.

Sephardim – Jews of Western or southern European origin (originally from Spain and Portugal).

Shoah – The Holocaust; extermination of European Jews (1938–1945).

Synagogue – Jewish house of prayer and communal center.

Tallit – Prayer shawl.

Talmud – Collection of rabbinic teachings that are binding Jewish law.

Tanakh – The Hebrew Bible.

Tefillin – Phylacteries or prayer straps.

Torah – Holy Book, Pentateuch, the five books of Moses; also used to mean the entire body of Jewish writings.

IMPORTANT TERMS IN TAOISM, CONFUCIANISM, AND SHINTOISM

Amaterasu – Sun goddess (Shintoism).

Chi (or Qi) – Vital life energy.

Ching (or Jing) – The essence of life (Taoism).

Feng Shui – ("wind–water") The art of living in harmony with the landscape and with nature (Taoism).

I-Ching – The *Book of Changes*; originated in pre-Confucian times

Jiba – A place in Japan where God is thought to have created humans (Shintoism).

Kami – Objects of reverence; may be gods, people, or places (Shintoism).

Li – Principle or law (Confucianism).

Shen – The mind of a human being (Taoism).

Shinto – Ritual location, temple or sanctuary (Shinto).

Tao – The unfathomable cosmic principle (Taoism).

Tenno – The emperor of Japan (Shintoism).

Tien – Heaven or God (Confucianism).

Torii – Large gates, usually painted red, into Shinto shrines (Shintoism).

Wu-wei – The principle of active non-doing (Taoism).

Yin and Yang – The opposing principles of the world (male and female, dark and light, etc.) and their union.

Literature

CHRISTIANITY

The Bible. Revised Standard Edition. New York: Oxford University Press, 1973.

Brosseder, Johannes, Ed. *Dialogfähige Theologie.* Neukirchen-Vluyn: Neukirchener, 2001.

Eco, Umberto and Martini, Carlo Maria. *Belief or Non-Belief?* London: Arcade Publishing, 2001.

Edwards, David L. *Christianity: The First Two Thousand Years.* Maryknoll, New York: Orbis Books, 1997.

Hann, Martin. *Die Bibel.* 2nd ed. Paderborn: Utb, 2005.

Kollmann, Bernd, ed. *Antikes Judentum und frühes Christentum.* Festschrift for Hartmut Stegemann on his 65th birthday. Berlin: Gruyter, 1999.

Küng, Hans. *On Being A Christian.* New York: Image/Doubleday, 1984.

———— *A Short History of the Catholic Church.* London: Modern Library, 2003.

Steenblock, Volker. *Kleine Philosophiegeschichte.* Stuttgart: Reclam, 2002.

Wilber, Ken. *Up From Eden: A Transpersonal View of Human Evolution.* London: Anchor Books, 1981.

Wilson, Brian and Smart, Ninian. *Christianity.* NJ: Prentice Hall, 1998.

ISLAM

Notes:

(1) Schimmel, Annemarie. *Muhammad.* Munich: Diederichs, 2002.

(2) Hughes, Thomas Patrick. *A Dictionary of Islam.* Chicago: Kazi Publications, 1994.

(3) Hofmann, Murad. *Islam.* Munich: Diederichs, 2001.

(4) Fiedler, Teja and Sandmeyer, Peter. *Die sechs Weltreligionen.* Berlin: Ullstein, 2005.

Additional Literature:

The Holy Qur'an. Text, Translation and Commentary. Translated by Abdullah Yusef Ali. Tahrike Tarsile Quran, Inc., 1998.

Arberry, A.J. *Sufism: An Account of the Mystics of Islam.* New York: Dover Publications, 2001.

Armstrong, Karen. *Islam: A Short History.* NY: Random House/Modern Library Chronicles, 2000.

Esposito, John L. *Islam: The Straight Path.* 3rd rev. ed. NY: Oxford Univ. Press, USA, 2004.

Mathewson Denny, Frederick. *An Introduction to Islam.* 3rd ed. NY: Prentice Hall, 2005.

Ruthven, Malise. *Islam: A Very Short Introduction.* New York: Oxford University Press, 2000.

HINDUISM

Notes:

(1) Prabhupada, Srila. *Srimad Bhagavatam.* London: Bhaktivedanta Books, 1989.

(2) Mensching, Gustav. *Die Söhne Gottes. Aus den heiligen Schriften der Menschheit.* Wiesbaden: Desch, 1958.

(3) Glasenapp, Helmuth. *Indische Geisteswelt.* Holle: Bertelsmann, 1958.

(4) Jung, Wolfgang. *Paranormal Deutschland e.v.* www.paranormal.de

(5) *Reise in Rajasthan.* www.rajasthan-indien-reise.de

Additional Literature:

Michaels, Axel. *Hinduism: Past and Present.* Trans. Barbara Harshav. NJ: Princeton University Press, 2004.

Narayanan, Vasudha. *Hinduism.* NY: Oxford Univ. Press USA, 2004.

Swami Bhaskarananda. *The Essentials of Hinduism: A Comprehensive Overview of the World's Oldest Religion.* 2nd ed. Seattle: Vivika Press, 2002.

Zimmermann, Jutta Maria. *Vedische Mantras. Begegnung mit dem Yoga.* Audio-CD. Stuttgart: Raja, 2002.

BUDDHISM

Notes:

(1) Mensching, Gustav. *Die Söhne Gottes. Aus den heiligen Schriften der Menschheit.* Wiesbaden: Desch, 1958.

(2) Schumacher, Stephan. *Zen.* Munich: Diedrichs, 2001.

(3) Han Shan. *150 Gedichte vom Kalten Berg.* Trans. and introduction by Stephan Schumacher. 5th ed. Munich: Diedrichs, 1992.

(4) Schumann, Hans Wolfgang. *Mahayana-Buddhismus.* Munich: Diedrichs, 1990.

(5) Dogen Zenji. *The Shobogenzo or The Treasure House of the Eye of the True Treachings.* Trans. Rev. Hubert Nearman. CA: Shasta Abbey Press, 1996.

(6) Braun, Hans-Jörg. *Das Leben nach dem Tod. Jenseitsvorstellungen der Menschheit.* Zurich: Gilomen. 1996.

(7) Ulrich, Hans E. *Von Meister Eckhardt bis Carolos Castaneda.* 2nd ed. Frankfurt: Fischer, 1987.

Additional Literature:

Dalai Lama XIV (Tenzin Gyatso). *The World of Tibetan Buddhism.* Trans. Geshe Thupten Jinpa. MA: Wisdom Publications, 1995.

David-Neel, Alexandra. *The Secret Oral Teachings in Buddhist Sects.* Rev. ed. CA: City Lights Publishers, 1981.

Han, Byung-Chul. *Philosophie des Zen-Buddhismus.* Ditzingen: Reclam, 2002.

Nhat Hanh, Thich. *The Heart of the Buddha's Teaching.* NY: Broadway, 1999.

Thurman, Robert A. *Essential Tibetan Buddhism.* San Francisco: Harper, 1996.

JUDAISM

Notes:

(1) Krauss, Rolf. *Das Moses Rätsel.* Munich: Ullstein, 2001.

(2) Mensching, Gustav. *Die Söhne Gottes. Aus den heiligen Schriften der Menschheit.* Wiesbaden: Desch, 1958.

(3) *Jüdische Geschichte und Kultur.* www.judentum-projekt.de

(4) Theo Ellesat, et. al. (2003) *Christen an der Seite Israels.* www.israelaktuell.de

Additional Literature:

Holz, Barry W., ed. *Back to the Sources: Reading the Classic Jewish Texts*. NY: Simon & Schuster, 1986.

Müller, Ernst. *A History of Jewish Mysticism*. New ed. NY: Barnes & Nobles, 1995.

Scheidlin, Raymond. *A Short History of the Jewish People*. NY: Oxford Univ. Press, 2000.

Schoeps, Julius H. *Neues Lexikon des Judentums*. Gütersloh: Gütersloher Verlagshaus, 2000.

—— *Theodor Herzl, 1860–1904: An Illustrated Biography*. Trans. from German. NY: Overlook Press, 1999.

Scholem, Gershom. *Origins of the Kabbalah*. Trans. Allan Arkush. New Jersey: Princeton University Press, 1991.

—— *On the Kabbalah and its Symbolism*. Trans. Ralph Mannheim. NY: Schocken Books, 1996.

Telushkin, Joseph. *Jewish Literacy: The Most Important Things to Know about the Jewish Religion, Its People, and Its History*. NY: William Morrow, 1991.

CONFUCIANISM

Notes:

(1) Felitz, Werner. *Konfuzius: Der gute Weg. Worte des großen chinesischen Weisheitslehrers Konfuzius*. Cologne: Anaconda Press, 2005.

(2) Mensching, Gustav. *Die Söhne Gottes. Aus den heiligen Schriften der Menschheit*. Wiesbaden: Desch, 1958.

(3) Govinda, Anagarika. *The Inner Structure of the I'Ching*. NY: Weatherill Publishers, 1981.

(4) Wilhelm, Richard. *Konfuzius: Gespräche (Lun Yü)*. Ditzingen: Dtv, 2005.

Additional Literature:

Bauer, Wolfgang. *Geschichte der chinesischen Philosophie. Konfuzianismus, Daoismus, Buddhismus*. Munich: C.H. Beck, 2001.

Baynes, C.F. *The I Ching or Book of Changes*. Trans. Richard Wilhelm. 3rd ed. NJ: Princeton Univ. Press, 1967.

Blofeld, John. *Taoism: The Road to Immortality*. Boston: Shambhala Publications, 2000.

Lee, Ming-huei. *Der Konfuzianismus im modernen China*. Leipzig: Leipiziger Universitätsverlag, 2005.

Oldstone-Moore, Jennifer. *Confucianism*. Oxford: Oxford University Press, 2002.

Van de Weyer, Robert, ed. *366 Readings from Taoism and Confucianism*. Cleveland: Pilgrim Press, 2001.

TAOISM

Notes:

(1) Wilhelm, Richard, ed. *Laotse: Tao Te King. Das Buch vom Sinn und Leben*. Trans. Richard Wilhelm. Cologne: Anaconda, 2005.

(2) Terhart, Franjo. First publication.

(3) Mensching, Gustav. *Die Söhne Gottes. Aus den heiligen Schriften der Menschheit*. Wiesbaden: Desch, 1958.

(4) Chuang Tzu. *Basic Writings*. Trans. David Butler. NY: Columbia University Press, 2003.

Additional Literature:

Bauer, Wolfgang. *Geschichte der chinesischen Philosophie. Konfuzianismus, Daoismus, Buddhismus*. Munich: C.H. Beck, 2001.

Chen, Hanne. *Daoismus erleben*. Bielefeld, 2001.

Chuang Tzu. *Wandering on the Way: Early Taoist Tales and Parables of Chuang Tzu*. Trans. Victor Mair. Honolulu: Univ. Hawaii Press, 1998.

—— *The Inner Chapters*. New ed. Trans. A.C. Graham. NY: Harper Collins, 1987.

Fischer, Theo. *Wu wei. Die Lebenskunst des Tao*. Reinbek: Rowahlt, 2005.

Lao Tzu. *The Complete Works of Lao Tzu*. Trans. Hua Hu Ching. Revised edition. CA: Seven Star Communications, 1979.

Wildish, Paul. *Principles of Taoism*. London: Thorsens, 1999.

Wohlfart, Günter. *Zhuangzi. Meister der Spiritualität*. Freiburg: Herer, 2002.

SHINTOISM

Notes:

(1) Novak, M. and Cerna, Z. *Japanische Märchen und Volkserzählungen*. Hanau: Dausien, 1997.

Additional Literature:

Laube, Johannes. *Oyagami. Die heutige Gottesvorstellung des Tenrikyo*. Wiesbaden, 1978.

Littleton, C. Scott. *Shinto and the Religions of Japan*. Oxford: Oxford University Press, 2002

Obayashi, Taryo. *Ise und Izumo. Die Schreine des Shintoismus*. Volume 6. Freiburg: Herder, 1989.

Ono, Sokyo. *Shinto: The Kami Way*. Tokyo: Tuttle Publishing, 2004.

MANDAENISM

Notes:

(1) Brandt, Wilhelm. *Mandäische Schriften. Aus der großen Sammlung heiliger Bücher Genza oder Sidra Rabba*. New facsimile edition of the 1893 text. Amsterdam: APA, 1973.

Additional Literature:

Rudolph, Kurt. *Die Mandäer*. Göttingen: M.Sandig, 1967.

Widengren, George, ed. *Mani and Manichaeism/Orthodoxies and Heresies in the Early Church*. London: Ams Press Inc., 1967.

BAHA'ISM

Notes:

(1) *Religionspädagogische Plattform im Internet*. www. rpi-virtuell.net

(2) Ackermann, Trudi. *Baha'i Liechtenstein*. www.bahai.li

Additional Literature:

Faizi, Gloria. *The Baha'i Faith: An Introduction*. New Delhi: Baha'i Publishing Trust, 1971.

Smith, Peter. *The Baha'i Religion: A Short Introduction to its History and Teachings*. Herts, UK: George Ronald Publishing, Ltd., 1998.

NATURE RELIGIONS

Brinton, Daniel G. *Religions of Primitive Peoples*. Facsimile reprint of 1899 edition. Adamant Media Corp., 2001.

Crowley, Vivianne. *Naturreligion. Was Sie wirklich darüber wissen müssen*. Munich: Goldmann, 2002.

Drury, Nevill. *Sacred Encounters: Shamanism and Magical Journeys of the Spirit*. London: Watkins Publishing, 2003.

Gill, Sam D. *Beyond the Primitive: The Religions of Nonliterate Peoples*. The Prentice-Hall Series in World Religions. NY: Prentice-Hall, 1981.

Porterfield, Amanda. *The Power of Religion: A Comparative Introduction*. NY: Oxford Univ. Press USA, 1997.

Picture credits

Beer, Günter 248

Corbis, 2 Images.com, 10 Magnus Johansson/Reuters, 12 Dave Bartruff, 13 Brooklyn Museum of Art (t., b.), 14 Blue Lantern Studio, 15 Brooklyn Museum of Art (l., r.), 16 Johanson Krause/Archivo Iconografico S.A., 17 Stefano Bianchetti (l.), Brooklyn Museum of Art (r.), 18 Stefano Bianchetti, 19 Christie's Images (l.), Historical Picture Archive (r.), 20 Bettmann, 21 Corbis (l.), Chris Hellier (r.), 22 Bettmann (l.), Karl-Heinz Haenel (r.), 23 Burstein Collection, 24 Bob Krist (c.), Hanan Isachar (b.), 25 Richard T. Nowitz, 26 Bettmann, 27 Christel Gerstenberg (t.), Bettmann (b.), 28 Bettmann, 29 Bettmann (c., b.), 30 Tom Bean (l.), Bettmann (r.), 31 Richard T. Nowitz, 32 Bettmann (l., r.), 33 Bettmann, 34 Dietrich Rose/ zefa (t.), Stapleton Collection (c.), 35 Bettmann, 36 José F. Poblete (l.), Francis G. Mayer (r.), 37 Paul Almasy, 38 Stapleton Collection (l.), Bettmann (b.), 39 Bettmann, 40 Bettmann (t.), Jerry Lampen/Reuters (b.), 41 Max Rossi/ Reuters, 42 Charles & Josette Lenors, 43 James L. Amos (t.), David Lees (b.), 44 Christie's Images, 45 Massimo Listri (t.), Bettmann (b.), 46 Robert Maass (l.), Paolo Cocco/Reuters (r.), 47 David Butow/Corbis Saba, 48 Historical Picture Archive (l.), Reuters (r.), 49 Summerfield Press, 50 Blaine Harrington III (l.), Bob Krist (r.), 51 Alessandra Benedetti, 52 Elio Ciol, 53 Bettmann (l.), Chris Hellier (r.), 54 Gianni Dagli Orti (l.), Archivo Iconografico, S.A. (r.), 55 The Art Archive, 56 Sandro Vannini, 57 Russell Underwood (t.), Charles & Josette Lenars (b.), 58 Günter Rossenbach/zefa (l.), Sean Sexton Collection (r.), 59 Patrick Ward (t.), London Aerial Photo Library (b.), 60 Brooklyn Museum of Art (l.), Ariel Skelley (r.), 61 Jonathan Blair, 62 Raymond Gehman (l.), Bettmann (r.), 63 Elio Ciol, 64 Peter Turnley, 65

Archivo Iconografico, S.A. (t.), Michael Mulvey/Dallas Morning News (b.), 66 Christian Charisius/ Reuters, 67 Jack Moebes (t.), Michael Dalder/Reuters (b.), 68 Brooklyn Museum of Art (l.), Wendy Stone (r.), 69 Bettmann, 70 A. Huber/U. Starke/ zefa, 71 Jacques Pavlovsky/Sygma (t.), Herbert Spichtinger/zefa (b.), 72 Kazuyoshi Nomachi, 74 Kazuyoshi Nomachi, 75 Kazuyoshi Nomachi (t.), Reuters (b.), 76 Frans Lemmens/zefa, 77 Kazuyoshi Nomachi (t.), Historical Picture Archive (b.), 78 Hanan Isachar (t.), Kazuyoshi Nomachi (b.), 79 Bettmann, 80 Brooklyn Museum of Art, 81 Kazuyoshi Nomachi (t.), Bettmann (b.), 82 Adam Woolfit, 83 Steve McDonough (t.), Krause, Johansen/Archivo Iconografico, S.A. (b.), 84 Massimo Listri, 85 Jennifer Kennard (t.), Marco Cristofori (b.), 86 Françoise de Mulder, 87 Roger Wood (t.), Reuters (b.), 88 Charles & Josette Lenars (t.), Roman Soumar (b.), 89 Setboun, 90 Burstein Collection, 91 Bettmann (t.), Archivo Iconografico, S.A. (b.), 92 Patrick Chauvel/Sygma (t.), Sean Adair/Reuters (b.), 93 Bettmann, 94 Kazuyoshi Nomachi, 95 Kazuyoshi Nomachi (t.), Earl & Nazima Kowall (c.), 96 Kazuyoshi Nomachi, 97 Atef Hassan/Reuters, 98 Kazuyoshi Nomachi, 99 Archivo Iconografico, S.A. (l.), Olivier Martel (r.), 100 Hanan Isachar, 101 Mohsen Shandiz/Sygma (t.), Bettmann (b.), 102 Kazuyoshi Nomachi, 103 Claro Cortes IV/Reuters (t.), Setboun (c.), 104 Damir Sagolj/Reuters, 105 Kazuyoshi Nomachi (t.), Ceerwan Aziz/Reuters (b.), 106 Kazuyoshi Nomachi, 107 Joseph Sohm/Visions of America, 108 Dave Bartruff, 109 Hanan Isachar (l.), Fayaz Kabli/Reuters (r.), 110 Kazuyoshi Nomachi, 111 Kazuyoshi Nomachi (t.), David Rubinger (b.), 112 Aaron Horowitz (t.), Robert Harding World Imagery (b.), 113 Gavriel Jecan, 114 Charles & Josette Lenars (t.), Najlah Feanny (b.), 115 Dean Conger, 116 Reuters, 117 Reza; Webistan (t.),

Peter Macdiarmid/Reuters, 118 David Lees, 119 Bettmann (t.), Danny Lehman (b.), 120 Gavriel Jecan, 122 Kazuyoshi Nomachi, 123 Paul W. Liebhardt (t.), Kazuyoshi Nomachi (b.), 124 Diego Lezama Orezzoli, 125 Angelo Hornak (l.), Lindsay Hebberd (r.), 126 Wolfgang Kaehler (l.), Adam Woolfitt (r.), 127 Brigitte Sporrer/zefa, 128 Jeremy Horner, 129 Bettmann (t.), Stapleton Collection (b.), 130 Paul C. Pet/zefa, 131 Steve Raymer (t.), Richard Cummins (b.), 132 Chris Lisle, 133 Luca I. Tettoni (t.), Blaine Harrington III (b.), 134 Bettmann, 135 Hulton-Deutsch Collection (t.), Christine Kolisch (b.), 136 Gavriel Jecan, 137 Archivo Iconografico, S.A. (t.), Jeremy Horner (b.), 138 Angelo Hornak, 139 Chris Lisle (t.), Angelo Cavalli/zefa (b.); 140 Michael Freeman, 141 Brooklyn Museum of Art (t.), Peter Guttman (b.), 142 Stapleton Collection, 143 Angelo Hornak (l.), Ted Streshinsky (r.), 144 Historical Picture Archive, 145 Paul Seheult/Eye Ubiquitous (t.), Arvind Garg (b.), 146 Eye Ubiquitous, 147 Arne Hodalic, 148 Corbis, 149 Sam Diephuis/zefa (t.), Michael Freeman (b.), 150 Chris Lisle, 151 Hulton-Deutsch Collection (t.), Frans Lemmens/zefa (b.), 152 Lindsay Hebberd, 153 Amit Bhargava (t.), Earl & Nazima Kowall (b.), 154 Jitendra Prakash/Reuters, 155 Lindsay Hebberd (t.), Arvind Garg (b.), 156 Utpal Baruah/Reuters, 157 Noshir Desai/ Corbis Sygma (t.), Steve Raymer (b.), 158 Lindsay Hebberd, 159 Jim Zuckerman (t.), Alen MacWeeney (b.), 160 Lindsay Hebberd, 161 David Sutherland (t.), Anders Ryman (b.), 162 Sophie Elbaz/Sygma, 163 Brian A. Vikander (t.), Hulton-Deutsch Collection (b.), 164 John W. Gertz/zefa, 166 Eye Ubiquitous, 167 Kevin R. Morris (l.), Sheldan Collins (r.), 168 Lindsay Hebberd, 169 Lindsay Hebberd (t.), Sakamoto Photo Research Laboratory (b.), 170 Frans Lemmens/zefa (l.), Macduff Everton (r.), 171 Yang Liu, 172

Archivo Iconografico, S.A., 173 Bettmann (t.), Charles & Josette Lenars (b.), 174 Christie's Images (l.), Earl & Nazima Kowall (r.), 175 Keren Su, 176 Robert Harding World Imagery, 177 Louise Gubb/Corbis Saba (t.), Andrew Wong/Reuters (b.), 178 Kevin R. Morris, 179 Liu Liqun (t.), Tibor Bognár (b.), 180 Catherine Karnow, 181 Bettmann (t.), China Span, LLC (b.), 182 Asian Art & Archaeology, Inc., 183 Lowell Georgia (l.), Macduff Everton (r.), 184 Fridmar Damm/zefa, 185 Michael Freeman (t.), Simon Marcus (b.), 186 Burstein Collection, 187 Bettmann (t.), Allen Ginsberg (b.), 188 Hans Georg Roth, 189 Kevin Fleming (l.), Jean Pierre Amet/Corbis Sygma (r.), 190 Ed Kashi (t.), Brooks Kraft (b.), 191 Michael DeYoung, 192 Bradley Smith, 193 Ashley Cooper (t.), Chris Lisle (b.), 194 So Hing-Keung, 195 Archivo Iconografico, S.A. (t.), Lindsay Hebberd (b.), 196 Leonard de Selva, 197 Bob Krist (t.), Rob Howard (b.), 198 Daniel Lainé, 199 Jennifer Kennard (t.), Earl & Nazima Kowall (b.), 200 Chris Hellier, 201 Michael Freeman (t.), Nathan Benn (b.), 202 Bennett Dean/Eye Ubiquitous, 203 David Bathgate (t.), Dave Bartruff (b.), 204 Robert van den Berge/Corbis Sygma, 205 Bettmann (t.), Angelo Cavalli/zefa (b.), 206 Arvind Garg, 207 Angelo Cavalli/zefa (t.), Reuters (b.), 208 Peter Guttman, 210 Historical Picture Archive, 211 Alinari Archives (t.), Ricki Rosen/ Corbis Saba (b.), 212 Gianni Dagli Orti, 213 Stapleton Collection (t.), Fine Art Photographic Library (b.), 214 Bettmann, 215 William Whitehurst (l.), Stapleton Collection (t.), 216 Arte & Immagini srl, 217 Historical Picture Archive (t., b.), 218 Dave Bartruff, 219 Nathan Benn (t.), Brooklyn Museum of Art (b.), 220 Eric and David Hosking, 221 Richard T. Nowitz (t.), John C. Trever, PhD./The Dead Sea Scroll Foundation, Inc. (b.), 222 David Turnley, 223 Bob Krist (t.), Fred Prouser/Reuters (b.), 224 Richard T. Nowitz, 225 Nathan Benn, 226 Bettmann, 227 Elio Ciol (t.), Bettmann (b.), 228 Bob Krist, 229 Richard T. Nowitz (l.), Stefano Bianchetti (r.), 230 Tim Page, 231 David Rubinger (t.), Historical Picture Archive (b.), 232 Peter Turnley, 233 Ted Spiegel (t.), Richard T. Nowitz (b.), 234 Archivo Iconografico, S.A., 235 David Rubinger (t.), Richard T. Nowitz (b.), 236 Owen Franken, 237 Peter Guttman (t.), Ted Spiegel (b.), 238 Richard T. Nowitz, 239 Historical Picture Archive (t.), Kevin Cruff (b.), 240 The Art Archive, David H. Wells (l.), Bettmann (r.), 242 David H. Wells (t.), David H. Wells (b.), 243 Randy Belinsky/Reuters, 244 David H. Wells, 244/245 David H. Wells, 245 Richard T. Nowitz, 246 David H. Wells, 247 Richard T. Nowitz (t., b.), 249 Ed Kashi (large photo), Seth Joel (small photo), 250 Les Stone/ Sygma, 251 Richard T. Nowitz (l.), Les Stone/Sygma (b.), 252 Les Stone/ Sygma, 253 Michael Freeman, 254 Yuriko Nakao/Reuters, 256 Bettmann (t.), Archivo Iconografico, S.A. (b.), 257 Jack Fields, 258 Setboun, 259 Michael S. Yamashita (l.), Nevada Wier (r.), 260 Kevin R. Morris, 261 Setboun (t.), Creasource (b.), 262 Setboun, 262/263 Setboun, 263 David Butow, 264 Archivo Iconografico, S.A. (t.), Keren Su (b.), 265 Historical Picture Archive (r.), Dave Bartruff (b.), 266 Burstein Collection (t.), Asian Art & Archaeology, Inc. (b.), 267 Leonard de Selva, 268 Macduff Everton, 269 Michael S. Yamashita (t.), Archivo Iconografico, S.A. (b.), 270 Burstein Collection, 271 Christie's Images (t.), Joyce Choo (b.), 272 Alain Nogues/ Corbis Sygma, 273 Archivo Iconografico, S.A. (l.), Betty Mallorca (r.), 274 Bettmann, 274/275 Bohemian Nomad Picturemakers, 275 Simon Kwong/ Reuters, 276 Macduff Everton (t.), Julia Waterlow/Eye Ubiquitous (b.), 277 Terry W. Eggers, 278 Tim Page, 279 Asian Art & Archaeology, Inc. (t.), Setboun (b.), 280 Stapleton Collection (l.), Simon Kwong/Reuters (r.), 281 Guang Niu/Reuters, 282 James Leynse, 283 Michael S. Yamashita, 284 Asian Art & Archaeology, Inc., 285 Bettmann (t.), Kimimasa Mayama/ Reuters (b.), 286 Peter Harholdt, 287 Anonymous/Sygma (t.), Chris Lisle (b.), 288 Gideon Mendel, 289 Michael Freeman (t.), Shunsuke Akatsuka/ Reuters (b.), 290 Murat Taner/zefa (l.), Yuriko Nakao/ Reuters (r.), 291 Yuriko Nakao/Reuters, 292 Archivo Iconografico, S.A., 293 Nik Wheeler (t., b.), 294 John and Lisa Merrill, 295 Hanan Isachar (t.), Corbis (b.), 296 Hanan Isachar, 297 Richard T. Nowitz (l.), Richard Hamilton Smith (r.), 298 Paul C. Pet/zefa, 299 Torleif Svensson (l.), Frans Lemmens/zefa (r.), 300 Rob Howard, 301 Mike R. Whittle/ Ecoscene, 302 James L. Amos (t.), David Samuel Robbins (b.), 303 Arne Hodalic

Fillery, Burga 253 (Graphics)

Index

312

The publisher wishes to thank Salim Abdullah,
Director of the Zentralinstitut Islam-Archiv-Deutschland,
Soest (Islam chapter) and Michael Lawton, Head of
the Liberal Jewish Community Gescher Lamassoret,
Cologne (Judaism chapter) for their useful advice on
the original edition of the present volume.

For their helpful comments and advice on the
American edition, we wish to thank Russell Cennydd
and Leslie Cohen-Gee.

This is a Parragon Publishing Book

Original edition: ditter.projektagentur Gmbh
Project coordination and picture research:
    Irina Ditter-Hilkens
Editing: Kirsten E. Lehmann
Design: Sabine Vonderstein

American edition produced by: APE Int'l. Richmond, VA
Translation: Sally M. Schreiber, Dr. Lizzie Gilbert,
    Markus Flatscher, Sue McRae, Mary Dobrian,
    Jennifer Taylor-Gaida, Christine Yoshida
Editing: Russell Cennydd, Tammi Reichel

ISBN: 978-1-4054-9046-7

Printed in Malaysia